D0906144

# THE STORMING OF THE MIND
## ROBERT HUNTER

# THE STORMING OF THE MIND
## ROBERT HUNTER

# THE STORMING
## ROBERT HUNTER

Doubleday & Company, Inc.
Garden City, New York
1971

# OF THE MIND

Copyright © 1971 by Robert Hunter

ALL RIGHTS RESERVED

Library of Congress Catalog Card Number 79 - 172519

Printed in the United States of America

For my mother, Augustine Bernadette Stein,
for much motherly tolerance and love.

# Contents

# ACKNOWLEDGEMENTS

This book would not have been possible without the assistance of: my wife, for emotionally "rolfing" me; my kids, Conan and Justine, for demonstrating again and again that they were born with their reason intact, and for resisting efforts to break it up; Fritz Perls, not only for helping to guide me through some deadlocked spaces, but also for encouraging the development of many of the ideas contained herein, for adding his own insights, and for suggesting the general outlines of a "gestalt sociology" of sorts (although, obviously, he can't be blamed for the results); Theodore Roszak for drawing my attention in a number of conversations to things I might have overlooked; the late Fred Hampton of the Illinois Chapter of the Black Panther Party for troubling, a month before he was shot to death, to debate some of these points (although Hampton would no doubt have disagreed with much written here); Fred Latrimouille for guiding me into rock music; Ross Lane for providing me with a lot of material; Ken Specht and Sylvia Spring for help at a critical time; Aaron Bruce for instruction along the lines provided by Conan and Justine; Pat Nagle and Bill Galt for sending me to the States; Stu Keate for subsidizing much of the research; Lee Pulos and Dave Berner, each in their own quite different ways, for turning me on to a lot of new experiences and possibilities; Sol Kort of the University of British Columbia extension department for a lot of important contacts; Mike Murphy of the Esalen Institute for some mind-stretching notions; and, naturally, many, many others.

# ONE CHILDHOOD'S END

Essentially, this book evolves from the "discovery" that a new form of human consciousness has come into being in the high-pressure incubator of mass technological society. This is the most central and crucial change taking place in our world today. In comparison to the importance of this change, all other changes – automation, the emergence of mass media, and even space flight – are little more than minor adjustments in the over-all mechanism. They are the details, the parts – not the whole.

"Something" is happening: we all sense that. Something strange. Something that has never happened before. Some sort of a transformation is taking place. The human race has entered a schizophrenic-like state from which it cannot possibly emerge without being re-shaped to the roots of its being. Without such a transformation, our chances of survival are just about nil. If the reflexes which have dominated our collective behavior through-out the whole of human history continue to determine our course in the future, the destruction of life on earth becomes, sooner or later, a statistical certainty. At this moment, as John R. Platt has put it, our chances of surviving even for ten or twenty years are only 50-50. "This is a shorter life-expectancy than people have ever had in the world before."[1] In short, the human race has found its way to the center of a steel trap so cumulative and depth-structured that there may be no way out – no way out, that is, short of some sort of spontaneous reorganization of our collective self. At first glance, such a hope seems pure pie-in-the-sky, no more worthy of serious attention than the notion that legions of angels or benevolent overlords from Alpha Centauri might descend to straighten things out.

Yet, on closer examination, we see that just such a spontaneous transformation is what is happening. And it has begun to come clearly into focus. It amounts to a "self-structuring hierarchical jump." Others would say simply that people are getting their heads together.

Many – still overwhelmingly the majority – would insist that society is degenerating, becoming hedonistic and irrational, and that shock troops from some bizarre Brave New World are parachuting into our midst, sabotaging the foundations of civilization.

This negative kind of reaction is inevitable. There is no question about whether a society would be capable of accepting a force growing within it which promises to replace it, or whether any society would be capable of accepting the need for its own extinction. The Romans plainly did not welcome the birth of Christianity with cries of "Right on!" It made no difference to them that the new vision was more integrated, more humane and less violent. The lions feasted precisely because Rome was incapable of choosing to bury itself in the interests of evolution. No society commits itself voluntarily to the back wards of history, stepping aside to make way for its successor.

The disjuncture taking place today is far more thorough-going than the one experienced at the time of the fall of the Roman Empire. It is a disjuncture more on the scale of the changes which marked the end of the Neolithic Age – except that rather than taking place during the course of several thousand years, the change is being wrought in virtually a single generation. In evolutionary terms, it is a cataclysmic change, a near-instantaneous mutation. It is happening at such a speed that there can be almost no hope of controlling it, any more than an individual can hope to control his own entry into the schizophrenic experience *after* it has begun.

This is an evolutionary leap – a *self-structuring* evolutionary leap – taking place almost with the speed of the transformation wrought on the children in Arthur C. Clarke's *Childhood's End* – probably the most prophetic science-fiction work of our time.

We have been trying to anticipate the *appearance* of the world of the future for so long that we have largely forgotten to consider how the spaces inside people's heads will inevitably be altered. Some fundamental readjustment must be made if we are to survive the massive restructuring of our physical environment which is now taking place, at a rate which is at the very least breathtaking. Loren Eiseley has remarked that "you can now literally be born in one age and die in another – all within a single lifetime."[2] That is fast change, indeed. By our previous historical standards, it is at least super-normal. By evolutionary standards, it is as unthinkably sudden as the change effected when atoms are split.

We accept – because we really have no subjective experience of it – the fact that in the last century we have increased our speed of travel by a factor of $10^2$, our speed of communication by $10^7$, our speed of data handling by $10^6$, our energy resources by $10^3$, our ability to control diseases by $10^2$, our power of weapons by $10^6$, and our rate of population growth by something like $10^3$ times what it was a few thousand years ago.

These are what are called quantum or order-of-magnitude jumps. Yet while we accept these phenomenal and unprecedented changes in our relationship to the physical world (often with only a shrug), we seem, at the same time, to be unwilling to accept even a marginal readjustment in relationship to our psychic, emotional, and moral environment. This is clearly demonstrated in the general reaction to marijuana. Even though it is only a minor mind-altering agent, it is viewed by many with all the knee-jerk reflexes of horror and antagonism that used to go into fear of communism. People who can accept an order-of-magnitude change in the speed with which we travel or communicate nevertheless seem incapable of accepting even a slight change in social attitudes. What these reflexes represent is not merely inconsistency; it goes far deeper. What they demonstrate is the inherently *unintegrated* nature of the consciousness which is now dominant in all highly technological nations.

By contrast, the consciousness now emerging, the holistic postwar consciousness, is essentially integrative. (See APPENDIX.) It represents a jump in terms of complexity of organization that at least approximates the kind of quantum leaps which have been taken in communication, travel, weapons, growth, use of resources, and population. It is a compensatory, homeostatic process.

The changes in our world have all been one-sided so far – a

massive and ever-accelerating (to say nothing of fundamental) – altering of our physical world, with little or no perceptible altering of our psychic world. Yet, as Ludwig von Bertalanffy has noted, "operating the colossal social structures of our time – from businesses to national states to mankind as a whole – with the ethical concepts of a nomadic bronze-age society of 3,000 years ago is like operating an atomic reactor with the technology of a bushman."

Today, in relationship to the advanced industrial world, many of even the most sophisticated among us – in cognitive, perceptual, and ethical terms – are little more than bushmen. We cannot help sooner or later accidentally causing the nuclear reactor to explode. The emergence of a new consciousness capable of grasping the complexity of our contemporary situation is a matter of biological necessity. It is, to begin with, a survival strategy, infinitely more complex than the strategy which allows flies to adapt to DDT, but no less spontaneous.

It cannot easily be understood in terms of adaptation to the hardware of the contemporary environment or that of the near future. It is not specifically an adaptation in the sense of adjusting to technology as insects did to insecticides; rather it is *a reorganization of the structure of consciousness*. Otherwise, super-technicians would be appearing *en masse* instead of hippies. Woodstock would have been a program staged by the American Association for the Advancement of Science, with kids bringing their slide rules instead of their dope.

A change in the structure of consciousness means that the evolutionary breakthrough is coming inside people's heads, not outside. It is an individual experience. What is happening is that individuals are entering this psychic world of the future one at a time, as though stepping through some magic looking glass. Once through, they are changed forever. A gap opens up between them and those who have remained behind which is possibly as great as the gap between *homo sapiens* and Neanderthal Man.

Today, in the air-conditioned living rooms of the industrialized world, two different evolutionary versions of humanity are striving to coexist. No society has ever had to contain such immense differences. No society before modern industrial society has found itself stretched like elastic over such an enormous fissure.

The kids are blowing their minds with dope, writhing ecstatically under stereo headphones, gawking at (as some would have it) or grokking (as they would have it themselves) both sunsets and television sets alike. In appearance, the new consciousness they have attained cannot help but appear bizarre and frightening, even degenerate, to those who were born in the age now ending. At the very least, it must appear berserk: as berserk, let us say, as Los Angeles even in the early 1950's would have appeared to a citizen of the Middle Ages: new, impossible forms of communication; strange obsessions and concerns; incomprehensible goings-on; mad manners of speaking; a complete breakdown in the "normal" (i.e., Middle Ages) way of life. It would appear sacrilegious, perverse, horrific. The pace would be terrifying, the rhythmn unreal.

We may understand the situation better if we put it as a fable:

One day, our children's faces suddenly changed color. It was a new color, one which had never been seen on earth before. *But* – the new color could not be perceived unless one's eyes changed in a certain way too. The normal human eye would not notice any change. The children's eyes had changed along with the color of their skins, and so *they* could see the change in each other and in themselves. They tried to explain this to their parents, tried to describe the new color. But the parents, whose eyes were the same as they had always been, could only shake their heads and insist: "You look the same as me. What are you talking about?"

The children tried to explain the new color by comparing it to the other colors with which the parents were familiar. They drew analogies. They spoke in metaphors. They tried parables. They even worked out formulas. But the best the parents could do was to try to imagine the new color as being maybe like this or maybe a bit like that, or perhaps some combination. But it was a new and completely different color, and because the parents' eyes had not changed in the necessary way, as hard as they might try they simply could not *see* it. Of course the parents couldn't accept this. They were left thinking that they had a pretty good "idea" of what the kids were talking about, but decided that they didn't need to see the new color. After all there were plenty of other colors and it couldn't be *that* different. Or more likely, they thought, the kids were suffering from some failure of the optical nerve. Maybe because they had watched too much television. Or – and this, the parents decided, was very likely – the kids were putting on an elaborate act just to get attention.

The kids, realizing that the parents, unless they did something to change their eyes, would never be able to see the new color, finally gave up. They stopped talking to the parents and began to talk just to each other. They watched as more and more kids came along with new eyes and the strange new skin. Eventually they would outnumber the adults anyway . . . .

The holistic postwar consciousness involves a perceptual change – and this inevitably affects *what is seen*. An eye trained to see things as being separate and unrelated, an eye trained to *divide*, cannot readily perceive whole systems or flows. Certainly it cannot directly perceive synergistic effects, which are always more than the sum of their parts. But an eye trained to see things in terms of patterns or gestalts, which automatically related things one to the other, and all into something more, confronts the world in a quite different way. The postwar generation, with its different eyes, sees the world differently, and as a result sees a different world. Its reality is another reality. Moreover, since the critical problems which now threaten our existence can only be understood in terms of gestalts, or wholes, or flows, or synergistic effects, the eye of the new generation is the only one capable of even *seeing* the problems. No solutions can be attempted until the problems are clearly perceived. Without being able to see the problems which have piled up around them, the older generation has had to fumble blindly, helplessly. Its failure to deal with the realities of our time is, in this view, not surprising at all. What is surprising is that it has managed to survive this long.

The great life crises of our time are *all* synergistic effects, or, as they have been called, "meta-problems." They are the results of the interactions of many lesser problems, producing an effect – such as total environmental collapse – which is impervious to attempts to correct it by concentrating on various aspects (or "problems") which are only part of the over-all meta-problem. The basic life crises on planet Earth right now, including the dangers of nuclear destruction, race wars, cultural conflict, overcrowding and ecological devastation, all fall into the category of meta-problems. Only, a consciousness is absent from the corridors of power, from the White House to the Kremlin – although, significantly, it has at least begun to make an appearance in some of the suburbs of technological society and in a few of the unindustrialized regions.

When an individual finds himself completely unable to deal with some fundamental life crisis, he is liable to experience a breakdown and become schizophrenic. In a gestaltian sense, societies may undergo similar "breakdowns." They may go "mad." We now know that these "breakdowns" are, in fact, attempts at *breakthrough*. Western society is at this moment going through just such an experience – we have entered a state of collectivized schizophrenia.

The notion is loaded with negative associations. It need not be. But in order to understand the value of this experience, we must let go of the *idée fixe* that schizophrenia is nothing more than a collapse. Powerful evidence has been accumulated in recent years (by psychiatrists such as Harry Stack Sullivan, R. D. Laing, John Perry and Julian Silverman) which indicates that schizophrenia is a healing process – what Kazimierz Dabrowski has called "positive disintegration." It appears to be "a natural reaction to severe stress, a spontaneous process into which persons may enter when their usual problem-solving techniques fail to solve basic life crises. . . . "[4]

The super-gestalt of a society may, under severe stress, similarly enter a schizophrenic state. Certainly the stresses graphically described by Alvin Toffler in *Future Shock* – "a fire storm of change" in which we are helplessly enveloped, driven like leaves in a hurricane – would qualify as being severe enough to induce just such a natural reaction. Anton Boisen describes schizophrenia as "an attempt at re-organization in which the entire personality, to its bottommost depths, is aroused and its forces marshalled to meet the danger of . . . failure. These acute disturbances tend either to make or break. [They] may send the patient to the back wards, there to remain as a hopeless wreck, or they may send him back to the community in better shape than he has been for years."[5] Schizophrenia is essentially an attempt to reorganize an individual psyche into a new perceptual, cognitive and intuitive configuration so that it may deal successfully with situations with which it had not been able to cope before.

In our society, the schizophrenic trip seldom works: it is not given a chance. Rather, the patient is zonked with tranquillizers and even shock therapy. The effort is all directed at preventing the metamorphosis. So far as social schizophrenia is concerned, however, there are – fortunately – no omnipotent psychiatrists around to block the process. Planet Earth is the asylum, and while many politicians and technicians are doing their best at the moment to head off the "acute disturbances," to tranquillize the patient, there are no Outside Authorities to back them up; there is no powerful machinery of State beyond the asylum itself upon which they can rely should the patients become too unruly, too determined to change.

Beyond the schizophrenia model, there is a deeper process at work here: self-structuring hierarchical growth. This will be discussed in the next chapter. For now, it is our present dilemma which must be considered, the life situation with which we are confronted.

Arthur Koestler has expressed it perfectly:

> All efforts of persuasion by reasoned argument rely on the implicit assumption that *homo sapiens*, though occasionally blinded by emotion, is a basically rational animal, aware of the motives of his own actions and beliefs – an assumption which is untenable in the light of both historical and neurological evidence. All such appeals fall on barren ground; they could take root only if the ground were prepared by a spontaneous change in human mentality all over the world – the equivalent of a major biological mutation. Then, and only then, would mankind as a whole, from its political leaders down to the lonely crowd, become receptive to reasoned argument, and willing to resort to those unorthodox measures which enable it to meet the challenge. It is highly improbable that such a mental mutation will occur spontaneously in the foreseeable future. . . . [6]

Koestler here recognizes the multidimensional nature of the trap in which we find ourselves. Not only are the meta-problems themselves completely resistant to our traditional problem-solving techniques, but the perceptions and cognitive and intuitive reflexes which we have at our disposal do not even allow us to *see* this failure; let alone clearly perceive the nature of the solutions now required. We are trapped, as it were, in an invisible prison, unable to see that we are, in fact, imprisoned by the limitations of our perceptions, and therefore more or less unconscious of the need to escape, to climb over the walls and move at will through other perceptual worlds wherein a new order of answers might be found. Unaware that we are trapped, bounded by very high walls, locked into complex cages, we fail – to begin with – to recognize our situation. This basic failure does not allow us to begin to act.

Having said this, one has only etched in the outlines of the trap in which we find ourselves. It goes deeper. If the trap were no more subtle, there would be an easy solution: education. People would just need to be re-trained or taught how problems evolve into meta-problems, how a "crisis of crises" emerges, how departmentalized and specialized problem-solving techniques fail to work when applied to problems which themselves are synergetic effects – the results of the interactions of different sets of problems, something more than the sum of all their parts. So long as we are dealing with the separate parts we cannot deal effectively with the whole. Such an educational program, involving as it must the re-shaping of our basic notions of specialization, would be formidable. It would also likely be futile.

The experience of the past shows clearly that an awareness which threatens a tolerable life-style to which they have become adjusted is automaticallly resisted by large masses of people. One of the great unofficial educational programs of the last decade – launched by well-informed scientists with relatively easy access to the most powerful educational tool in history (the mass media) – was the effort to teach people the need for nuclear disarmament. The effort failed in its essential objectives. The lessons about racial equality, similarly taught through the mass media, also had pathetically little effect on the population at large. Lester Grinspoon, a psychiatrist, in a paper titled "The Unacceptability of Disquieting Facts," has explained why:

> People cannot risk being overwhelmed by anxiety which might accompany a full cognitive and effective grasp of the present world situation and its implications for the future. It serves a man no useful purpose to accept this truth if to do so leads only to the development of very disquieting feelings, feelings which interfere with his capacity to be productive, to maintain his mental equilibrium.[7]

The real problem is therefore not ignorance or even apathy. In the dense informational environment of mass society, true ignorance of the dimensions of the problems we face can only be achieved through the purposeful exclusion of facts which keep intruding at every turn. Apathy itself is purposeful. It is really avoidance, a "positive" act. Rather than risk having their equilibrium overwhelmed, great numbers of people chose existentially to look the other way: to escape into the banality of television serials or movies or sports activities. This deliberate, even though perhaps largely unconscious, avoidance amounts to a process of "self-apathizing."

In the context of individual psychological survival, it serves a highly functional purpose. In any long-term social or racial sense, it is suicidal. But the self-apathized individual, convinced (perhaps rightly) that he cannot' himself deal with large long-term issues, must concern himself with his own immediate survival – in terms of being able to carry on – and one way to do this is to screen out the disquieting facts which might, in a day-to-day sense, incapacitate him. Thus, as someone has remarked, once the crack of doom sounds it becomes just another noise. Moreover, as the crises pile up, as doom becomes several possible dooms, as the threat of environmental collapse is stacked up on top of the threat of nuclear war, the need for self-apathizing becomes greater. Individuals become more resistant to disquieting facts, not less so. They work out, in fact, fairly generalized reflexes with which to reject information of a negative character.

"Efforts at persuasion by reasoned argument" become even more futile. It is a recognition of this basic situation which has led to the rejection of the liberal position, which pins its hopes on education, which insists rather dogmatically that *homo sapiens* is only "occasionally blinded by emotion." Yet the only successful liberals are those who indulge in manipulation (which is not quite the same as "rational argument") as unreservedly as their opponents.

In the past, in an evolutionary sense, self-apathizing was not too dangerous a survival tactic. In terms of the over-all survival of the species it didn't really matter. We did not have the power, after all, to obliterate ourselves overnight. Consciously, we were incapable of choosing to commit suicide and there was no way we could do it unconsciously. No power had come into existence which could spread death over every continent. If a given tribe or race found its situation intolerable and great numbers of individuals became self-apathizing, it was a matter of no real biological concern. The tribe might die out or be conquered or remain in the power of some other tribe, but the survival of the whole species was not threatened as a result.

Today, the situation is fundamentally different. We are living with the Bomb, bacteriological weaponry, pollution. Self-apathizing becomes, in any biological sense, truly irrational – as irrational, let us say, as the behavior of a family out on a picnic confronted by a hungry tiger. If, after having observed the approach of the tiger, the family chose to stay put, to keep on munching away at their goodies, and as a result were eaten themselves, we would have to conclude that they had behaved in an irrational manner.

Reflexively, despite the deluge of books, articles, radio reports, television programs, masses of people are choosing to avoid the individual risk of being overwhelmed by the bad news. Put all these "rational" (in terms of purely individual survival) decisions together and they produce a behavior pattern which is *collectively irrational*. In the information-soaked society of mass communications, avoidance of disquieting facts is hard work. One must be determined indeed to succeed at it.

The only rational choice at this stage is to recognize that the basic conditions of life have changed. That squirrels of bad news – threats which formerly could only wipe out an unadaptive fraction of the species – have evolved into tigers which can wipe us all out. Under the new ground rules of survival, the "family" must get up from its picnic. It must fight or run. Whatever the decision, it must interrupt its feast in some drastic, radical manner. We see that, in view of our present situation, the only rational people around are revolutionaries – people who are choosing to quit the picnic of day-to-day individual survival.

This is the reason why such groups as the Black Panthers appeal so enormously to well-educated, literate members of the Establishment. These literates recognize – however dimly – that the revolutionary blacks are *sane* and, moreover, perfectly rational. It is their heritage from the Age of Reason that compels literate people to admire (however secretly) such objective, detached, even *scientific* analysis as that offered by revolutionaries such as Eldridge Cleaver.

Unfortunately, the revolutionaries are in the position of rational men trying to convince irrational men by *reasoned argument* of the nature of a problem facing them mutually. It can't work. There are too many who, in our modern context, have chosen avoidance and hence irrationality as a basic mode of self (ego) survival. And these choices are all made subconsciously, so they cannot even be pointed to or trapped in a snare of words.

Human behavior is infinitely more complex than we assume. We point to a "cause" of such and such behavior, we find evidence that this is in fact *the* cause, and we are contented, or at least ready to defend our findings to the end. Yet human behavior is vastly complex, involving not single causes of a given action but whole clusters of interacting causes each with various degrees of power, but each equally valid since its removal or sudden increase in power would alter the whole structural pattern which results in a single effect or form of behavior. In short, it is impossible for the rational ones among us – the revolutionaries – to peel and poke and dig through all the complex interacting levels of "cause" to reach even the single effect of "apathy" in time to avoid the consequences of our collective irrational and self-destructive behavior.

Our only hope would seem to be some sort of spontaneous change in human mentality, as Koestler suggests. Precisely the equivalent of such a mental mutation is what is happening right now, whether Koestler recognizes it or not.

We begin our analysis with the assumption that "apathy" is now irrational but "passivism" has now become rational, if only because within nations as well as between them balances of power now exist, which was not formerly the case – in the days when it did not matter so much whether power was balanced or not. In those days, we did not have the power to exterminate ourselves as a whole species.

We will not be able to fake it this time. Either we will achieve a complete reorganization or we will perish. The kind of phoney victories of the past – of "christianity" over "paganism," or communism over czarism, or American republicanism over British monarchism, will not suffice. The complete reorganization is something the revolutionaries, in the position they are in, cannot offer. Only a spontaneous, organic – in short, honest – change can work: the equivalent, as Koestler suggests, of a spontaneous change in human mentality. *This* is what is happening.

It is not happening in a vacuum. Strong "integrative" tendencies are everywhere evident, from the rise of what John Kenneth Galbraith calls technostructures to the emergence of first other-directed, then autonomous, social types in the large urban sinks, which have become the new evolutionary stages. A process which I have described in an earlier book as Large Scale Integration is at work – it is, in fact, the same process, a self-regulated revolution, which John Platt terms a self-structuring hierarchical jump.

Specific integrative tendencies have been identified in almost every field of human activity, from education to science to interpersonal relations. On a grand scale Teilhard de Chardin has attempted to encapsulate these tendencies. Something very much like his Noosphere of accumulating knowledge and consciousness would appear to be taking form, enveloping the planet. The town-planning has least been done and the downtown section of Mc-Luhan's Global Village constructed. More mystically, one might say that, in evolutionary terms, God is passing a break-boundary in terms of becoming aware of Himself. What we see happening before us, on a grand scale, is what Arthur Koestler has called the Integrative Tendency joined in a penulimate battle with the Self-Assertive Tendency, which until now has dominated the behavior of groups of human beings throughout the course of history.

Yet, even put together, these strong developments in the direction of higher, more integrated levels of human organization can do little more than temporarily restrain the persistent and deeper-rooted negative trends which threaten our extinction. Somehow, they must "come together," congeal, become focussed, if the overwhelming force of habit is to be overcome in time.

This book suggests that these integrative tendencies *have* begun to come into focus, that a new holistic consciousness – a higher order of human consciousness – has made its appearance. Many of the kids who are called, and call themselves, "freaks," are in reality *mental mutants*. They have mutated through an auto-evolutionary process triggered by technology, particularly television, and further stimulated by the use of psychedelic drugs. This new consciousness has, so far, gone through two distinct stages in its development, has entered its critical third stage, and the direction of the fourth stage is now evident.

In the last year, the emergence of this new consciousness has been celebrated by Charles A. Reich in *The Greening of America.* R.D. Laing has written, too, about what he calls the achievement of an "RUA" level of perspective. Alvin Toffler has written, in the negative, about the forces which are producing the change. Theodore Roszak has likewise written, from a purely academic vantage point, about the emergence of a counter culture, in which this new consciousness makes its most spectacular appearance. The new consciousness is not quite news, but this book offers a substantially different analysis from any of those just mentioned. My own experience with and in what Roszak calls the counter culture is too different from what he describes for me to accept his highly academic offering. His experiential qualifications are unimpressive, and his anti-technological bias determined almost everything he had to say. As a "picture" of the counter culture, his book, *The Making of a Counter Culture*, is almost surreal. What he did was to impose his own academic, highly literate viewpoint on the raw material of the young people who are part of the "counter culture." As an expression of the anti-technological position of the liberal academic community, his book is virtually a manifesto. As a study of the new consciousness, it makes no attempt to move off the university library turf. It is bounded by Roszak's own filter so tightly that almost nothing else gets into its pages. As a "guide to our times," as one reviewer termed it, the book offers little that could not have been said ten or even twenty years ago. Basically, it is a guide to another time, a time now passed. The subject matter – the new consciousness – provides only the loom on which a rather standard literary-artistic tapestry is woven.

Precisely what is missing is any comprehension of the new consciousness that extends beyond liberal academic expectations of it. Its biological or evolutionary meaning is not grasped at all. And the actual dimensions of the change being wrought seem, in Roszak's book, not even to be guessed at. As for strategies, the book offers nothing much more than a hope that somehow something will happen, thanks to these rather uneducated and hopelessly illiterate kids, that will beat up on the Machine, getting even for all the ways in which it has itself been beating up on the academics for so long.

Finally, the greatest weakness of the book lies in the fact that it is written from an American perspective and seldom gets beyond the border.

Even more misleading, in its way, is Charles Reich's attempt to write about the new consciousness in *The Greening of America.* He comes closer, far closer, than Roszak. Someone turned Reich on. His descriptions of what he calls the "higher, transcendant reason" of the new consciousness are at least accurate. He knows whereof he speaks. So thankful is Reich for being turned on that he spends most of his time lavishly praising his liberators, the students and heads who made it possible for him to perceive the emergence of the new consciousness, who "brought him in." But the substance of his book, finally, is his neo-Marxist analysis of the American Corporate State, or, as Roszak would have it, The

Technocracy. Beyond the interpretations and descriptions of being high, Reich begins to falter badly.

He chooses to break the different levels of awareness or consciousness in America down into Consciousness I, "the traditional outlook of the American farmer, small businessman, and worker who is trying to get ahead," Consciousness II, which "represents the values of an organized society," and Consciousness III, "the new generation," which has begun to develop "a new consciousness appropriate to today's realities and therefore capable of mastering the apparatus of power and bringing it under human control...."[8]

So far as Consciousness III is concerned, Reich makes sense. As for I and II, they are so highly arbitrary, political, and narrowly American that they only serve to confuse things and in fact to obscure the real nature of the new holistic consciousness by measuring it against false models. I and II are actually part of the same type of consciousness. Once they are extracted from the nationalistic confines in which Reich is developing his ideas, these "two levels" break down into a single level. Both represent, in the more general context of Western civilization and, more specifically, technological society, the same type of consciousness: that which Herbert Marcuse describes as being "operationalistic." To describe the new consciousness as Consciousness III is to accept Reich's definitions of Consciousness I and Consciousness II. And these may only be accepted if one allows that the new consciousness is a peculiarly American phenomenon. It is not. Reich makes the mistake of assuming that it is, or at least of letting his arguments develop *as though it were*.

Inevitably, his discussion swerves into the same dead end as Roszak's. It becomes a statement of the academic liberal's wishes about society. The last portion of *The Greening of America* amounts to a list of "shoulds." This *should* be done, that *should* be done, the kids *should* try this, people *should* do that, society *should* feel this way, government *should* act in such and such a manner.

"In a very real sense," he admits, "it is misleading to give a name to the new consciousness, such as Consciousness III." It is, but not precisely for the reasons he gives – that it is not static or fixed. It is misleading, more to the point, because the other two kinds of consciousness which he identifies as preceding it are not what he claims them to be. And, further, because the kind of labelling he does is no less misleading than the academic interpretation which Roszak brings to his examination of the counter culture. Both men are Americans, assume that the evolutionary change will be wrought in America, and that, in the end, the most important question in the world is whether America will succeed in transforming itself or not. They are, in their own way, super-patriots.

Viewed from outside America, the drama being acted out there can be seen as being critical and pivotal – but it is not the whole story, it is not the whole struggle, and while it would seem indeed to have begun unfolding in America, there is nothing to suggest that it will end there.

At the onset, I stated that this book evolved essentially around the "discovery" that a new form of human consciousness has come into being. (It is no discovery to the millions of mostly young people whose consciousness it is.) The "discovery," however, has so far been dealt with only from within the hurricane of the United States, where it is difficult to be cool about it or to look at it from any larger perspective. Missing so far has been any strategic appraisal that takes into consideration all the highly-industrialized nations (where the process is also at work). Also missing has been any serious consideration of what will happen if the American revolution in consciousness is successfully *blocked*.

Prime Minister Pierre Trudeau of Canada has warned that other nations – particularly Canada – must brace themselves for a tremendous shock wave if America does stumble into an open civil war. But nobody has given any warnings yet about the effects on other nations if the Second American Revolution does *not* come, or if it fails.

And so far, the essential nature of the new consciousness seems to have been missed. Without this basic understanding, no strategic analysis of the chances of success, the effects of failure, or even the conditions which are favorable or otherwise to the emergence of the new consciousness, is really possible. If the new consciousness is rejected or repressed in America, can it surface elsewhere? To date it has only caused disturbances *within* nations. At what point will it begin to affect international order? Where is the likeliest breakthrough point? That point is not necessarily situated in America, and one wonders where it is. Finally, there is a critical difference between the sort of revolution which the emergence of a new consciousness makes inevitable and the kind of revolution which has, in the past, been the only kind. To understand the revolution of the new consciousness strictly in the inherited revolutionary terms of the past is to make a fatal tactical error.

The new consciousness itself must be the initial subject of our search for some understanding of the nature of the changes taking place around us. Most attempts to do this have so far been too narrowly political, too myopically American. Mainly, they have been the expression of relatively fixed viewpoints *imposed* on the emerging consciousness, without getting underneath it into its organic nature. Once the essential nature of the change in consciousness is understood, we may proceed to consider some of the new political strategies which will have to be developed to bring its perspective to bear. And which *are* being developed by a whole new breed of revolutionaries, using tactics which have never been possible before, weapons which have never existed before. So truly revolutionary are these tactics and weapons that they are not even recognized for what they are. Moreover, it would appear that there is no defence against them. But, first, the *kind* of consciousness which is now assembling its arsenal, and some idea of how this consciousness came into existence. . . .

# TWO THE URBAN LAUNCH PAD

As with human behavior, social processes are infinitely more complex than most of us have been trained to admit. No single "cause" is ever adequate to explain a single effect. We may *say* the Russian Revolution was triggered by ... (pick a cause). The Reformation came about because ... (pick a reason). The first landing on the moon was achieved due to ... (pick a process, a man, an organization, even an interacting series of processes, legions of men, whole dynamic sets of organizational activities). None is the full story.

To attempt to list the "causes" of the change in human consciousness which is taking place in the pressure cookers of the industrial world is to move in the direction of a revised and updated History of Man. Such cannot be our purpose. Rather, we may follow the direction clearly indicated by science: toward simplification; toward simpler and more general explanations. When Newton worked out a formula ($F$ equals $ma$) which accurately predicted pendulums and projectiles, he swept all previous long-winded theories of motion into the ashcan. In terms of explanations of the dynamics of change, social or otherwise, such a simplification of theories was achieved in late 1970, when the American biophysicist John R. Platt synthesized the idea of "hierarchical growth." Borrowing heavily from the work of theoretical physicist David Bohm, Platt noted:

Sudden changes of structure are among the more startling features of living systems. Until recently, they have not been much looked at from the point of view of a general systems theory. Nevertheless, they may include such dramatic phenomena as falling in love, acts of creation, evolutionary jumps, social revolutions or reformations and, in general, the sudden formation of larger integrated systems from malfunctioning or conflicting subsystems . . . . The universe should not be regarded as made up of "things" but of a complex hierarchy of smaller and larger flow patterns in which the "things" are invariant or self-maintaining features of the flow . . . . Such flow systems can undergo sudden transitions to new self-maintaining arrangements which will in turn be stable for a long time. Bohm identifies the "quantum jump" of an electron, from one steady state of an atom to another steady state, as being a pattern-restructuring of this kind . . . . There is a similar restructuring, by growth, of a complex structure to larger hierarchical patterns with the passage of time, like the growth of large crystals from a mass of small ones under heat and pressure. The growth may not be uniform but by successive small steps as each crystal rearranges suddenly. Likewise in the biological world, a group of children – or a group of industrial organizations – brought together may rather suddenly develop leader-follower relationships and a defined pattern of roles throughout the group. In general, the growth picture is that of a hierarchical structure with stable pattern from the lowest levels (molecules, enzyme cycles, cells) up to the level $i$ (say, the organism), which grows to a new structure because it comes in touch with new and different materials or information or another organism. This can make the pattern unstable at level $i$ until there is a resolution (conflict, cooperation) with restructuring either by breaking apart or by a new organization at the $i$ plus $1$ level to make a new stable pattern encompassing the larger experience or the larger system. . . . The area of social evolution exhibits the most dramatic and large-scale restructurings of this kind that we know about, such as the sudden collective restructurings that occurred in the Reformation and in the Industrial Revolution. These changes go deeper than ordinary political revolutions because they are not simply an exchange of power from one group to another, but a thoroughgoing change in philosophy, personal attitudes and ways of work and economic organization in every part of society . . . . The largest of all these changes, in its speed and scale and its long-range evolutionary implications, is the world transformation through which all humanity is now passing . . . . It is no distortion to speak of this world reorganization of all our patterns as a "quantum jump," or as a sudden collective change of awareness or flash of understanding for the human race.

Platt notes that such hierarchical jumps have at least five common characteristics:

*Cognitive dissonance.* Bits of data are accumulated which do not fit the old patterns, assumptions or predictions. At first these new observations or discoveries are dismissed. But they persist and accumulate. Finally, a confrontation comes with the old system. It is recognized as being fundamental. A simplification from some entirely different point of view suddenly snaps big parts of the problem into a new, clearer picture. Cognitive dissonance is a precondition for any kind of personal growth – doubts must appear, anxiety, even a desperate thrashing-around as the individual attempts to avoid the restructuring which is taking place, transforming him. Similarly, social dissonance takes place as a transformation begins in a culture or nation. Such dissonance is everywhere evident today.

*Overall character of the dissonance.* Although, initially, the doubts and new bits of data may crop up in one area or field of activity, similar difficulties soon make their appearance in other areas. Eventually they are recognized as being fundamentally the same, not uniquely the "special" problem of a given area as they were orginally considered to be.

*Suddenness of the restructuring when it comes.* Platt explains: "The reason for the speed is that the change is prepared everywhere at once. Even though individual elements of reform seem weak, when they reach a certain critical density and begin to join forces, the old order finds itself overwhelmed from without and betrayed from within, from directions it never guessed. The new self-maintaining patterns, like new vortex patterns, are self-reinforcing to each other as soon as they touch, because they can form the beginnings of a better-integrated system with a speed of understanding and communications and economics that the old malfunctioning system cannot match."

*Simplification.* Older, complex patterns of behavior or awareness are snapped into a new focus, rendered more easily accessible. These represent permanent steps forward.

*Interactions jumping across the system level between the old subsystems and the new super-system that is in the process of being formed.* Dissonance or conflict between the malfunctioning subsystems cannot be resolved by changes that take place only at their level of operation. A buildup of one of the conflicting subsystems leads only to a counter-balancing by another sub-system. Thus, workers in an office cannot solve a problem which is caused by their boss unless they go over his head. The changes must be effected at a higher level of organization. In disarmament talks, "peace talks," and such, we see precisely this process at work. A successful transformation may only be achieved by "going over the bosses' heads." A jump from the national "system level" to an international "super-system level" needs to be affected.

The new consciousness may, therefore, be understood simply as the result of a self-structuring hierarchical leap, coming spontaneously at a time when tremendous pressure is being exerted for the adoption of new survival strategies. *The least of this pressure will be political.* At its source, the pressure can be seen clearly to be nothing less than biological. We are speaking of an evolutionary change, a change which will affect all history from here on. While we may understand the mechanism or process by applying the useful concept provided by Platt and Bohm, nothing has been suggested yet to explain what *activates* this mechanism. It is the force behind the re-structuring which is taking place to which we must finally address ourselves – and will, in the concluding chapters of this book.

Rather than attempting this just yet, let us try to make the concept of hierarchical growth itself a bit more "real." It is an over-all process, a synergistic effect. It will manifest itself in many different ways, reacting directly to many different pressures. All will be "part" of the over-all process. Within the general process of this kind of growth, some forces will be working directly and with considerable effect, while others can be seen to be nibbling at the edges of the situation, rather than emerging as major forces in the creation of the new consciousness.

To illustrate, let us consider just one fairly central factor in the over-all equation of change: the increased density of the urban environment.

It has been estimated that the average urban dweller comes into contact with more people in a single week than the average feudal villager did in a lifetime. While this is generally viewed as being a bad thing, little has been said about what a liberating experience it can be.

Formerly, individuals were locked at an early age into a fixed set of relationships, beginning with immediate members of their family. Expectations were built up about the individual by these others and much of his behavior consequently was directed to-ward fulfilling these expectations. In order to be accepted, approved of, and rewarded with recognition, the individual had no choice but to remain carefully within the narrow boundaries of the role thus assigned to him. The ancient – and not so ancient – world was composed of such nuclear groups. Individuals easily won recognition, and approval, on such simple grounds as family name, tribal connections, and the sharing of common experiences, territory, customs, and prejudices. One had to "do" nothing but live up to the expectations of one's nuclear group. Banishment or exile awaited the cousin or son or daughter who deviated. In a tightly-locked world of nuclear relationships such an exile could be a terrible punishment.

One of the great positive effects of urbanization is to reverse that situation radically. Now one may change, refuse to live up to a certain set of expectations, reject the ground rules of one's clan or church or whatever, and "move on." The diversity of an urban environment guarantees that all but the most weirdly eccentric will be able, sooner or later, to find a new group of peers.

On a grand scale, this process became visible in 1967, when hundreds of thousands of American kids found that they could escape the expectations of their families and communities, try on an entirely different life-style – and yet be spared the pangs of exile. Places like Haight-Ashbury awaited them. And when they tired of The Haight, or outgrew it, or became disillusioned, there were other subcultures, other worlds, into which they could attach themselves. Individual growth was no longer inhibited by fear of aloneness. The brake had been removed. One could outgrow family, friends, community, and still find another "family," another set of friends, another community, and even then not have to worry – because these, too, could be outgrown. Thus, growth became possible on a gigantic scale. Unending growth. People might meet, hook up, and become friends or lovers at various stages in their own personal development, but they connected only if their growth trajectories happened to be parallel. Once these ceased to mesh, at the next stage the individual could be certain of finding other individuals on whose "wavelength" he happened to be.

It has been remarked that technology removed the limits on the growth of cities. But a more critical effect by far has been the removal of limits on personal growth. A man who knew he was going to be living in the same village for the rest of his life dared not "change," because the village would not change, he could be certain – and the result of his changing would mean only that he would become an outcast. In the modern megapolis, there are few real outcasts.

We may measure the swiftness with which this change has come about by a simple reference: most young adults today remember their parents as being each "one person." Mom had the same personality, the same tastes, throughout the entire time that her children were growing up. Her image is fixed. As a rule, the same applies to the modern young adult's recollection of his or her father. Now, however, psychologists are beginning to fret about the stresses placed on the tots of today who must deal with "escalating parents," parents whose personalities keep changing, who are growing, expanding their consciousness, changing location, rearranging their patterns of friendship on the basis of whatever "wavelength" they have achieved. The psychologists need not worry unduly. The tots of today will be so free of the restraints which were formerly exercised against individual growth that, even by the wildest psychedelic standards of today, they will be out of sight.

We see here, in this single example, evidence of hierarchical growth. In relation to high population density (which is not anchored to any unchanging technology, as was the case in the past) a structural change takes place in the attitudes of people toward each other. Relationships may be entered into and dissolved with ease. Less is "expected" of such relationships, but then less is demanded in turn of the individual. He need not freeze his development at any one stage or level. He need not avoid risking a personality change. He need not fear "trying on" a new life-style. He need not avoid situations or experiences which might set him apart from his friends of the moment.

The family is "breaking down" in the industrialized nations only because, at the moment, the family demands that every member maintain his position in relation to all the other members, that no structural changes take place. Mainly, parents impose their own expectations on their children and feel, when the children reject these expectations, that something is amiss, that the relationship has gone on the rocks. It need not. All the parents need do is release the hammerlock they have automatically applied on their children's personalities and behavior. The children are going to break it anyway. The hierarchical growth which has taken place is self-structuring in the sense that the children, having adapted to the radically different real life situation which they experience beyond the home, are incapable of resisting their own tendency to grow. Growth, after all, is a biological imperative. In the past, psychic, emotional and even spiritual growth was repressed. The ground, in effect, was barren. It has now, thanks to urbanization, become rich and fertile. With the limits removed, young people spontaneously relax: they are not afraid of going through changes, or trying new experiences; they have no built-in inhibitions against personal transformation. The new self they may accidentally or otherwise acquire is not likely to find itself alone. And as a "youth culture" takes shape, it exerts a tremendous gravitational drag. It becomes a new social moon dragging youngsters in tides away from the beach on which they were born. It is a vortex. Not only need they *not fear* change – because the possibility of exile has been eliminated – they know in advance that whole new cultural worlds, new families, new brothers and sisters, are out there waiting. The pressures which in the past tended to work against the individual who wanted to move out from under the heap of his immediate family, friends, and community, are now working in the opposite direction.

This is one factor in the structural change. It exhibits all the characteristics which have been attributed to self-structuring hierarchical growth, from cognitive dissonance (the quarrels that develop between parents and restless children), the suddenness of the restructuring (one morning, like the girl in The Beatle's song, "She's Leaving Home," the kid is gone), right through to the interactions jumping across the system level (the kid effects the change by finding a way of integrating himself into a larger system, namely the "community" of all the other kids he will come into contact with as he pursues the experience of his own unrestricted growth). There are many such examples to which we could point.

However, it should be sufficient to concentrate on what is perhaps the single biggest factor in the triggering of this spontaneous change in consciousness which has taken place. We must look for a common denominator, some radical change which has affected everyone, something so pervasive that its effects have penetrated society from top to bottom. This will be the prime factor in the change. Without doubt, that factor is the mass media. We may, at this point, extend our discussion beyond the outline suggested by the theory of self-structuring hierarchical growth. For, within the context of this general process, many other processes are at work. These are sub-systems in the over-all system of transformation. Their effects, while being integral parts of the whole, are much more specific and measureable. They may also take, as we shall see, some unexpected turns. New balances are being struck. Adjustments are being made. Disequilibriums are being compensated for.

# THREE WHO PUT ALL THOSE LIGHTS IN YOUR HEAD?

The mass media have done something to the minds of all of us, yet much of the analysis of recent times has tended to obscure it. Our experience of "the world" and "world events" is one dimension removed from reality, not only because we experience the world and its convulsions through the filter of the media, but because decades of exposure to newspapers, movies, radio and television have blurred the distinctions between the real and unreal. Mass media have created another level of experience, halfway between the real world of direct perception and the nonexistent world of fantasy. So pervasive has been the influence of mass media that this "halfway" world has come to be accepted as real. It is in relation to this half-real world that we measure ourselves, define our positions, take our cues for response. Yet it is a world *which does not exist*, except, by now, in the *minds* of the millions who are plugged into the mass communications web.

The mass media are milked at every turn, and have become a waste basket containing little more than fantasy and abstraction. Virtually no one is ever quoted in a newspaper who is not peddling something: a viewpoint, a product, an idea, a party, a platform, a prejudice, a dream, a nightmare. Unless one has something to offer (to sell, in fact) there is simply no point in being quoted. By default, the pages of the newspapers have fallen into the hands of manipulators. No one becomes "newsworthy" who is not attempting to manipulate. The more successful he is in his manipulations the more "newsworthy" he becomes. The news page is an arena in which wills are constantly struggling with each other for control of public opinion.

Very little "pure" information moves through the pages of newspapers. Some does: results of a census, a poll, the bare bones of some scientific theory or other, a new recipe, instructions for tending a garden. Accidents, disasters, crimes will continue to be reported. Everything else, however, everything that is of political or social importance, is invariably propelled into print on the basis of the intent to manipulate. Whether the cause is "good' or "bad" is quite beside the point.

Television and radio, it goes without saying, contain virtually no pure information. Statistics, tables, lists, and such do not lend themselves to these media, and so their presentation of "news" has come to be concentrated to an even greater degree on those areas in which the objective is manipulation.

At the heart of the mass communications process today stands not the teletype, the printing press, or the cathode tube, but the public relations firm. Everyone who "uses" the media has some ulterior motive. No one comes before the camera or microphone to express anything but a position intended to have an effect. Unless one wants to achieve an effect, there is simply no point in exposing oneself to the public. The media, in short, are understood to be machines, instruments for injecting ideas into the minds of other men. Thus, no matter how "objective" a given newspaper is, its contents are all colored. The "news" itself is not objective, for the newsmakers themselves are manipulators. Politicians, governments, industries: all offer "information" which is geared to meet their own individual aims, none other. And to the extent that the "information" is tailored, preselected, biased, rearranged to fit into one context or another, it reflects no reality. Almost entirely, we are confronted with lies and distortions.

It is the biggest open secret of our time that every manipulator, whether a salesman, a politician, or a "spokesman," will have at least two opinions – one for public consumption, the other private. It is the "public" opinion – the lie or, at best, the distortion – which gets aired in the mass media. The off-the-cuff stuff never reaches the newspage or the airwaves. That is, the *truth*. The public arena is dominated entirely by lies, distortions, and fantasies. It is, not partially but *in essence*, an unreal world.

Looking more closely, we see that there is a symbiotic relationship between the news media and the entertainment media. The problem is not just that the news media are unable to deliver the real world into our homes and heads, but that the entertainment media have made us less *interested* in the real world.

We have, all of us, lived amazing lives. We "remember" a thousand action-packed adventures, a thousand dramatic confrontations, a thousand heart-wrenching moments: those we witnessed on the screen. These were emotional experiences. We tensed as the hero walked into the ambush. We froze in horror as the monster slithered around the corner. We wept when the heroine died. Certainly, we were only sitting on our asses – but, to the degree that these movie or television (or at an earlier stage, radio) productions were well staged and well directed, we had an emotional response. Those emotional responses were real. Chemically, we reacted. Some part of our psyche was affected, and while all the deaths, horrors, battles, kisses, and sorrows were false, our response was, in some degree, genuine. It made an impossible-to-measure but nevertheless real psychic impression. Our memory banks gradually began to fill up with false memories, memories of experiences we never had, but which, because we had vicariously experienced them, nevertheless left tiny claw-marks in our minds, miniscule tears in the tissue of our patterns of response. Heroes left their footprints on our brains. No one has yet measured the extent to which our behavior patterns are shaped by sets of emotional responses, but certainly it will be acknowledged that our responses will be based on our experiences, or on the types of stimulation to which we have been exposed. Those of us who have been living at least a portion of our lives in front of a movie or television screen will have had our emotions so frequently stimulated by unreal (vicarious) experience that we will have acquired the habit of responding to the unreal as though it were real. Moreover, the unreal experiences to which we have been exposed were calculated to stimulate us. Thus, the "reality" presented on a screen is always sharply etched. In real life, we might not immediately recognize a threat – but on the screen the threat will be accentuated to the point where it is impossible to miss it. Every situation presented on the screen is similarly high-lighted. Makeup has been added at every point. All the emotional features have been underlined.

A schism now opens in the back regions of the mind wherein

memories are contained. I am not referring so much to visual
memories, which can be sorted out fairy easily. (After all, we will
know whether we have been to the Sahara Desert or Mount Ever-
est or not.) I mean the emotional memories, those flickers to
which we cannot necessarily attach a picture or even a sound, and
which function to establish patterns of response, patterns which
will form the nucleus of larger, more generalized behavioral patterns. Or which may, at least, come into conflict with those patterns of response based on *real* experience. Either way, we are
substantially interfered with in the process of responding emotionally to any given situation. This interference ("emotional static") is reinforced by a corresponding conditioning of the mind to
accept unreal situations. Presented with the choice between an
easy, high-lighted, exciting "reality" and another – less well-produced, lacking even the essential ingredient of a plot – most of us
have opted, without realizing it, for the glossy package. Unlike all
those generations who lived before the onslaught of the mass
entertainment media, we have a "choice." And we are *conditioned*
to react to slick, simplistic realities. We may, under stress, retreat
into just such a reality by ducking into a theater or flicking on the
TV. Our ability to distinguish between the real and the unreal
gradually disintegrates. Our memories are not intact as they were
in other eras; we do not remember only those events we actually
witnessed or were a part of, we do not remember only those
individuals we actually met, we do not remember only those an-
guishes and ecstasies which were truly ours – rather, those memories (which in earlier times were the *only* memories) are now mixed
up at random with all the "false" memories (and their corresponding emotional reverberations). As the memories recede into
the background, both the memories of real events and the memories of unreal events, they necessarily blur. The distinctions become less and less clear.

We are, as a result, that much more vulnerable to the tailoring
of news. We have grown accustomed to staged realities, to acted
behavior. We are, in these fundamental ways, less accustomed to
distinguishing between the fake and the authentic. There are so
many actors lodged in our memories that we have come, in some
part of us, to accept the actor as being the person he portrays. The
fact that a man is acting in real life will not "jar" us simply
because we will be familiar, and comfortable, with a person who
acts. The well-directed politician will be that much more "real" to

us. The easy reality presented by the press release will not automatically stink, because, after all, we have swallowed many easy realities and a groove has been worn in our minds along which packaged reality may pass without causing us to automatically spit it out. We are used to the *point* of every confrontation being made evident to us. We are used to having our realities underlined for us, situations being spelled out. We have grown somewhat passive. The news media fortify this ever-increasing passivity by attempting to do the same, and by presenting the viewpoints of only those people who are attempting in one way or another to high-light or underline some facet of experience. Forced to work less for an understanding, the muscles of our minds grow soft. A "false consciousness" comes into existence, dwelling in the by-now almost completely unreal world of the mass news media, feeding on the even less real world of mass entertainment media, and reacting – in real terms – on the basis of false information.

Technological man as a result is becoming, in essence, not more intelligent, but more stupid; less able to distinguish between real and unreal; more and more susceptible to manipulation.

As the mass media become more pervasive, our experience of life becomes more cluttered with second-hand information. Lives which, before the onslaught of the mass media, were experienced entirely in the real world are now increasingly saturated with vicarious experience. Technological man is presented with so much packaged experience that he has acquired a taste for it. When experience does present itself directly he tends strongly to "package" it himself, to make it more digestible. He has grown accustomed to the "fat" being skimmed off. There is so much competition for his attention that the competitors have learned to peel away the "excess information," to present him with a sharply-defined "reality." Anything less, they know, will be ignored or, rather, lost in the shuffle. The real world *out there* is a world of fragments, headlines (which at most are boldface lumps broken off from the whole), information bits, data points, slogans, flashes, tatters of thought and shrapnel from the exploded grenades of ideas (*always* taken out of context).

Literally, technological man has been injected with so much distilled "reality" he has become addicted to it; he goes about his business in a world of fantasy, doped into believing that the events he perceives through the mass media are real. In fact, they are not.

To the degree that they are well high-lighted, dramatic, well-produced, crisp, tight and "factual," they have been fashioned by the *consciousness of theater*, which is different not only in degree but in kind from the consciousness of reality. The world is a stage for technological man as it was for no other man in no other time. The consciousness of theater lies at the center of all world events: the politician is conscious of himself as an actor, industry is geared to the production of marketable fantasies, the individual is conscious of himself as a costumed character. Image, public relations, appearance, salesmanship, presentation, pitch – here is the substance of the reality of technological society.

Contrary to much opinion, there is nothing irrational about this world of simplified realities which has come to dominate so much of our consciousness. Not *despite* but *in accordance with* the imperatives of rationality has it come into existence. What is involved from the international to the interpersonal level is manipulation. Manipulation always serves a function. Few worlds are more functional than the world of theater. Every word, every gesture, every action is designed to produce an effect. No actor steps on stage to experience himself or to arrive at any conclusions: he is there to take part in a performance. The cultural magnetism exerted by superstars can be traced to the degree to which we have all been affected by the consciousness of theater, the result in large part of our having acquired complex sets of false memories. We have become self-conscious as no other people in history were. There is always a camera at least potentially lurking in the background. At any moment we may be called upon to set forth our views. We will be measured according to our ability to turn in a great performance.

Much of this has been understood as alienation, yet what it really represents is the transplantation of the heart of technological rationality into the breast of modern man, the unconscious adoption of what has been called the "operationalistic mode of consciousness." Before we can continue, it will be necessary to review briefly what is known about this mode of consciousness.

The mainspring of the technological or industrial society is technique. Technique is the totality of methods rationally arrived at and having absolute efficiency (for a given stage of development) in every field of human activity. Its characteristics are new – the technique of the present has no common measure with that of the past. Technique spreads across the planet through a process of self-augmentation; that is, anonymous research advances in different fields pile up, overlap with advances in other fields, converge, produce new interdisciplinary advances, which in turn overlap again and give birth to new hybrids, and so on. . . .[10]

Herbert Marcuse notes that the very rationality of technique subverts Reason. He means Reason in the classical Greek sense, which was later watered down to the word "intuition." Marcuse argues that our rational technological society draws its power essentially from the *concept of length*. This produces the "operational" point of view, known as operationalism in the physical sciences and behavioralism in the social sciences. For the physicist, all that is required in order for him to function effectively, is that he know the length of any and every object. The concept of length, for the physicist, means that everything can be measured and related to a set of operations or functions. His sense of what is going on in the universe is thereby restricted to that which can be measured. Anything else is unreal, by which is meant: unmeasureable. Having chosen to limit his awareness to only those things which can be measured, the physicist has effectively divorced himself from any generalized awareness of larger processes which cannot as yet be brought into the framework provided by the concept of length. Similarly, in the social sciences, we see that behavior or aptitudes which cannot be related to a set of measureable operations are unreal or irrational. The behaviorist reduces his concept of man in exactly the way that a physicist reduces his concept of nature, to a kind of quantifiable object – at best, an *object d'art*, at worst, a bio-electronic perpetual motion machine.

The operational mode does away with any dialectic, any conflict between our sense of what is real and what is unreal, true or false, good or evil. Once one has adopted the operational mode of thinking, there is no dichotomy. Simply, what can be measured and related to a set of operations is *real*, and what is left over – anything which cannot be canned and analyzed – is *unreal*. Within the context of the operational mode there is no room for dialectical thinking, or, as the ancient Greeks would have it, Reason. The effect of the operational mode is to reduce our awareness of the world around us by increasing our awareness of details, thus literally not letting us see the forest for the trees.

Adoption of the operational mode has far-reaching effects on our habits of thought. We no longer allow ourselves to use as tools in our thinking any concepts which cannot be hitched to a measurement and a set of operations. For instance, religion (or metaphysics or spirituality or ethics or empathy) is relegated to a niche in our hierarchy of technological operational values about roughly equivalent to that of a variety show. And certainly, "awareness" – that is, awareness other than operational awareness – has about as much positive value in the technological scheme of things as diarrhoea.

Marcuse notes that we live in a rationally totalitarian society. "The scientific method which led to ever-more-effective domination of nature thus came to provide the pure concepts as well as the instrumentalities for the ever-more-effective domination of man by man *through* the domination of nature."[11] *Technically*, autonomy is impossible and determining one's own life is likewise an impossibility. This amounts to loss of freedom which "appears neither as irrational nor as political, but rather as a submission to the technical apparatus which enlarges the comforts of life and increases the productivity of labor."[12] The rationality of pure science is value-free and is described as being neutral, but this neutrality has a positive character – it can be bent to practically any end.

Long before the Industrial Revolution, even before alienation made its large-scale debut at about the end of the Middle Ages, and before the word "adjustment" slipped into common usage, societies were held together by a process known as *mimesis*. That is, an immediate identification of the individual with his society, an immediate *automatic* identification. In highly industrialized societies this process of mimesis reappears. But the difference today is that mimesis is largely the product of a sophisticated scientific management and organization. Public relations aims ideally at mimesis, and works *against* introjection – which suggests the existence of an inner dimension which is distinguished from and often antagonistic to the external "reality." The idea of inner freedom or autonomy designates a private space – the space inside our heads – where we may remain ourselves. Technology invades this private space, replacing opinion with public opinion, introjection with mimesis. Technological society is total – it saturates us with packaged opinions and attitudes. No matter how determinedly "autonomous" we may try to remain, the fact is that much of it filters through even our strongest defences, and we find ourselves – – quite unconsciously – adopting mental stances and attitudes which are not very distinguishable from public stances and attitudes.

Now we may see the extent to which we have all been affected. We accept the world of preselected fragments of reality as being real because this is an easier world to deal with than the one which we experience directly, which is not so brilliantly produced. We tend in our behavior and responses to react to the unreal world because it is easier to extract meaning from it – simply because the meaning has been underlined for us not only by the people who package it but by the people who have taken part in it and who are attempting, by virtue of their ability as actors, to hold our attention, to convince us of something, to sway our opinion, to convert us to some cause or other. It makes no fundamental difference whether the "cause" is the purchase of a new car or the adoption of a new political viewpoint. Techniques are being applied. And these techniques, which dominate the whole pervasive universe of public opinion and world events (the universe *out there*), are in essence no different from the techniques which have become the mainsprings of industrial excellence. As the universe *out there* increasingly takes up room *in here* (in the private space inside my head and yours) its imperatives come to dominate our consciousness. These imperatives are derived from the concept of length to the extent that they serve a function, that they are "rational," that they are related to a set of operations (which may be a political campaign, a sales pitch, any sort of a cause). Propaganda is pure operationalism, no less so than entertainment. The success of either is readily measured at the polling booth or the box office, and it is first and foremost with an eye to success that their creators direct their attention. The reality they concern themselves with is strictly defined in accordance to what can be measured, what set of operations is involved, and how the aims to which these operations are related may be served most efficiently.

Here we have the psychic world of mass technological society – a world where what is "real" is what can be measured, and where what cannot be measured is trimmed away, treated as though it did not exist; where the logic of domination which serves so well to make machines function has penetrated the sphere of human relations almost totally. Technological man conceives of his behavior as a form of mechanical stress which needs to be applied. He understands that he has a role to play. Yet a role is a function, not an identity. The extent to which we conceive of ourselves as having roles (rather than being) is the measure of the degree to which the operational mode of consciousness has taken hold, passing from the purely technical sphere into our own individual consciousness through the "conductor" of the mass media (themselves shaped by the operational mode). It is a trap whose dimensions are practically bottomless. Consciously, there is probably no way of avoiding being contained in it. The trap has closed. It grows more elaborate every year. The harder we struggle to get back in touch with reality, the more desperately we thrash around in search of the "rational" (which we cannot help, at this stage, but equate with "reality"), the deeper we sink into quicksand. It would seem to be a hopeless situation.

# FOUR CHECKING THE BULLSHITTERS' QUEEN

But what we have been examining so far is only a *primary effect*. It is an effect which has been felt, not surprisingly, in America as nowhere else. It was the first psychic shock wave of modern technology.

Coming rapidly into focus now is a secondary effect. The essential human problem posed by technology (in terms of perception and awareness) was how to cope with false, escapist consciousness (conditioned acceptance of "staged" realities). As this consciousness grew more sophisticated, it became less detectible, until it finally reached the point where the lines between the commercials and the newscasts dissolved. All news had become, at its root, a commercial. All politicians and public personalities had become actors and actresses. The decisive properties of any debate had become, not their content, but their presentation. All demonstrations were staged.

The highest compliment which might be paid an individual was to call him "real." Those states which are hardest to attain are those we most value. However, "realness" too could be faked. Much energy went into its manufacture. In terms of operational logic, it was not a contradiction to speak of "projecting a *real* image." The object was still manipulation.

The *secondary* effect, which we must look at closely if we are to understand what is now happening in technological society, involves a greatly heightened ability to distinguish between real and unreal, between the genuine article and the fake. It is mainly the young, and particularly the very young, who have acquired this ability. The older individuals in mass society, for the most part, are still snagged by the primary effect of technology upon their perceptions and modes of awareness. That is, they have been drugged by the mass media and are still wandering around in a stupor, unable to distinguish clearly between reality and unreality. And if they are unable to tell the difference between an acted-out response and a genuine response, between calculated behavior and spontaneous behavior, between a staged situation and one which has not been designed with a view to achieving an effect, it is only because they have lost the capacity to make such distinctions in terms of their *own* behavior.

It will be assumed that if the older members of mass society have had their perceptions interfered with by technology, the young will be even more thoroughly affected. They will be that much less capable of making critical distinctions.

Nothing could be further from the truth. Technology makes its greatest impact where familiarity with it is least highly-developed. It is the innocent mind which is most vulnerable to its effects. The evolution of the modern communications web has been rapid, so rapid that few of our citizens have had time to make an adjustment to it. Most of them had finished learning how to react to society before it had become a *mass* society. Their minds were shaped at a time when incoming information was still mostly "pure." That is, they got their information directly, through immediate perception. Something happened – they witnessed it, reacted to it, incorporated it into their memory, and worked out a pattern of response based on that tucked-away information. It wasn't until after the Second World War that television made its large-scale debut, and the consciousness of theater really began to dominate the selection of information for mass consumption, with the result that people who had information to offer (viewpoints, products, or ideas to sell) began to tailor the presentation of themselves and their information.

The individual whose sense of reality had been shaped before the onslaught of orchestrated, choreographed, scripted, made-up and acted-out "reality" was simply not prepared to cope with this kind of manipulation. Accustomed to believing what he was seeing, hearing what was being said, he had no built-in defences against the producers and managers. Appearances had always been deceptive, but never so deceptive *in essence* as they were to become once an actual stage had been moved into every living room and everyone who wished to communicate through the medium of that stage had learned that appearance was everything in the new world of mass communications. The individual whose perceptions were shaped before mass communications had spread itself over the whole face of society *automatically* accepted the information passed on to him by his eyes and his ears. Accustomed as he was to direct experience, no sorting mechanism existed in his mind to distinguish between "real" information and "unreal" (or second-hand, distorted) information. So far as the automatic processes of his mind were concerned, all the information was real. He did not recognize that the information reaching him through the mass media had passed through a filter and that it had been engineered to have an effect on him. Neither did he automatically realize that his memories (those which might be the sparks igniting emotional responses) were in part false, that is, based upon vicarious experiences. Many, it is true, would be intellectually aware that something of this nature was happening, and so they could construct intellectual defences against it, but that meant they had to be consciously on guard. Their "guard" was frequently down. They could not keep it up all the time; much got through, working upon their minds whether they liked it or not.

Of course, public relations had not come into existence purely as a response to television. The bullshitters have always been with us. However, until the arrival of mass media – and particularly television – the bullshitter's chance of fooling anyone had remained about constant: he had to *appear* in front of people in order to manipulate them. Once mass media was a fact, he no longer had to do that. The power to manipulate took a quantum leap, comparable to the invention of the guided missile. Just as men could now kill from a distance so great they could not even see their target, so, thanks to mass media, could they bullshit from a tremendous distance. The power to affect minds had moved up into the megaton range. So long as the would-be manipulator had to appear in front of his intended victims, they could at least experience him whole. That is, they had a chance to react to him intuitively, calling into play a vast reservoir of sensory and psychic equipment. The media screened all this non-verbal information out. And once the manipulator had learned the tricks of projecting himself (or rather, his image), his power was magnified, *while there was no corresponding magnification of the mental and emotional defences against him.*

All of us give off what are now called "vibrations." Our vibrations are a synergistic effect – something more than the sum of our spoken language, facial expressions, intonation, gestures, posture, smell, and the rhythm which regulates the interactions between all these signals, plus something less easily grasped: almost an electrical field, a heaviness or buoyancy, an impression which bypasses our cognitive processes and finds its way into the deeper layers of our consciousness. This psychic "scent," or sixth sense, is vastly underrated in our literate, mechanical culture. Since, unlike the functioning of the eye or ear or nose, it does not lend itself to easy measurement and is not readily related to a set of apparent operations, it has tended to be dismissed as being "unreal." (The logic of operationalism at work.) The concept of synergy, after all, has until recently been little understood in the West. It refers to the behavior of a whole system unpredicted by the behavior of any of the separate parts of that system. That is, we may add up the functions of the five senses and still not be able to account for the behavior of the whole being, simply because the *interaction* of those five senses produces a reaction which is more than the sum.

Through the mass media an *image* may pass, but not a whole person. The power of the image increases as the definition drops. The more that is left out of the whole person, the greater the magnification of what remains. So, while we might react to a part, we could not react to the whole. The importance of that *part* was magnified all out of proportion for the simple reason that we were forced to take it as being representative of the whole. Having seen the face of a politician or salesman, having heard his voice, we then had to arrive at an emotional judgement on the basis of virtually no more information. It was as though we had been presented with a picture of his toenail and were being forced to judge his ability to play billiards. Further, all manipulators had learned to control their images. While few – if any – were capable of controlling the synergistic effect of the workings of their whole being, almost all could control the few facets which were all that passed through the media. As for those of us on the receiving end, our basic defence against manipulation had always been our power to react to a whole person. It was not the power of reason at work, it was the simple power to "pick up vibrations," that is, to experience another person directly, totally. Little of this experience translated itself into sequential logic. Or at least the "logic" we used to explain our reactions was almost invariably a rationalization of what was, in fact, a deeper, surer knowledge. We could get the "feel" of a person, a hunch, a reaction. Our intuitive faculties were at work. They could, by and large, be trusted. What mass media really did was banish these intuitions from the communications process. Our intuitive ability to determine the degree to which we were being conned was lost to us, since we were unable to get the whole story, only a scripted "chapter" of it. (A man's face, say, or his voice.) What we call, for lack of a better phrase, our sixth sense, had been thrown right out of the game. It was as though our queen had been taken off the board and our opponent had been given two queens to use against us. Add to this the fact that we had all been exposed to decades of cinema and radio, that we had acquired not only false memories, but false *models of behavior.* Not only were we always, in a part of our heads, "remembering" the highlighted dramatic scenes from one favorite movie or another, thus coming to be more comfortable amid well-staged "realities" as opposed to dreary rambling ones, feeling literally more "at home" when the lighting was right, the parts well-acted, the script well-written, but also we were increasingly susceptible to the "personality" which came closest to being a composite of all the Humphrey Bogarts, Errol Flynns, and Cary Grants we had ever known and admired. Style was now a bigger factor in the equation of communication than ever before, yet style was the least substantial factor of all. It was, of course, perfectly in harmony with images.

But what is happening now?

Let us not underestimate the adaptability of human beings. The pre-war generation was the first to be confronted by modern mass media. The rules of the game of communication had been changed almost overnight. Suddenly the odds were all in favor of the "house," the decks were all stacked; the pre-war generation, unaware of the new rules of the game, found itself losing consistently and there was not much that could be done about it.

The *post*-war generation, however, grew up in a different environment. Mass media were already an established fact. Margaret Mead has observed that young people who were born after the Second World War are natives in the modern world and older people are the "foreigners." Like foreigners, they are being bilked of every psychological penny, being played for perceptual suckers at every turn. If the older generation is more or less incapable of resisting the subtle intrusions of mass society into their minds it is only because they were trained in modes of perception which did not allow for the differentiation between "pure" and "filtered" sensory information, which did not autolmically sift through memories, shuffling the false ones to one side and the real to the other.

The young have acquired a whole new set of perceptual responses. They have learned to differentiate, to sift, to distinguish the real from the unreal, the genuine from the phony. Little if any of this is conscious. These are automatic responses. Just as the previous generation had to learn a new set of automatic reactions in order to be able to cope with the automobile (and *did* learn those reactions, easily), so this generation has learned a new set of reactions with which to cope with mass media and, in a broader sense, with mass society. What is involved is a quantum leap in perceptions, comparable to the leap in the ability to manipulate engineered by mass media. The ability to cope with manipulation has risen in a steep curve to the point where it has not only caught up with the power of the media to distort, it has passed beyond and is now far ahead.

The odds are no longer in favor of the house. A new generation of players has arrived which *allows* (without even having to think about it) for the odds, and which plays so incredibly well that it is the house which is in trouble.

At every new high-tide mark in our history and evolution it is assumed that human beings have exhausted their capacity to adapt and grow. Thus most technology is understood to be working upon passive creatures, shaping them as though they were clay. Yet, biologically, it has been shown that a process of homeostatis is at work in every animal. Each has an internal equilibrium; each seeks to maintain its balance. The evolution of the human animal has, since the acquisition of the larger brain, been increasingly concentrated on his mind. While man must still achieve a physical balance in relationship to his environment, more essentially he needs to achieve a *psychic* balance, to work out an equilibrium which is a dimension removed from purely physical harmonies. The impact of mass media was equivalent, in evolutionary terms, to the onset of the Ice Age, which disrupted all established physical relationships in the affected hemispheres, broke up ecological harmonies and patterns, forced mass migration, wiped out certain species, and drove others, in the battle for survival, to adopt whole new strategies, tactics, stances, modes of habitation. Mass society has worked no less catastrophically upon the human species, except that now the disaster is visited upon the hemispheres of our brain, and it is our established psychic patterns and harmonies which have been smashed. The primary effect of technology is upon the ability to distinguish between real and unreal in terms of human relations, and the secondary effect is the adaptation to the new environment. In retrospect, we may see that the "disaster" was a good thing: it forced the adoption of new modes of consciousness which were superior, certainly better suited to the new environment, with a much higher survival value. We have been forced to move, not slowly, as we would otherwise, but rapidly ahead. Rapid adaptation, it goes without saying, is a disruptive, bloody, agonizing business. Many, if not most, are bound to be hurt. And, finally, a whole species – that species which had adapted itself to the world as it was before the disaster – cannot avoid being wiped out. The survivors will be, very definitely, a new breed.

The young are that new breed. Psychically, they have a very different shape. They have acquired the ability to have a *whole* reaction to another person on the basis of only that fragment of his being which passes through the mass media. They have "caught up" with the media. In a sense, they can tell from the picture of his toenail whether a person will be a good billiards player. They can tell from his voice or his face (no matter how well rehearsed his performance is, no matter how well-scripted his speech) whether he is being sincere or not. They have "righted" themselves in relation to the mass media, learned to compensate for the blurring of reality, to absorb false memories, false models of behavior, and still not list to one side. They have learned, in effect, to "swim" in the currents of mass society. They know the terrain, know where to go for food (to "feed their heads," as the song so accurately goes) and know, also, what is poison for their psyches. Bad vibes. Good vibes. The extent to which these expressions have become commonplace is a crude measure of just how far the new consciousness has gone in its development.

As for the players who not long ago had two queens at their disposal, few of them are even aware that the new consciousness has come into being. They continue to function as though nothing had changed. They cannot help but interpret the behavior of the young in terms of their own frames of reference, and in those terms the behavior of the young will of course appear perverse. After all, they are not responding according to formula. The best laid-on acts do not go down with the young. The very best scripted speeches are not accepted. The best of the old-style actors are booed from the stage.

Yet the manipulators continue to go through the motions. Why?

For one thing, few of them are conscious of just how operationalistic their behavior has become. In the grip of the primary effect they cannot understand human relations except in terms of cause and effect, mechanical stress, sets of operations, measurements and, finally, dominance. Technological logic demands that every action must produce an effect, must be geared to accomplishing something, making something start or stop. To the people whose consciousness is bounded by the operational framework, life literally has no meaning without an "objective." They are *mission-oriented*.

A machine is useless without a function. So pervasive has been the influence of technology upon modern man he cannot conceive of himself without a function. *Being* is not enough. Experiencing is not enough. Being conscious is not enough. Living, in the end, is not enough. Unless what he is doing is something that can be measured and related to a set of operations, modern man feels impotent. So the old-style manipulators continue to go through the motions of manipulation (of themselves as well as others) because they can conceive of nothing else to do. They have been well programmed. The power games (which can be measured, etc.) are still *real*. Status (which can be measured, etc.) is still real. Wealth, influence, fame, conquest . . . and so on, are all wedded to the operationalistic mode of consciousness. If Richard Nixon seems a machine, it is precisely because at bottom he conceives of himself as a machine. He *must work* – on himself as much as on others. The Protestant Ethic and the First Industrial Revolution are the mind and the body of technological man, at least of technological man who is still under the influence of the primary effect.

The spectacle with which we are presented today is pathetic at times. We see the bullshitters going about their business as though they still had the power which mass media initially handed over on a platter. So much are they under the influence of the mass media drug that few of them are aware themselves of just how unreal their behavior is, how thoroughly their perceptions and thought processes have been divorced from reality. The young who stare at them, aghast, can scarcely believe their eyes. To them, the old boys on the tube, in the legislature or congress, are transparently phony. In a sense, the young have acquired X-ray vision – they had to in order to "see" through the wall the media had raised between what was real and what was not. The old men, suddenly naked, may at times sense their nakedness, but mostly they will continue to interpret the hostility of the young in terms most flattering to themselves. ("The young are ungrateful, Communist, surly, lazy, rude.") They have too much invested – – a life style, nothing less – in their own consciousness to begin to concede that it is indeed a false consciousness.

There is a further dimension to this process of perceptual compensation for the effects of mass media. The adjustment which had to be made in order to balance the relationship between sender and receiver was close to astronomical. In order to perceive directly through the media (especially television), in order to pick up the basic outline of the whole person at the other end, perceptions had to be refined at their roots. One had to be able to get much out of a fragment of information. In order to catch up with the media, that fragment had to be seen so clearly that the essential nature of the whole person could be discerned. The psychic "eye" had to become, in a sense, a different optical device, just as the telescope or microscope is different from the human eye, yet is derivative. This new refined means of "super perception" came into being to meet the psychic requirements for balance in relation to the uneven pressure exerted by mass media. It was designed, so to speak, to zero in on distant planets and galaxies. (In terms of perceptions, mass society poses problems for the observer similar to those confronted by an astronomer – the bodies being viewed are so distant.) However, when not being used to view the "stars," it is turned on relationships which are immediate. Their essential nature too is vastly magnified. And so, in terms of personal as well as public relations, a change takes place. The young experience each other more directly, automatically picking up all sorts of data their parents are likely to miss. And it is not just each other, but their parents as well, whose being is experienced so much more clearly and precisely.

Finally, having said all this about the mass media and the double whammy effect they have had on the two most recent generations of human beings, it must be noted that we have been looking over our shoulder at media effects of the past, and looking around us at media effects of the present. But a *third effect* is now becoming apparent. The role of media is undergoing a profound change. For the very people who have made the compensatory perceptual leap are now taking up cameras and beginning to use the media consciously, with an intimate understanding of their powers and effects. So far, media have been used blindly by manipulators to further their own interests. Both the first and second effect of mass media were accidental. The third effect will be no accident. The energies of media are being harnessed. Media have never been neutral, any more than a great river roaring down to the sea is neutral. But the tremendous natural power of media has not been brought to bear, except for the trivial purpose of getting people to buy toasters or to vote for given candidates. This is equivalent to building the Grand Coulee Dam for the exclusive purpose of manufacturing ballpoint pens. A far greater project is now underway, to which we will turn our attention in the concluding chapter of this book. Some other things need to be said first.

# FIVE THE TRIPLE-DECKERED GENERATION

Much of what has been said so far about "the young" needs to be qualified.

Generally, we are referring to the post-war generation, which tends to be thought of as a lump, a single package delivered more or less by the same robot stork. "The young feel...." "The young think...."

The young, it goes without saying, are at least as sloppy in their conceptions of themselves as a group as are their critics. The assumption persists that the young are more or less of the same mold. Certainly, in relation to the pre-war generation, the young can be seen to be a different breed. The differences between the pre- and post-war generations are so marked that most of us have got hungup considering the obvious. Overlooked have been the very considerable differences in perceptions and types of consciousness *within* the context of the younger generation.

When we refer to the post-war generation we are referring to a group of people whose only common denominator is that they were born after the Second World War had ended and the technical apparatus which has created modern mass society had been more or less assembled and put to work. That was more than twenty-five years ago. In that period, the average time lag between a technical discovery and its general use has shrunk to nine years. The transistor was not discovered until 1948. The integrated circuit appeared ten years later. And in 1969 came large scale integration. Herman Kahn has argued that if the difference between the First World War and the Second represented one "generation" of technological changeover, then the period since the Second World War has been marked by no less than four complete technological overhauls. The post-war generation, it follows, has not been uniformly affected by technology. Its oldest members will have been affected to a lesser degree, and in different ways, than its youngest members.

We need not look for great differences in the perceptual modes of the pre-war generation. There will be some – those in their old age will not have been affected as much by the primary effect of mass media as those in their fifties, forties, and thirties. In fact, the very old in our society – those whose formative years were spent outside the ambit of mass society entirely – are closer in many ways to the young than the middle-aged. It was upon the middle-aged that the full weight of mass society fell.

The post-war generation, however, has been affected by more basic changes in a shorter period. If there are four technological "generations" standing between us and the Second World War, we might reason that there are likewise four "generations" of psychic adjustments involved, producing not one homogeneous "younger" generation, but *four*. So far as the fourth and latest stage is concerned, not much may be said about it since it is still concerned with learning to walk and talk. The other three "stages," however, have achieved a fairly high level of definition. And if we look closely we may see that the spectrum of 'youth" *does* break down into three broad wavelengths.

To begin with, we must do away with thinking which limits itself strictly to pre-war and post-war catagorizations. Those who were born during the war must be included as part of the first stage of the younger generation, since, at least in North America, they will be no different from those born immediately after the war insofar as they will not have any real memories of it. (Of course, in Europe, even thirty-year olds will have some personal recollections of the war – but it was involvement of the most passive kind.) These individuals, like those who were part of the baby-boom which followed the war, had at least reached school before the full effects of the first post-war technological re-tooling took place. The first commercial radio station had opened in 1920, so they were all affected by that. The first commercial television station had opened in 1939, but it was not until the late 1940s that it really became a *mass* medium. It was in 1939, too, that work began on the first digital computer slated for commercial use. But it was not until 1944 that the famous Mark 1 was completed and it was not until 1954 that the electronic digital computer came into wide-spread use. The transistorized portable radio – a significant stage in the shaping of the new consciousness – arrived that same year.

It would be a mistake to attempt to relate the three rough apparent stages of the younger generation too precisely to the technological timetable. For one thing, the effect of a given technology (such as television or the automobile or the radio) on an individual will depend a great deal on his social position. The rich and the upper middle class will have access to all three of these innovations before the middle class, the working class, and the poor. There is considerable staggering of the effects of given technologies as one moves down the social ladder, with the poor invariably being the last segment to be affected. Geographical considerations will have to be kept in mind. And in over-all terms of "technological society," the breakdown comes country by country as well as region by region and class by class. Some innovations have more direct application in social terms than others. The laser, for instance, even though operational since 1960, has had no discernible psychic effect. No one yet speaks of the "Laser Generation." Furthermore, the stages to which I am referring were not the products so much of any single technological innovation, but rather came into being as a generalized reaction to a large combination of factors, certainly not all technological. The introduction of rock music, for instance, was a factor whose importance is scarcely appreciated, yet which played a crucial role. The civil rights movement, which represented in America the first real shaking-up of a system which had automatically been taken to be "right," was likewise a major factor. Much psychic furniture was abruptly shifted around. But in both these cases we see that there is an interaction between technology and society – neither rock nor civil rights could have had much of an immediate effect without a television set, a radio, and a record player in every home.

Finally, it must be added that no single "stage" is going to be any more absolutely fixed in one mold or another than any of the "types" to which psychologists are constantly referring.

Some members of the first stage will have acquired all the capabilities of members of the third stage, and many in the third stage will not even have achieved the degree of perception common-enough at the first stage. We can see, too, that there are many individuals in their thirties, forties, fifties, sixties, even older, who will have perceptual equipment at least as highly-developed as anything possessed by any youngster alive. The potential for a vastly-heightened over-all awareness has always existed. Very primitive people will frequently display intuitive talents far outstripping anything which, until recently, we have known in the West. The operational mode of consciousness "reined-in" those senses which could not be accounted for in terms of its logic. Those of us (mostly in the mechanized West) who were most affected by operationalism had become "perceptually-deprived." To some extent, the adaptation to the pressures of mass society has been a matter of bringing us back "up" to a certain perceptual level, at least in terms of our ability to see what is going on around us. However, it remains that in the West the purely operational awareness *sufficed* until the advent of mass society. It seemed, after all, to work very well - and, in terms of mechanisms, no doubt about it, it did. The psychic imbalances produced by mass society proved too much, however, even for the cast-iron operational mode, and something finally gave. The strains imposed on the operational (rational) consciousness were too great. All along, the purely rational mode had been too small a vessel to contain human consciousness, and it was only by bending and pulping the larger consciousness that it could be made to fit. Once mass society had taken shape, however, the load was simply too great. And so, in stages, like contractions in a birth process, the new consciousness began to come into being.

At the first stage we see that it is ragged, spotted, poorly put together. The compensatory heightening of perception in relation to mass media began to take place, but the actual numbers of those involved was so small they could not help but think of themselves as misfits. They were, after all, the first wave to come in. The banks were solid - they had not yet been eroded. The first stage found itself hitting concrete and bounced off, making scarcely a dent. Having made the compensatory perceptual leap, their consciousness had escaped from the influence of the primary effect; they could "see" through the operationalistic mode and the false consciousness it had created, but there was little they could *do* about it. Like Allen Ginsberg, they could see that some "sphinx of cement and aluminum (had) bashed open their skulls and ate up their brains and imagination." They could see

Moloch! Moloch! Nightmare of Moloch! Moloch the loveless! Mental Moloch! Moloch the heavy judger of men.

Moloch the incomprehensible prison! Moloch the crossbone soulless jailhouse and Congress of sorrows! Moloch whose buildings are judgement! Moloch the vast stone of war! Moloch the stunned governments!

Moloch whose mind is pure machinery! Moloch whose blood is running money! Moloch whose fingers are ten armies! Moloch whose breast is a cannibal dynamo! Moloch whose ear is a smoking tomb!

Moloch whose eyes are a thousand blind windows! Moloch whose skyscrapers stand in the long streets like endless Jehovahs! Moloch whose factories dream and croak in the fog! Moloch whose smoke stacks and antennae crown the cities!

Moloch whose love is endless oil and stone! Moloch whose soul is electricity and banks! Moloch whose poverty is the specter of genius! Moloch whose fate is a cloud of sexless hydrogen! Moloch whose name is the mind![13]

But this first stage had no base, no tradition, no literature. There was no way it could launch a frontal assault. Most gave up, contented themselves with reading Ginsberg, Kerouac, et al, and either finished university or dropped out. Frustrated at virtually every turn, they sank for the most part into discontented apathy, from which many of them were never to emerge. This was the Beat Generation. Today, their members are in their late twenties, some are in their early thirties. A few, of course, are older.

The second stage arrived at a time when a base had, at least tentatively, been established, when something of a tradition had been fashioned, and when, certainly, a great body of Beat literature existed. Moreover, the heightened perception was better defined. The counter culture was already a fact of life. The second stage, unlike the first, had a more-or-less autonomous sense of identity, a much greater awareness of its position in relation to the dominant culture. The wall by this time had at least shown signs of cracking – thanks, not to the Beats, but to the assaults engineered by the civil rights movement. More confident, confronted by apparently less overwhelming opposition, the second stage possessed far more power than the first. It was not to be so easily dismissed.

If the 50's had been the period during which the first stage was making its presence known, the 60's were to be the parentheses in which the second stage would find itself roughly contained, its strength and energy growing steadily until, near the end of the decade, it had peaked. In rapid succession came Haight-Ashbury, the March on the Pentagon, the Chicago Democratic Convention, Hair, Woodstock and Moratorium Day, all these running parallel to the black assault on the racial Maginot Line. The second stage, unlike the first, could and did launch a frontal assault.

But it was still too soon. As the 70's opened, it was evident that this second incoming wave had likewise been turned back, although at tremendous cost. America had not been able to dismiss this second wave as it had the first. It had had to fight it off like a mad dog. But the old order by this time knew for certain that it was threatened and it knew from what corner the attacks were coming. The possibility of a civil war was definitely one of the cards in the deck. Things had now become serious.

Robert Frost, like all good poets also a psychologist, once wrote: "There's nothing I'm afraid of like scared people." Scared people pull the triggers of guns when there is no need to. Scared people swat the flies of their nightmares with ICBMs. By the time the energies of the second stage had peaked, there were plenty of scared people in America. And if by the time the 70's had arrived fear was a smog which had thickened in America to the point where people seemed unable to see beyond the end of their block, it was a smog which had come to affect the vision of the counter culture as much as it did the great white whale of the Silent Majority. Certainly, the whale felt itself under attack from bearded Captain Ahabs of the New Left and Queequeg-like characters wearing FREE HUEY buttons. The whale had become edgy, interrupted in its feast, unnerved by oil slick on the water, Red Tides and gritty air, a dull sense of something being terribly wrong. But if the Silent Majority was jittery, its nervousness was little more than a twitch in its tail compared to the fear that by then clogged the throats of the Ahabs. The counter culture was convinced that Moby Dick was sounding. The next noise would be that of the splintering of doors being kicked open by jackboots. America's counter culture was breathing deeply, as though each breath might be its last. And now we perceive the outlines of the third stage as it begins to emerge.

The battle lines are drawn. They weren't at the time that the second stage was arriving. This is an important difference. The first stage had run into a wall of incomprehension and confidence – the old order felt secure and so did not trouble itself much with trying to find out what was going on. The Beats could be dismissed as perverts; and thus they could sneak into the nation's consciousness through the back door. Their relative success (after all, they established a literature and a tradition, even a base in the universities) encouraged the second stage to try the front door; whether the front door of a university administration building or the Pentagon, it made little difference. The assault was much more open and direct. Its goals were more explicit. Furthermore, the perceptual mode of the second stage was sharper, the new consciousness was more intact and sure of itself.

The third stage begins to appear at a time when the situation has altered. The old order is alert. It has picked up its gun and is manning the turrets. It knows – and it did not know before – that it is being attacked and that the attack is deadly serious. It is prepared to repel the attack or go down, Davey Crockett fashion, trying. It has already shown its willingness to break bones, bash skulls, and to kill. The third stage has been watching the beating the second stage has been taking. Unlike the second, it is wary and nervous.

It is this third stage our attention must be focussed on now, for this is the critical stage, the "generation" on whose behavior the future depends.

These three stages have been developing elsewhere, more or less following the pattern of response so evident in America. In the hinterlands of technological society the first stage "bounced," just as it did at the center. The second stage hurled itself in the other advanced industrial regions (Western Europe, Canada, Japan, Czechoslovakia) with the same self-confidence and energy against the old order, and it too, for the most part, crashed – although not without shaking and cracking the wall. In France the wall all but buckled. The reactions through Technology Land were more or less the same – the first wave was too novel to be taken seriously and, since it lacked real muscle, it was dismissed. The second stage was shaken off, although not without a fight. The behavior of the third stage in all regions, and the reaction to it, will be crucial. Where it manages to break through, the countries involved will begin to move ahead rapidly in terms of social evolution and growth. The new consciousness has much to offer. Where it is rejected outright, or hammered into near-oblivion, stagnation will set in.

Although the ways in which the greatly-heightened perception manifests itself have been pointed to repeatedly (we are, in fact, obsessed with these manifestations), little has been written about what, *essentially*, is involved.

Virtually no appreciation of the fundamental *intactness* of this consciousness can be gained so long as we stick to the frames of reference provided by either the academic or scientific cultures. Its nature, if it is to be understood at all, must be approached through other lenses. Common themes run deeply through all its manifestations, and by following these common themes to their root we may approach the kind of awareness they so accurately reflect, an awareness which is finally truer and deeper than any which has yet been incubated within the confines of a single culture.

It would take, as suggested earlier, a revised and updated History of Man to cover *all* the manifestations of the new consciousness and the contexts out of which these various facets emerged. Legions of scholars might gratify themselves for years undertaking such a project. Astrology and the *I Ching* would have to be dealt with at least as exhaustively as Zen and computer technology, for each of these is a component in the character of the new consciousness. Rather than attempting to do this, let us focus on two of the most highly-visible facts – rock music and drugs – and attempt to get to their roots. They tend generally to be dismissed as "aberrations," breakdowns in the glittering machinery of the Twentieth-Century mind, except of course by those who experience them directly. Like urbanization, both these phenomena contribute to personal liberation, a liberation which is far more fundamental than any merely political experience of transcendence.

Further, as we shall attempt to show, neither drugs nor rock music represent anything more than an opening gambit, a cathartic "first step," an initial readjustment. Neither is an end in itself. The steps beyond both drugs and rock music have, in the last year or so, been taken. We must finally concentrate on the steps *beyond* if we are to see the larger picture or to understand what is happening to mankind. But let us not get ahead of ourselves.

# SIX A MUCH NEEDED ASS-SHAKING

It is not enough to listen to the *sound* of the new consciousness. We must consider the experience of it, what it does to the psyche through the medium of the body.

Like urbanization, it liberates.

The rock phenomenon is complex. It cannot be viewed in isolation. Unlike jazz, out of which it only grew in part, rock has virtually no common heritage with the past. Rather than directing our attention to the literate "message" it contains, let us begin at the point where it departs from the past.

There are at least two contrasting ways of handling time: monochronic and polychronic. Edward T. Hall has suggested the monochronic time-sense is a characteristic of low-involvement peoples, "who compartmentalize time; they schedule one thing at a time and become disoriented if they have to deal with too many things at once."[14] Polychronic peoples, on the other hand, possibly because they are so much more involved with each other, "tend to keep several operations going at once, like jugglers." Low-involvement peoples, who need to separate activities, also like to screen themselves from one another. Polychronic people don't use the screens – they need to establish contact, physical or otherwise.

Of course, the way in which one experiences time will be characteristic of one's whole perceptual method. A mechanical, operationalistic culture, grounded in the concept of length, requires monochronicity in order to function every bit as much as a fork requires a hand. Here we can begin to appreciate the fundamental nature of the assault unleashed against the Western psyche by rock music. For unless one automatically compartmentalizes time, one's ability to function amid schedules is seriously impaired. A hole opens in the otherwise air-tight perceptual structure of the cage which is technique and rationality, the cage in which the Western psyche has grown perverse, like an old monkey locked up all his life, his sex habits thrown out of whack, his movements so long constrained that he has lost his curiosity. Rock music punched a hole in the cage. Something got out. Not only a new rhythm but a new style that came with it. The world was suddenly not so bleak and fixed.

Simply, *poly*chronicity is clearly a better deal than *mono*chronicity, just as a bowl of fruit beats a single apple. Eldridge Cleaver put his finger on the dimensions of the shift: writing of whites trying to learn the Twist, he says they presented a startling spectacle as they entered the dance floors in droves:

> They came from every level of society, from top to bottom, writhing pitifully though gamely about the floor, feeling exhilarating and soothing new sensations, release from some unknown prison in which their Bodies had been encased, a sense of freedom they had never known before, a feeling of communion with some mystical root-source of life and vigor, from which sprang a new awareness and enjoyment of the flesh, a new appreciation of the possibilities of their Bodies. They were swinging and gyrating and shaking their dead little asses like petrified zombies trying to regain the warmth of life, rekindle the dead limbs, the cold ass, the stone heart, the stiff, mechanical, disused joints with the spark of life . . . it afforded them the possibility of reclaiming their Bodies again after generations of alienated and disembodied existence.[15]

Yet it was not just their bodies they were reclaiming. It was, too, a whole perceptual (and finally conceptual) mode. The girdles were coming off, not only from around the pelvis but around the mind and the senses.

Blues and soul sounds had been echoing from the basement for generations. Some jazz had been brought up into the light, but a lot of it went straight into the head, bypassing the body. Now a rhythm had got going which set the body in motion, springing it from the rack of the punch clock to which it had been chained in the wake of the Industrial Revolution. Rock music did more than liberate the body from blueprint dancing, it liberated at the same time (though at first less obviously) whole territories of the mind.

The mind is only separate from the body on paper. Successful psychotherapy can change the rate of production of enzymes in your liver. Chemically, we are one creature from head to toe, and the brain, like any other organ, is an island washed by that chemical stream. Changes in the rhythms of our bodies produce changes in the rhythms of our minds: we not only move and feel differently, we sooner or later come to perceive differently, to *think* differently, and, finally, to *act* differently. Suddenly, we have less aversion to grouping, to contact, to involvement. The strung-out streets, neatly dissecting each other at ninety-degree angles (once a sign of orderliness) now appear as coldly abstract as the pages of the geometry texts from which they were copied. We are scrambled in our perceptions (our realities) not just at the surface, but somewhere near the primary root of consciousness. What constituted order in the old reality now represents the cutting edge of chaos, an edge as technically perfect as a butcher's axe, but one which nevertheless chops through the organic nature of events and things, making hash of them; thus, the old "order" is seen to be disruptive, it creates chaos under the guise of rationality. And what was formerly perceived as being chaotic – free movement, organic groupings, random flowing, spontaneity – now can be seen to be part of a higher, more substantial order.

Only from the relative position of the old perceptual framework does this seem like madness, just as the workings of a modern steel factory would look like the end of the world to a child yanked from the Upper Amazon and set down in the middle of it.

Something in this order of psychic change was finally involved in the assault of rock – the transformation was by no means the work of rock music itself, but the rhythms let loose were critical, at least as critical as the work wrought upon the sensorium by television. TV may have cut with all the delicacy of a laser beam at the fine threads holding the literate mechanical mind intact, but rock and roll, from its onset, pounded those who were hearing right out of their grooves. As they learned to swing their hips and asses, so they learned to reach out. Their ears, left all but covered with cobwebs from training in communication which was as light on involvement as it was heavy on content, suddenly were blown clear. Minds protected by a suit of armor hammered out of the alphabet and the ruler now found themselves being stabbed through large undefended openings.

More was getting in from the outside. The moat was being filled in, the castle gates were swinging out, the walls were being stormed. Whether any given individual knew it or not, the proud flag bearing the Western motto – "I" – was being hauled down and something still as strange as an untranslated hieroglyph, a more complex sense of oneself-among-many – broadly: "US" – was going up in its place. And what was involved was not just a rhythm and a style, but a whole technology.

The gramophone had found its way into relatively few homes, and in those to which it did what was played on it was dictated by those in the family, the parents, whose character and awareness was most fixed. By the time rock music arrived, a dramatic and unprecedented shift had taken place. The power over the choice of auditory information had moved largely downward into the hands of those who were *least* fixed, most capable of responding to something new. There was that much less chance of the message not getting through. And, of course, the spreading-around of the sound via recordings was only secondary to how it got spread by radio (and to a much lesser, almost nonexistent degree by television). What the importance of the invention of the portable radio was is anybody's guess, but it was probably considerable. If affluence meant that the buying power of the young, for the first time in history, was colossal, it also meant that for the first time in history a sizable portion of the economy would be directing its energies right past the wage-earner, traditionally the key to the whole buying-selling system (and, perhaps just incidentally, the key therefore to the political system as well). As that sizable portion of the economy grew, it became, inevitably, *dependent* on its market.

Youngsters, for the first time, exercised influence directly on society, through the medium of the all-important economy. While it remains that the youth market is manipulated, the actual effect of the manipulation, in terms of directions being chosen, is minimal. The producer must mainly follow the lines of development, in tastes, attitudes, beliefs, etc. Or, at the very least, to succeed he must seek out the advice of representatives of the class he is appealing to, and so individual young people (affected like their counterparts, and so therefore "representative," no matter whether seeking to exploit themselves and others or not) came quickly to have a "voice" in the shaping of society.

The vote, by itself, means nothing. What count are the crude forces and lines of tension which broadly shape the way votes en masse are used. Economic muscle is collectively a more direct means of influencing events and taking part in the decisions about what direction a given country will take, even if that muscle is never weighed in at a polling booth. The new rhythms and style liberated by rock music came thus to have a major effect on society in almost no time at all: a society after all takes the shape of what it contains only to the extent that those contents express themselves in the actual machinery, that is, where the wheels turn. The economic sphere remains the largest single wheel, and it was this wheel whose turnings were most immediately affected by the new style. If little of that style has found any political expression, it is only because the *whole* has been much more directly affected than this one part, the lesser wheel of politics. It is a wheel whose control is vested, by the barrier of voting age, in the hands of that portion of society least affected by the new perceptions. The ever-growing portion (still a minority, but inevitably a majority) which *was* affected is now only beginning to hit the political sphere. And while the economy and, to a less specific but more generalized extent, society as a whole, literally cannot afford to ignore the demands of this new style, the political sphere *can*, and does, and will continue to ignore it until, like the last sealed compartment in a sinking ship, its doors, too, burst in from the pressure.

In terms of the rate at which the new perception has spread around, the portable radio, symbol of affluence, has functioned much as the radio operating on the portable battery did during the Algerian war. It became, not a modern technique for getting news, "but the obtaining of access to the only means of entering into communication with the Revolution, of living with it."[16] To be sure, many of those affected were only vaguely aware of a "Revolution" taking place. They understood that society was "unreal," that is, it functioned in an absurd, erratic, transparently phony and even dangerous manner. What they did *not* understand was that, basically, society did not appear anywhere near as phony and absurd to the people whose perceptions it reflected. What is called the "alienation of youth" is actually the measure of distance between the new perceptual mode, which has broadly been acquired by youth, and the old mode of perception:

it is a tremendous distance. And rock, as it continues to evolve, widens it every year.

For if the distance between a kid shaking his ass to Elvis Presley and his Perry Como-loving mother was astronomical, consider how much greater the mileage logged between a kid today grooving on The Who, the Chambers Brothers, The Doors, the Jefferson Airplane, The Band, Jimi Hendrix, Ravi Shankar, and a mother who may *still* be in the Perry Como space.

The first effect of rock was to impress the same basic rhythm on a whole generation throughout Technology Land from West Germany to Japan, with America and Canada and England and France and Mexico, to mention a few, in between. There was no moment in history prior to this when a similar event took place. The rhythms and styles had differed from country to country, more so from race to race. True, there were peoples in different countries who were broadly monochronic and others who were polychronic, and the split was not simply racial: Southern Europeans had less need to compartmentalize than Northern Europeans, but in North America it was after all the Northern Europeans who had shaped and still ran society. The technical capacities which the West had developed were intrinsically wedded to the monochronic style. Now, abruptly, an alien rhythm was being broadcast across the political and national spectrum, moving young bodies from London to Berlin to San Francisco in another way. It was a basic rhythm, more organic, beginning with the beating of a mother's heart to which a child finds himself geared long before he's born. Before the onslaught of rock (delivered by technology), one could identify Germans, Frenchmen, Englishmen, Americans, Italians, and Swedes before they opened their mouths. Their bodies spoke a language almost as distinct as their tongues. They were built, moved, acted and reacted after a definite mold. Today? Look at a young Swede or American or Frenchman or Englishman. Tell-tale physical characteristics remain, traces of nationality can be detected if one looks carefully at the manner of dress; but the movements? Their bodies betray a different rhythm, itself only now a symptom of the changed perception, the out-of-the-mousetrap mind, and that rhythm is not something peculiar to any nationality. The political boundaries have been transcended.

To the extent that our attitudes are shaped by our experience, consider how different the experience of a youngster in the industrially-advanced nations is from that of his parents. The postwar generation is the first to have faced manhood in a mass society, which is the first society to provide the opportunity to look into cultures other than one's own, the first to offer, holus-bolus, through the mass media, an "overview," a greater-than-nationalistic picture of the world.[17] The modern young man thereby comes to measure himself against a more complex set of behavioral standards. He *can't help* but see (in some region of his mind) that being a good American or good German or good Englishman is not necessarily the same as being a good human being. This shift in the center of psychic action from the national stage to the global results in a proportionate expansion of the dimensions of the problems of self and sense of identity. When there was not much conflict in concepts, which was bound to remain the case so long as one's experience of the world was bounded by borderlines, identity was shaped easily and effortlessly.

Mass society presents no such opportunity for instant self. One's center is not so cheaply made. If it is to come together at all it must, in a mass or global society, come from the four corners of the world. This represents a leap, in terms of identity, of tremendous magnitude. Instead of being fashioned by one culture, stamped in other words with a single set of parental characteristics, the postwar generation has been fashioned by many cultures. The mass media has a compound eye, and it is through this eye, not the eye of any one nation, that the postwar generation viewed the world from childhood onward. What began to develop was a world-view, not a nation-view. No longer was one's identity shaped in a single mold: to have been born after the Second World War, to come to manhood, to arrive at some sense of self, meant to achieve a center which was closer to the real center of human experience, *all* human experience, than it could ever have been so long as it was wielded to any one political, racial framework.

There was no way to avoid this, since the young in mass society lived all their lives not "at home" but in the world. Mass media blew a hole in the shelter of the home and the child grew up with all the winds and storms blowing through his livingroom. He lived, for all intents and purposes, "outside," in the world. It got into his head right at the start, and as his style, his perceptions, his impressions, his feelings and finally his self came together, they did so around a different psychic skeleton, one which had been shaped by those winds blowing through the livingroom. Parents might still have tried to live as though the temperature had not changed, as though the workings of the cultural thermostat had not been thrown out of whack by gusts blowing in daily from outside, but these children, the first in history of whom this could be said, were not really living in a culturally-regulated interiorized environment. Their experience was of the world, a global neighborhood, rather than a single backyard. How could they be other than more complex? How could their standards help but be different? In earlier ethnocentric cultures, it was a life's work to grow to the point where one could begin clearly to see the whole world, the whole multi-faceted context of one's essential humanness. Now, abruptly, one *began* in the world, and the problem, if one's goal was still to succeed in the local environment, was to *get back down* there. That problem was called alienation, surely the most negative possible way of describing what was really the most hopeful of developments. Alienated from what? From the constrictions which too-narrow a cultural definition inevitably imposed on its members. If it was difficult, finally impossible, for the postwar generation to relate to the dreams of its society, it was only because that generation knew from the start these dreams were nothing if not small and unimaginative, tightly reined-in, solidly blocked-off and nailed down to the Procrustean bed of a single cultural concept of man, even of consciousness. The question, "Who am I?" had become more complicated.

Rock music poses the question beautifully. It is a global sound. Its basic rhythms sluice through the dams that societies raise around themselves. It draws, in its more advanced forms, from a repertoire of sounds previously compartmentalized one from the other. Among the ground-shaking collisions of an Africa whose ear is still to the earth, one hears the liquid notes of Polynesia, high precise explorations in the rarified upper regions of the ancient psyche of India, mathematical voyagings of European scholars, the quiet of America of the plains with the cacophany of the traffic jam hurled across it, Germanic broodings, Mediterranean hedonism, Mexico, even traces of China. It is sound, like technology, grown from many roots, and striking therefore across the lines between the gardens in which those roots are lodged. No wonder then that it bruises the ears of men whose world is smaller than all the worlds from which it draws; the sound is built on a scale larger than the scale of minds and perceptions which are contained in the acoustical chamber of any one society.

The proposition may be easily tested. Who can fail to see that as the narrowly nationalistic consciousness rises on a curve of intensity, aversion to the new sounds of rock also sweeps upward? So too does love of the purely local idiom. Working the other way, we find that receptiveness to rock increases in roughly direct proportion to the degree of one's liberation from the single-culture context.

The deeper one gets into the pit of technological culture, into the attitudes of people who are most affected by mass society, who are closest to its center, and who are therefore most representative of the future taking shape around us, the more pervasive one finds the influence of rock to be. Teenagers in the industrial West now spend an average of two hours a day listening to these sounds, two hours a day with this sound-wind of the whole world blowing through their heads. And it is among the upper middle class that the furthest explorations in these new sounds are most popular, that same upper middle class which is the firstborn of technological society.

It does not matter much that for the most part the lyrics may go unnoticed. Contemporary rock communicates essentially along lines that poems seldom move and essays ignore completely. It pole-vaults the wall of conceptualization and explodes among the machineries of perception, seldom directly affecting the way we think, but almost always affecting our rhythm, which may prove to be the key to those reflexes which go into the making of feelings, and, in turn, responses, attitudes, biases, selections, all the subconscious interactions which at their extreme pole crystalize in thought.

The critical importance of rhythm in the formation of societies has been largely overlooked, yet even at the extreme pole of cognition, in the "pure" realms of abstraction, we see certain essential rhythms. As we move down the ladder of consciousness, further and further from abstraction, we find that the influence of rhythm grows steadily stronger. In fact, it is one of the mainstrings of consciousness, certainly the key to the identity of any given culture. The science of the language of the body is still too young for much to be known about muscular expression of cultural differences, but we do know that every emotion expresses itself in the muscular system. Further, the muscular system is not capable of rationalization. Unlike the mind, the body doesn't kid itself. Every emotion is expressed directly, honestly. The elaborate complex of needs and fears which largely controls the psyche, controls also the way in which information is received and the way in which it is presented. That is, our mental responses are subject to so much intellectual interference, so many rapid decisions based on objective needs (to not create a disturbance, to cover up revulsion or love, to impress or cajole or control others), that it can seldom be honest.

Our psychological reactions, in short, are mainly *social*. They draw upon information about what is going on *out there*, gear themselves to that information, and express not *our* emotions but the *relationship of our emotions to those around us*. Physiological reactions, on the other hand, are strictly internal. The emotions we express physiologically are those which we actually feel, rather than being those which we feel in relation to our environment, with the extra confusing factor added of the need to react in accordance with the dictates (real or imagined) of a social context. The formula for psychological response is therefore different (it has several other ingredients mixed into it) from the formula for physiological response. Similarly, the rhythm which those responses follow (the whole orchestrated interplay between all the "separate" responses which, when viewed as a whole, betray a pattern) is bound to be different in the head rather than the body. It is into the head mainly that social instructions are broadcast.

At the body level, instructions are likewise being received, but it is in the upper region that instructions can be abstract at all. Body language, it must be understood, is a universal language, an older language, one spoken in a million dialectics by animals. Before man learned to speak he understood a body language. Sounds may have been a part of it from at least near to the very beginning, but sounds primarily the result of mechanical stress being applied. The vocal cord is an instrument played at first by muscular response. Grunts. Groans. Screams. Wailings. Purring. Simpering. Moans. Sobs. These are the roots of speech, of cognition. Up until the point is reached that these sounds are organized into smaller, more precise units of expression (words), they remain in the control of the internally-geared muscular system. When they begin consciously to be organized into ever-more-complex systems and sub-systems of expression, the final fully-elaborated system being a language, they begin to be controlled by the mind.

As the system evolves, the role of the mind becomes ever more pervasive until, finally, a point is reached where control of expression and response presents "political" problems for the whole being. If the body was the motherland of language, it was a motherland which discovered and colonized the brain. In time, the brain grew sophisticated enough to want to set up its own independent state of being, which it did – with the result that the responses and expressions controlled by the brain have a different style, a different rhythm, even basically a different philosophy. The brain, after all, is a colonized subject which grew away from the mother country and quickly surpassed it in sophistication and technology. It learned to fly into space, social space, where it came into contact with other spheres of influence.

The body remained behind, still speaking and understanding only the old language of the muscular system. Smells and the essential quality of sounds, the signals emanating from other muscular systems – appeals, warnings, threats, attractions, whatever the message – these were still the keys to response. Obviously, the two states still talk to each other. Much of the life-style of the mind influences the body and on many occasions, when the mind does not work quickly enough in producing a response to a situation, the body seizes control. In a pinch, it is almost invariably the older, seasoned wisdom of the body which prevails.

Only recently has any great awareness developed about the language of the body. Hunches may frequently be traced to its territory. "Instinctive" reactions. "Gut" feelings. Listen to your body, the modern therapist says. Listen to the *sound* of your voice, for the vocal cord is only partially under the control of the mind. Consider it a disputed territory, for muscular responses still control its foreign policies. Actual words will be selected according to the bias of the mind, but they will be delivered by an organ whose work, whether quick or plodding, harried, exhausted, elated, angry or frightened, will be done in accordance to instructions from the body.

The importance of rhythm can easily be appreciated. Rhythm is the regulator of response, the dictator of the relationship between responses. To the extent that the final pattern will be determined by these basic relationships, rhythm plays a formative and crucial role. Few thinkers have understood this as well as Havelock Ellis:

> All human work, under natural conditions, is a kind of dance.... Karl Bucher has argued that work differs from the

dance, not in kind, but only in degree, since they are both essentiallly rhythmic, for all great combined efforts, the efforts by which alone great constructions such as those of megalithic days could be carried out, must be harmonized. . . . The dance rhythm of work has thus acted socialisingly in a parallel line with the dance rhythms of the arts, and indeed in part as their inspirer. . . . Bucher has pointed out that even poetic metre may be conceived as arising out of work; metre is the rhythmic stamping of feet, as in the technique of verse it is still metaphorically called; iambics and trochees, spondees and anapaests and dactyls, may still be heard among blacksmiths smiting the anvil or navvies wielding their hammers in the streets. Insofar as they arose out of work, music and singing and dancing are naturally a single art. A poet must always write a tune, said Swinburne. Herein the ancient ballad of Europe is a significant type. It is, as the name indicates, a dance as much as a song, performed by a singer who sang the story and a chorus who danced and shouted the apparently meaningless refrain; it is absolutely the chant of the sailors and is equally apt for the purpose of concentrated work. Yet our most complicated musical forms are evolved from similar dances. The symphony is but a development of a dance suite, in the first place folkdances, such as Bach and Handel composed. Indeed a dance still lingers always at the heart of music and even in the heart of the composer

It is, however, the dance itself, apart from the work and apart from the other arts, which in the opinion of many today, has had a decisive influence in socialising, that is to say in moralizing, the human species. Work showed the necessity of harmonious rhythmic cooperation, but the dance developed that rhythmic cooperation and imparted a beneficent impetus to all human activities. It was Groose, in his 'Beginnings of Art,' who first clearly set forth the high social significance of the dance in the creation of human civilization. The participants in a dance, as all observers of savages have noted, exhibit a wonderful unison; they are, as it were, fused into a single being stirred by a single impulse. Social unification is thus accomplished. . . .

Thus, in a large sense, dancing has possessed peculiar value as a method of national education. As civilization grew self-conscious, this was realized. 'One may judge of a king,' according to ancient Chinese maxim, 'by the state of dancing during his reign.' So also among the Greeks; it has been said that dancing and music lay the foundations of the whole polilical, military as well as religious organization of the Dorian states.[18]

Today, the "peculiar 'value" of dancing has extended itself far beyond the national level. The global sound reaches a global audience, introducing a global rhythm. A "wonderful unison" comes into being, and responses, both collective and individual, from Berkeley to Berlin, begin to fall literally into step with one another. It is only at the far extreme of consciousness, at the level of politics, that these new fundamental harmonies express themselves poorly. Otherwise, in preference for life-style, aversion to certain groupings of ideas and personalities, and the political systems whose expression they are, these new harmonies, most overwhelmingly evident among the young, express themselves in unison almost flawlessly. And even at the ideological level, they are beginning to come together. The New Left is only at the beginning of a complex political evolution which will eventually express the global rhythm at least as accurately as national political systems now express earlier separated ethnic, racial and linguistic rhythms. Contemporary rock easily transcends the linguistic barrier: whether sung in German, French, English, or Swahili, any given popular song remains the same. Rather than dictating the contours of the rhythm, language is now pushed back into a crease in the folds of the sound. It loses its power to shape, and thus the mind, master of language, loses a large part of its grip on the rhythms of those who use it. The fact that young minds are still penned off from one another by the walls of language no longer means they still remain isolated: rock, if anything, is the Esperanto of body language, constructing a new common means of muscular expression, putting bodies in harmony with one another right across the lines of race and nationality and language. In earlier periods when cultural cross-pollination was still a rare and traumatic affair, something of the rhythm (and finally the character) of one society rubbed off only slowly on another. It took thousands of years for the personality of China to reach into Europe, hundreds for Europe to rub off on Africa and hundreds more for the reverse to happen. Now a rhythm has come into focus which is something more than the sum of them all, and in a single generation it spreads itself across the whole complex of those nations which have become a part of the global communications web. The internalized harmonies of India penetrate right to the heart of Europe and America, whose style is meanwhile thrusting itself deep into the mind of the Orient. English groups become popular in the United States as well as Germany and Japan, simply because the rock sound has no single national focal point, but rather stems from some point closer to the center of what is essentially a human, not an ethnic or racial, rhythm. It is a rhythm which by now is far from the jungle. If it contains harsh irregularities, metallic twangs, ricochets more like bullets coming off a steel wall than like anything in "nature," if turbines come through more clearly than tom-toms and parts of it clang like robots out of their crates and crunching through broken plastic, this means only that the rhythm and the sound are of their time; man, too, is a long way from the jungle. His world is not less real to him because of it; it is simply a different world.

The "loudness" of much rock, the volume at which it is played, is taken to be symptomatic of just how awful this different world is. Traditionally, we are most critical of those things which seem to us to serve no useful function. The usefulness of a thing is defined of course by the context in which it finds itself. In literate society *volume* has no place; in fact, the most functional and essential communicating which gets done in technological society takes place in near-perfect silence. (Memos, agreements, contracts, instruction manuals, blueprints, plans, schedules, programs, menus.) At the heart of the technological order stands the mute computer, surrounded by acres of filing cabinets (quiet as gravestones) containing sheets of paper whose message passes directly into the brain through the window of the eye. Critical data steals through the nervous system of society with only the whisper of static or the faint rustling of paper. Newspapers and books are noiseless; in television it is the image which is the root. Rather than truly being a noise chamber, technological society is increasingly, in terms of noise, a vacuum. It is only at the secondary level of communications that sound comes into play at all – verbal communications are liable, after all, to lack precision. It is not just that such communication is slow, it is also cumbersome and balky. Where we see it being used, we find ourselves looking into the older rooms of society. It is the foreman or the sergeant who barks out his commands. The architect and the general communicate through symbols, codes, graphs, maps, charts; they plot curves, analysis systems, calculate, process, use logic and mathematics; their essential messages are too complex to be transmitted by word of mouth, except at the component level. Fragments of the whole message may be passed on in this fashion, but these are only lesser bits broken off from the critical whole. The requirement of sound for communication rises as the importance of the message sinks, until, at the bottommost level, it is close to essential. ("All right, you guys, on your feet.") At the extreme opposite pole, the most characteristically technical and rationalistic end, planning comes more and more to be the dominant reality. Planning functions to reduce the need for verbal communication. If everyone operates according to plan, no words need be exchanged at all. If the road has been designed well, if the map is good, if the situation has been properly structured, no time need be wasted with words. The less sophisticated a task, the greater the role of words in its completion. *The machine itself may be noisy, but the means of communication which make it run grows ever less dependent on the spoken word.*

We see here the process of homeostasis at work. The loudness of contemporary music is a compensatory device, rising on a curve at the very time that the most functional communication is rapidly becoming inaudible. It is as though the whole being of technological man had sensed that his ears had been put out to pasture. In the new hierarchy of the senses being engineered by the requirements of technique, the ear has been displaced from high office, thrown out into the cold.

But it is not just technique in its most obvious forms which is at work here. Consider the social character which is shaped in the dense environment of the city. David Reisman has described it as being other-directed; that is, a kind of psychological radar is created. People rubbing up against each other in large numbers must learn, in order to survive, to pick up signals quickly and accurately. No longer can they afford to walk like bulls through the china shop of emotion. Increasingly, they must be sensitive to signals which are transmitted not by word of mouth, but by expression, movement, attitude, posture, mood, and position. In a city one must be slicker in one's relationships, one must pick up vibrations, learn to distinguish between situations and personalities in ways which were never necessary so long as population density remained below a certain level. Density increases the proximity of events, multiplies relationships, intensifies pressure, crams the package of daily experience full of more and more goods, until the point is reached where the need for a more effective means of packaging comes into being; in short, a new perceptual mode, *a more efficient* (relative to its environment) consciousness. There is less "space" available, not only in purely physical terms but in terms of time and the amount of psychic latitude one has at one's disposal. We rub not only shoulders but minds; we live not only cheek to jowl but personality to character. Our sense of identity, no less importantly than our bodies, is placed in a container where it has relatively less room to move, to be alone, to rule over itself, to exist without being affected, influenced, shoved around, molested, squeezed, jabbed, poked, and trampled.

It becomes a question of survival. The kind of consciousness which could get along nicely by utilizing only one awkward form of communication will not long survive, except by toughening its hide, in the dense psychic environment of the city. A greater range of responses is needed, an ability to select quickly the data one needs from a starburst of information. Minds which are not skillful bog down in great psychic traffic jams. The demand for a more sophisticated means of direction becomes overwhelming, and it is clear that purely verbal communication, in this context, is about as useful a vehicle as a horse and buggy downtown at rush hour. The new vehicle must have built-in automatic controls, radar, curb-finders, windshield wipers, a horn, a radio . . . and so it does. This is how far the invisible evolution of perceptions had been pushed on the urban stage. Verbal communication is now buried far down in the body of the vehicle, just as the wheel is buried in the car.

Again, the ear has slipped in rank. Little wonder the young dare to abuse it. They sense its relative valuelessness. Much of what they "hear" is not words; rather, they hear the weight, the intensity, the pitch, the structure of the whole verbal package. They are concerned with the thing as a whole, simply because one of the effects of increased density is to force the adoption of bulk means of perception. It is a logistics problem. There is so much more information, there are so many more relationships, so many more events, and the information and relationships and events are moving so much more quickly in so many more directions, one simply cannot keep tabs on every individual item.

Mass producers of goods are forced to deal with their products and customers alike *en masse*. Goods are shipped in bulk. The units of measurement get progressively bigger, always because so much more of everything is being handled. Psychologically, the same process is at work. The person who met only two or three hundred different people in his life could afford to concentrate on the smallest units of the communication he was to share with them. But the person who will meet thousands, who will have to deal with hundreds in a given day, cannot afford to handle his communications one piece at a time. He deals with bulk shipments of information, his contact with others is something which can only be measured by the gross or in reams. The situation calls for new equipment. A way must be found to handle all this communication by the ton rather than the ounce. And the way, simply, is to deal with messages in bulk. The urbanized youngster, who has learned to do this – to pick up on the gist of a message (the nitty-gritty, yes!) and to pay virtually no attention to the small pieces which went into its making, cannot help but become impatient or bored with the one-step-at-a-time process. The logic of verbal communication is the logic of the artisan; he can afford to spend much time on one item. In mass society so much must be communicated and is communicated that one can no longer expend a tremendous amount of effort on a single bit. A language of fragments develops. It is a language which recognizes that *all* verbal communication is fragmentary (that is, it expresses only a portion of the message, and frequently scrambles even that). Increased sensitivity to the other ways in which the message is being communicated – body movement, facial expression, mood, etc. – means that one does not have to put so much effort into the construction of elaborate verbal edifices. One may rightly gloss over great tracts and instead scan in search of the overall contour or pattern. Thus, the message is not ingested by the mouthful, but rather swallowed whole. And anyone who receives information in this manner will come to offer it the same way. A fragment of a sentence will suffice to express what he wants, since the way in which he delivers it is what counts. The medium, in this case himself, his whole person, is indeed the message.

Clichés have always been used to encapsulate a larger consciousness. They are the really large notes in the currency of language: expressions of a common awareness (or at least a common-ly-held belief) so well-constructed they come, like any tool which works well, to be used in every home. Because they *are* used so often, like knife or a spoon, we dismiss them as being of little value. Yet, let us note, it is only the truly literate who find the cliché to be irritating, even threatening. Naturally. Because, for them, language has become the absolutely critical means of expression. They have a vested interest in its soveriegnty. Their status is tied very closely to their ability to work with words. The bias in favor of carefully articulated language runs deep but only within the literate sphere of awareness, which is the same region within which technique took root. As the ability to communicate in more-than-words develops, as we escape (or are driven out of) the purely operationalistic area of consciousness, the status of the word-artisan diminishes. Clichés, by default, become more numerous and more pervasive, if for no other reason than the fact that clichés – so far as verbal exchange is concerned – *are ideally suited to bulk shipments of information.* They are large packages. All the other extra-literate means of expression may as easily be employed in the utterance of a cliché as the utterance of an elegant sentence. More, the cliché does away with the blurring of the essential message which careful articulation inevitably entails. The same clichés, or combinations of clichés, may be used, but more expression (non-verbal) is put into them. Consider the ways in which "Wow" may be used: it may be stretched out appreciatively to cover a range of reactions from vague comprehension to awe, striking the match of love, affection, approval, pleasure, amusement, or a dozen other specific emotional responses (or any combination of them) at any point in between. The length of the sound, the tone, the pitch, the variation: all will be critical components of the message. Sticking with this one current cliché, "Wow," we find too that it can as easily move into whole other regions of response: excitement, boredom, anger, fear, alarm, disgust, amazement, incredulity, sympathy, misery, ecstasy, frustration, etc. This one word, if its essential character can be heard, plays eloquently upon the whole gamut of emotions. Similarly, a host of other clichés can be used. And for people accustomed to experiencing communication in the large context of a whole person, a whole situation, it may be a more direct and useful form of communication than any which would make use of tremendous numbers of words. In the absence of an awareness of the other dimensions of human interaction, words assume a great importance, but as that other awareness comes back into focus, the nuances of the spoken word are relieved of their duties by the richer nuances of the language spoken by the whole organism.

Studies have already revealed as much. Words account for only seven percent of our communication between ourselves. Facial expressions account for fifty-five percent. Vocal information (intonation, stress, tone of voice, frequency of pauses and length of time spent talking) accounts for thirty-eight percent. Albert Mehrabian, an assistant professor of psychology at UCLA, found by using an electronic filter on tape-recorded conversations that it was possible to make words themselves unintelligible – but the vocal contents, the intonation and stress remained. When people were asked to listen to the filtered tape, they easily and readily detected the amount of friendliness or hostility contained in the conversation even though they had no idea of what words were being used. Posture, Mehrabian found, is used to indicate both liking and status. As the other ninety-three percent of our communications becomes more conscious, we may not unnaturally expect to see the role of words regulated to a position more in keeping with their actual effect. Clichés will come more and more to be the dominant reality of conversation as lump sums of information are traded, mostly non-verbally, in place of the old loose change of verbiage.

Rock music is a conductor bearing these more-than-literate impulses from one young person to another at least as well as electricity now transmits the messages that corporations exchange among themselves. Joy, anger, horror, boredom, bitterness, love, togetherness, all these and more, are communicated from body to body, mind to mind, and the message is primarily in the music. Only a fraction of it is in the words, which are, at any rate, used as they are in poetry – and poetry has always left more "spaces" to be filled in than prose. The essential message is always the feeling which is passed on. Words are only *added*. Even those lyrics which are expressive are hitched to rhythms without which most of the message would be lost. Its loudness, we may now see, balances the silence which is gathering at the heart of communication in Technology Land. Its volume is in proportion to its size and, as a lifter of bulk packages of non-verbal information, it has grown into an enormous brute, one which does not hesitate to land heavily upon the ear simply because the ear has been demoted, the ear is being made to do heavy menial tasks now, the ear is out in the fields and toiling.

A part of its job now is to pick up heavy loads and stack them quickly. In fact, the cliché "heavy," used to describe any message which is densely-packed with many-levelled meanings, is a precise tool of expression. "Heavy" lyrics, "heavy" rhythm, "heavy" characters. Such are simply multi-levelled. To identify something as being "heavy" is to recognize its multi-levelled character.

We may recall at this point one of the chief characteristics involved in a "self-structuring hierarchical jump" – namely, *simplification*. The unexpected, and sudden, accumulation of a whole new complex of interlocking clichés (heavy, far-out, hype, wow, stoned, freak, vibes, etc.) represents exactly this sort of thing. These clichés of the new consciousness encapsulate, as accurately as Newton's formula for pendulums and projectiles, the long-winded explanations of events which preceded them. The new consciousness has achieved a simplified, swifter, and more economical means of communication, ridding itself of the need for laborious explanations, tortuous literate communication, and cumbersome attention to detail. Two youngsters may exchange more information by saying simply to each other, "Such and such is a heavy scene," than two adults may exchange in an hour of analytical discussion. It is *real* information in terms of recognition of a basic situation.

Finally, one of the most important points about rock music is the fact that it cannot be understood simply as entertainment. A rapport exists between a rock star and his young stoned audience which transcends mere fun. The rock star is a teacher, a guru, and only incidentally an entertainer. The messages of such groups as The Beatles, The Rolling Stones, Moody Blues, etc., and particularly stars such as the late Jimi Hendrix, is that of *leader* and *followers*, not merely entertainer and fans. These "stars," Bob Dylan, for instance, enjoy a relationship with their audiences which formerly only existed between political leaders and their constituents or priests and their flocks. The rock star cannot be understood so long as one thinks of him as being merely a variation on the theme from Al Jolson. The rock star communicates in his music, and very specifically in his lyrics, a *parable*, a lesson, a message, instructions about awareness and how to deal with the world. The audience follows the lesson as aptly as the students of philosophers once did in Greece. Except that this is happening not only in a "head space," but in a body space as well. It is happening in a more ecstatic, multi-leveled fashion.

Not only have the basic ideas been shaped into words (which is all that written or purely verbal communication can accomplish), but the words have been taken a step further and shaped into sounds. The shaping of the words, with the ideas contained therein, into eloquent sound patterns represents an advancement in communication. We are speaking of *human* communication, rather than the communication of machines; which is what more and more of us, thanks to our technological and educational bias, have come to understand as being communication, not realizing the dimensions of humanness which have been lost in the process. Rediscovery of the multi-dimensional sensory communication which can happen between people, passing through the superior medium of music, is what modern music is all about. Had it not been for mass media like TV and radio, "rock" would only have been something listened to by those with very sophisticated sensitivity to music. It would, literally, have been confined to the intellectual chamber room. Mass media brought it to the masses, but only that section of the masses (the youngsters, mainly) who are capable of "getting the message," understanding what the message is all about.

The message is this: open up your senses, shed your old skin, prepare yourself for an evolutionary leap out of sight. The human race is irreversibly embarked on a "trip." You will need to be a lot freer, a lot more flexible, a lot faster in all your mental and emotional reflexes in order not to freak out as the trip gets underway. It is a simple message.

# SEVEN

# THE ACID QUEEN

The human mind cannot be conceived of as a glass or window through which information passes without bending or being distorted. Rather, external phenomena are filtered through a pre-existing structure. This structure itself is shaped by experience and conditioning and expectations which are themselves, to varying degrees, learned. This filter – or "reticular system," as it is more precisely called – discriminates. It accepts and rejects information, sifting through the daily barrage of sensory input like a kind of organic pre-programmed computer. The philosopher, J. Bronowski, has written about what he calls the "interlocked picture of the world" which the brain constructs. This picture is *not* the way the world looks but rather our way of looking at it. All perceptions, after having been picked up by the senses, are graded (interviewed, if you like) and screened by the reticular system before being forwarded to the mind.

Accordingly, we automatically distinguish between what our experience has told us is relevant and what is irrelevant – or non-functional. This filter is itself shaped by the environment in which the individual finds himself. The signals and messages he chooses to pick up are those he has been trained to catagorize as being of some importance to his survival. Others will be deflected. Accordingly, it is not the "eye" of the artist which permits him to detect nuances where the non-artist will see nothing – it is simply that the artist will not automatically screen out information which, to the other, is of no value or importance.

It is likely that LSD attacks this filter, rendering it more porous, opening up tunnels which would otherwise remain sealed. The effects of LSD are therefore of deep significence. One's reticular system is finally the product of one's whole cultural milieu. No culture could ever remain "intact" if the mental filters of its members were not synchronized with the larger, more generalized cultural filter. When LSD disrupts the functioning of the filter, it removes the individual from this over-all cultural context. It drives him not "out of his mind," but out of the *filter* surrounding his mind.

On the basis of its morality, priorities, prejudices, goals, ideals, and fears, any given society will roughly impress a similar set of mental reflexes on its members. Thus, people who grow up in a given society tend strongly to agree upon certain concepts basic to the structure of the society. Depending upon the technology and philosophy of the society, its degree of sophistication, their views will be approximately representative. And to the extent that the society is incapable of achieving some kind to overview – of transcending its own nature, its own habits, its own assumptions – so too will the perceptions of the individual be limited and inhibited. The cultural point of view, which is converted into a perceptual method, is internalized, and each individual becomes a walking micro-culture. Any device or system which tends to break down the structure of the individual micro-culture assaults, in the most direct and specific way possible, the very foundations of the over-culture, the partial and culturally-limited point of view – which members of a given society share, if they are to have any common impulse or behavior pattern at all. Or, more to the point, if they are to be controlled, managed, organized, or led.

A Czech doctor once said that LSD inhibits conditioned reflexes. To the extent that it does that, it removes the individual from the context of his culture. It takes him – however temporarily – away from the familiar board, renders the normal rules of the game useless, and opens him up to a radically-altered perception.[19]

To a lesser degree, regardless of the differences in the chemical process whereby the effect is achieved, this is also the secret of marijuana, hashish, peyote and so on: not really that they "expand" the mind, but that they widen the doors of perception, as Aldous Huxley said, sometimes just slightly, although at other times not only is the door (the preconditioned mental filter) knocked right down, but a whole wall may be demolished, and sensory data previously blocked out comes pouring in. One stands exposed, literally, to the elements, suddenly naked.

Few cultures have ever had as much of a vested interest in compartmentalized perception as technological society. Specialization insists upon informing individuals deeply but narrowly. And the *organization* of specialists from different fields has become the key to technological success. The "partial and culturally limited point of view" which has grown up in the West takes its shape mainly from the incubators of Aristotelian logic, Christian dualism and the concept of length. These great formative roots have in common an insistence upon division and fragmentation. Aristotelianism gave us a subject-predicate language, "with its tendency to treat objects as in isolation and to have no place for relations."[20] Christianity, of course, insists upon the theology of God and the Devil, absolute Good and absolute Evil, Heaven and Hell, the Spirit and the Flesh. We have already noted the effects of the concept of length. Together, they provide the conceptual blueprint for the Western psyche – a blueprint the outline of which has been blurred by electronic media, physics and the tremendous insights offered by Gestalt therapy and general semantics, but which remains nevertheless the operative design.

It is worth noting, as several writers have pointed out, that what is existentially astonishing about the LSD experience is the "discovery" that, mentally, most of us have been operating within the confines of a quite narrow and sharply restricted level of consciousness. The dualistic image of the world, which is our culturally limited way of viewing things, is "real" only along the avenues of this one wavelength of consciousness. It is the Oneness of the universe which becomes apparent once the dualistic image to which the reticular system is harnessed has been dissolved or broken down. Again, this discovery can be made through less potent (and dangerous) drugs.[21] *It can also be made without recourse to drugs at all.* For the consciousness which the drug experience offers is not unique; it is not "new"; it is not unnatural; there is nothing "freaky" or "far-out" or weird about it all, except in the context of contemporary society. The fact that such a holistic consciousness should be seen as being irrational reveals nothing except the degree to which Western civilization itself has become unnatural and freaky.

What do you "see" while stoned, whether on pot or acid or any other "hallucinogen," that isn't already apparent to a mind not locked in a conceptual cage? The attraction felt by drug-users for ancient Oriental philosophies and religions is no mere coincidence. Through their drug experiences they have come to see a reality not split by Aristotelian logic or Christian dualism or operationalism. They see things as they were always seen long before the concrete perceptual foundations of the West were poured. The "culturally-limited" point of view stamped upon generations of Europeans and their colonizing children is suddenly seen, through the medium of drugs, to be the product of a "narrow and restricted level of consciousness." To those minds most conditioned by the Western version of consciousness, the attitudes induced by drugs seem appallingly regressive: the idea that "primitives" and "savages" and "barbarians" and "heathens" might have had a better grasp of reality than their white conquerors does not go down well. It makes white supremacy a cruel joke. It makes what we have been conditioned to think of as "civilization" something very close to a farce. Just incidentally, it renders every established political context meaningless, at least as meaningless as the artificial contexts established by economics.

The real fear behind the generally hostile reaction to drugs is that the insights offered by these drugs might be more valid than the insights offered by established authority, that what is called "hallucination" and "illusion" might in fact be a greater (wider, deeper, more profound) perception of reality than the ordinary. Suppose that while stoned you *do* see things more clearly and directly. Suppose that ordinary (that is, culturally-conditioned) perception is something like partial blindness, imperfect, distorted, incomplete. And now allow just the *possibility* that drugs might open your eyes wider, that you might be able through the medium of drugs to perceive things in a more complete manner, that you might be able to activate repressed or dormant perceptual faculties within yourself. . . . Immediately, one can appreciate the threat these drugs represent to the established order. It is an order dominated by people who have learned the tricks of surviving and flourishing inside it. If it may be thought of as an elaborate machine, it is a machine which some people have learned to operate, and these people, naturally, have risen to positions of power based on their ability to operate the controls. They understand this machine. They have a mechanic's love of its familiar intricacies. *Anything* which suggests the existence of another, more complex and pervasive machine, one whose functioning is not understood by the people who have learned to work the old machine (or reality) is threatening to them in the extreme. If a greater reality emerges and claims the minds of men, what becomes of the lesser reality? It will be consigned, inevitably, to the garbage heap. And with it, also inevitably, will go all those who depended on it for their power and authority.

The fear of drugs is deep-rooted, but it has nothing to do with worries over whether young minds might be corrupted or ruined or that people will get intoxicated; after all, alcohol is not so feared. As for fear of young minds being ruined or somehow "lost" to society, this is at the very least a transparent rationalization. If the danger of "losing" young citizens was the authentic cause of the reaction to drugs, then automobiles would be far more loathed and hated than pot or acid. Who can argue that the automobile does not claim more young "minds" (along with their bodies) every weekend in North America than do drugs in a year? No, the parent who will turn the keys to his car over to his teenage son, but who will fly into a rage if he finds a single joint of grass in that same son's room, is reacting to a fear that runs far deeper than concern for anyone's well-being other than his own. Instinctively, many in our society have sensed what is going on: namely, that the premises and assumptions upon which this social order was built are being shaken at their roots, and that drugs, in some mysterious way, are a critical factor. The people who advocate their use, or who, more simply, *use* them, *are* in some fundamental way *different*. They come, rather literally, from another world. They are foreigners, aliens, members of another tribe. The reaction to them is almost as ferocious as the reaction to immigrants in earlier times.

It was presumably an understanding of this which prompted Eldridge Cleaver to write that the conflict between the generations today is deeper, even, than the struggle between the races. Although it is much more than a purely generational conflict, there are proportionately far fewer older people who perceive the "greater reality" than there are young ones.

This great reality is, to begin with, ecological. Ecology, after all, is merely one of the first of our Western sciences to escape the clutch of Aristotelian logic. Of necessity, it abandons subject-predicate methods in favor of relational methods, extends the concept of the organism-as-a-whole to "organism-as-a-whole-in-environments," is non-anthropomorphic, and concerns itself with whole systems in a functional (rather than merely additive) non-linear manner.[22] The orders and relations recognized by ecology are "higher;" that is, they are more profound. Peter Henry Liederman notes that we are moving from the Dialectic Age to the Ecological or Global Age. The "greater reality" is becoming increasingly apparent. "Western philosophy has taught us to think of everything in terms of dualisms, diametrically opposed, competing opposites. However, the philosophical base of Western thinking may be undergoing drastic change, for in science, politics, economics, and even religion, it is becoming less and less popular to view everything in isolation from the total system surrounding it."[23]

But ecology recognizes, as yet, only purely physical relationships and harmonies. The task of exploring further non-physical relationships has fallen to such embryonic sciences as parapsychology. J. B. Rhine has been able to verify experimentally the reality of psychokinesis, extra-sensory perception, precognition, clairvoyance, and telepathy. Evidence is beginning to accumulate that plants have emotions, that there is a "pool" of vegetable consciousness which functions telepathically across great distances and possesses memory. Experiments by Clive Backster indicate that every living cell has "primary perception," which implies a mind of sorts. (A test tube sample of human sperm was able to select its "daddy" from a group of men.) Amoebas, mold cultures, fresh fruits and vegetables, yeasts and blood samples have all shown "emotional" reactions recorded on the galvanic skin-response section of polygraph instruments, and the "power of prayer" to affect the growth of plants has been repeatedly demonstrated.[24] The literature which almost overnight has become available on these new "paranormal" frontiers of the mind is staggering. While it is true that much of it can be dismissed as being exploitive and sensationalistic, it remains that empirical data is accumulating at a tremendous rate. Much of the serious work being done is going on in the Soviet Union, although Soviet scientists take the position that psi results (which many of them acknowledge) must stem from some unknown physical source of energy.

J.B. Rhine, after forty years of experimental work in the field of parapsychology, was able to put it sweetly: "If a man criticizes us honestly, I know that he just has his windows cut to a certain size and can't see any further."[26] *And can't see any further.* Here, perhaps, is the edge which splits our society so cleanly into fundamentally different camps. On the one hand: the predominantly-older individuals whose perception is filtered through a pre-existing operational structure, the result of previous experience, conditioning and internalization of culturally-patterned points of view. And on the other: the mainly younger individuals whose reticular system has been softened in a variety of ways (electronic media would be one) so that it is not so tightly bounded and fixed, in terms of what they are able to perceive; and for these individuals the traditional Western mode of consciousness is but one wavelength on the spectrum of perception. *Other* wavelengths are more apparent to them.

The consciousness which emerges once the walls fashioned by Western science and religion have been dissolved or penetrated by drugs is not by any means a peculiar consciousness. The extent to which it is in harmony with the teachings and intuitive knowledge of other times and places (pre-technological and non-Aristotelian) has been clearly revealed by various studies, perhaps the most definitive one of which was reported by Willis Harman in *Main Currents of Modern Thought*

> Through the psychedelic experience persons tend to accept beliefs which are at variance with the usual conception of the "scientific world view." In a current study (by C. Savage, W. Harman, J. Fadiman, and E. Savage) the subjects were given prior to and immediately after the LSD session, a collection of 100 belief and value statements to rank according to the extent they felt the statements expressed their views. Subsequent personality and behavior-pattern changes were evaluated by standard clinical instruments and independent interviews. It was found that therapeutic consequences of the LSD session were predictable on the basis of the extent to which subjects indicated increased belief in statements such as the following:
>
> "I believe that I exist not only in the familiar world of space and time, but also in a realm having a timeless, eternal quality."
>
> "Behind the apparent multiplicity of things in the world of science and common sense there is a single reality in which all things are united."
>
> "It is quite possible for people to communicate telepathically,

without any use of sight or hearing, since deep down our minds are all connected."

"Of course the real self exists on after the death of the body."

"When one turns his attention inward, he discovers a world of 'inner space' which is as vast and as real as the external, physical world."

"Man is, in essence, eternal and infinite."

"Somehow, I feel I have always existed and always will."

"Although this may sound absurd, I have the feeling that somehow I have participated in the creation of everything around me."

"I feel that the mountains and the sea and the stars are all part of me, and my soul is in touch with the souls of all creatures." "Each of us potentially has access to vast realms of knowledge through his own mind, including secrets of the universe known so far only to a very few."

Note that in accepting these statements the individual is in effect saying that he is convinced of the possibility of gaining valid knowledge through an extrasensory mode of perception.[27]

Dr. John Beresford, who has described the discovery of LSD as possibly the most critical event in human history, remarked: "Take it once and you know that all you've known about consciousness is wrong."

The point here is simply to emphasize that the consciousness which comes into focus through the medium of drugs is basically no different from the consciousness manifest in various ways in most, if not all, peoples who have not been snagged by the inherent limitations of Western thought-processes. Those belief and value statements just quoted might have been uttered as readily by ancient Chinese, aboriginals, Bantu tribesmen, Eskimos, American Indians, devotees of the Uphanishads, Buddhists, Taoists and Zen masters, as they were by Westerners who had taken LSD. And those beliefs and values, while sounding strange coming from the heart of Technology Land, were by no means strange to these other peoples. What was strange, even frightening and insane, to *them* was the Western brand of logic, which was clearly exploitive, atavistic, and egocentric.

"It is my personal belief, after thirty-five years experience of it," wrote Sioux Indian doctor Charles Eastman, "that there is no such thing as 'Christian civilization.' I believe that Christianity and modern civilization are opposed and irreconcilable, and that the spirit of Christianity and of our ancient religion is essentially the same."[28] Dr. Eastman here put his finger on the crack which has now widened to the point where it is breaking the established Western churches apart. This Sioux would seem to be closer in spirit to a modern white pothead or acidhead (and a lot of others, all of whom could be loosely grouped together under the heading counter culture) than these whites are to their own elected representatives, the administrators of their universities and, certainly in many cases, to their own parents.

Ted Hughes has noted that the fundamental guiding ideas of our Western civilization derive from Reformed Christianity and from Old Testament Puritanism, which are based

> on the assumption that the earth is a heap of raw materials given to man by God for his exclusive profit and use. The creepy crawlies which infest it are devils of dirt and without a soul, also put there for his exclusive profit and use. By the skin of her teeth, woman escaped the same role. The subtly apotheosized misogyny of Reformed Christianity is proportionate to the fanatic rejection of Nature, and the result has been to exile man from Mother Nature – from both inner and outer nature. The story of the mind exiled from Nature is the story of Western Man. It is the story of his progressively more desperate search for mechanical and rational and symbolic securities, which will substitute for the spirit-confidence of the Nature he has lost. The basic myth for the ideal Westerner's life is the Quest. The quest for a marriage in the soul or a physical re-conquest. The lost life must be captured somehow. It is the story of spiritual romanticism and heroic technological progress. It is a story of decline. When something abandons Nature, or is abandoned by Nature, it has lost touch with its creator, and is called an evolutionary dead-end. According to this, our Civilization is an evolutionary error. Sure enough, when the modern mediumistic artist looks into his crystal, he sees always the same thing. He sees the last nightmare of mental disintegration and spiritual emptiness, under the super-ego of Moses, in its original or in some Totalitarian form, and the self-anaesthetising schizophrenia of St. Paul. This is the soul-state of our civilisation. But he may see something else. He may see a vision of the

real Eden, 'excellent as at the first day,' the draughty radiant
Paradise of the animals, which is the actual earth, is the actual Universe: he may see Pan, whom Nietszche, first in the
depths, mistook for Dionysus, the vital, somewhat terrible
spirit of natural life, which is new in every second. Even
when it is poisoned to the point of death, its efforts to be
itself are new in every second. This is what will survive, if
anything can. And this is the soul-state of the new world.
But while the mice in the field are listening to the Universe,
and moving in the body of nature, where every living cell is
sacred to every other, and all are interdependent, the housing speculator is peering at the field through a visor, and behind him stands the whole army of madmen's ideas.[29]

So the "greater reality" is an ecological consciousness, coupled
with an intuitive awareness of the existence of super-sensory phenomena; it is, further a pantheistic consciousness well-understood
by non-technological peoples, not bounded by an Euclidean, Aristotelian or Newtonian conceptual framework, a "native" (i.e.,
non-literate, less rigidly structured) sensibility. And it involves, as
well, a kind of existentialism: that is, the awareness that man is a
creature with no excuses. Meaning is something we invent or create for ourselves; everything we do, whether we are willing to
acknowledge it or not, we *choose* to do. Authoritarian religions
flourish in direct proportion to the unwillingness of great numbers
of people to assume responsibility for what they are and what they
do. Reliance on a higher moral authority – an anthropomorphic
authority, at any rate – is no different from reliance on a parent
for guidance. It is evidence, simply, that one has not grown up or
learned to stand on one's own feet; it is, in an adult, a form of
regressive behavior. The great sense of reality involves an awareness of more complex orders, higher levels of interaction and influence, but it does not allow that these be grasped solely
through metaphor or allegory: it demands that they be perceived
directly. The responsibility for bringing one's behavior into harmony with these more pervasive orders of existence remains with
the individual.

Through the medium of drugs, many people achieve a comprehension of this reality. Others are "there" to begin with, and
many others find their way to it through other media, such as
creative activity, various kinds of existential group therapy, Ges-

talt therapy, General Semantics, yoga, meditation, etc. These other routes are most arduous, yet when they *do* finally break the
mind out of its cage, the effects are more lasting and indelible. *By
themselves*, drugs can awaken individuals to a higher consciousness, but they cannot keep anyone there. If we may conceive of
"normal" consciousness as being a kind of stupor, then the individual whose only means of awakening involves recourse to drugs
is in the position of a person who must have cold water dashed in
his face repeatedly to keep him on his feet. There is more than a
bit of Pavlov's dog in all of us. Inevitably, through habitual activity of any kind, whether dependence on drugs or an alarm clock or
cold water or hot coffee, we get programmed, and to the extent
that we are programmed we are that much less free and that much
less capable of creative behavior; we are also that much less able
to respond in new ways to new situations.

The drug experience cannot be understood in the absence of an
understanding of the events and experiences onto which it impresses itself. For people who are genuinely turned on, drugs are
incidental. Being turned-on is a state of being which exists to
varying degrees, or at least in its embryonic form, *before* one
comes into contact with drugs; one's consciousness may be liberated by drugs only to the extent that it was ripe for liberation to
begin with. The answer is not to be found in drugs; drugs may
make the *questions* clearer, or even pose them. But what answers
there are can be found only in existence, in the experience of one's
being. Turned-off people generally remain turned off, no matter
how many drugs they ingest.

Psychedelics are devices which can be made use of by individuals whose psychology is properly geared to the era we are entering, just as automobiles are devices used (sometimes well, sometimes badly) by people geared to the age we are just leaving. The
risk factor is probably about the same. And let us not forget the
reactions of horror and loathing with which the automobile was
greeted when it made its debut. Simply, if we do not consider it
immoral to drive to the supermarket in the jockstrap of a mechanical monster, why should we consider it immoral to be carried
somewhere else in the arms of a psychopharmacological angel?
Drugs lend themselves to the kind of psychic adjustments which
are involved in being turned on, just as cars lend themselves to the
state of mind which derives some value from mobility.

We may understand the drug phenomenon better if we think in

terms of the need for equilibrium. It was not until the advent of mass media that the operational mode of consciousness could penetrate every level of experience. At every point of contact with the world *out there* we found ourselves confronted with engineers. Our emotional responses had been fiddled with, tickled, trained. Every commercial sought to control these responses. Every government announcement had been designed to impress itself upon us at the deepest level possible. Subtle (and often not-so-subtle) manipulation had become the overwhelmingly dominant characteristic of the mass society in whose currents we found ourselves washed. Manipulation is pure operationalism. Almost nothing was said or done "in public" without a reason. The whole public sector had been turned into a fantasy world. Not incidentally, but fundamentally. And not despite "rationality," but strictly in accordance with the functionalistic imperatives inherent in our concept of rationality. It was to this world that we related ourselves, incorporating its distortions into our own systems. Even our "spontaneity," in part, had become based on emotional responses patterned on false memories.

Yet in its natural state, human consciousness possesses a "center," which is not a single point of identity but a psychic ecosystem of sorts. It was this system whose equilibrium had been massively disrupted by the full-scale intrusions of technological rationality, and it was this system which needed to right itself in order for identity, the touchstone of consciousness, to retain some basic intactness. Just as physically we require nourishment (real food) in order to survive, so psychically, we require real, substantial experience, real events, real people. Certainly, we still have much of that. But the servings of real experience, in relative terms, had shrunk drastically in comparison to the unreal experience with which we were daily confronted. The psyche was to become undernourished, its internal equilibrium was disrupted, and in order to regain that equilibrium, to replenish itself, the psyche had to make some large re-adjustments. It had to become more adept at distinguishing real from unreal, in order to reject the toxic food of unreal experience. And it had to find ways of improving its immediate perception of things and events. Drugs, insofar as their *use* (as opposed to their *mis*use) assisted in the process of cleansing the doors of perception, enlarging them at any rate so that they were no longer contained within the artificial operational frame, were admirably suited to one of the essential psychic requirements of the times.

Let us back up a bit at this point and see if we can get a little closer to what is meant by a "psychic center."

To begin with, not very much is known about the "mind" except that it is assumed to exist somewhere inside the brain. That does not narrow the search very much: exploring the brain is like sending a rocket into space; it is a bottomless universe. One might ask, where in the midst of the uncharted region am "I"?

There are roughly twelve billion nerve cells inside the brain. Each is capable of transmitting and receiving impulses from other nerve cells. Some of these cells may have as many as ten thousand transmitting terminals each. In comparison to the complexity of the workings of these cells, the most sophisticated computer is nothing much more than a toy.

Roughly, the brain is made up of the left and right cerebral hemispheres, each covered by a deeply folded cortex. Each cortex has a temporal lobe having something to do with hearing, an occipital lobe relating to seeing, a parietal region having to do with skin sensations and muscular activity, and the crucial frontal lobe which gives us the power to plan. Among other things, the brain also contains large tracts known only as "Silent Areas" about which nobody knows very much. Our sense of consciousness is assumed to be housed in the cortex, popularly known as the seat of the intellect. But when Wilder Penfield of the Montreal Neurological Institute explored the cortex of his patients during brain surgery by "tickling" different parts of it with an electrode, he discovered that the person being tickled could not be "found" there. "I" was always somewhere else. As science writer N. J. Berrill puts it,[30] people make use of the cortex, and may even in part be embodied there, but they remain "elusive even though fully at home. . . ." The question of consciousness is two-fold: What is it and where is it? We know almost nothing of the nature of thought and little of the relationship of mind to brain. "One of the few things which is known is that the activity of the brain is almost pure energy, primarily electrical. All cell activity is accompanied by electrical charges." Marshall McLuhan has defined automation as being "a nonspecialist kind of energy or power that can be used in a great variety of ways." This definition could as easily be applied to the mind, which could also be referred to as a "total synchronized electric field." Or, as Jung has described it, "a question mark arbitrarily confined within the skull." Science writer Berrill sums up most of what *is* known about the mind by saying, rather lamely, "consciousness, thought, the mind itself, are the expressions or creations of the sum total of the activities of twelve billion cells, each with multiple extensions and connections. Together they seem to embody pure energy of an electrical nature."

Our thoughts, our sense of identity itself, somehow emerge out of the seemingly random interplay of forces within this given area. How? No one knows. Why? Again, no one knows. Nevertheless, we take this most central of mysteries for granted. It seldom, if ever, crosses our "minds" that we do not know what our "minds" are. "I" exist and am conscious of being conscious, and it is possible to assume functions, to take on responsibilities, on the basis of this thinnest of threads of information.

Our "center" is therefore not a given point, but a whole effect. The impact of mass media and technological rationality can now perhaps be better understood. Just as the whole eco-system of the earth can be disrupted by the addition of certain compounds, so that the system loses its equilibrium and begins to collapse, so too can the "mind" be affected. The acquisition of false memories, false sets of responses, etc., disrupted the internal harmonies of the psyche in just such a fashion. The mind of technological man had become polluted. Well, everyone knew this. But few realized just how far the pollution had gone and how dangerous it was. The earth, obviously, had suffered the effects of pollution for thousands of years without its atmospheric balance being decisively affected. It was not until the Industrial Revolution that man's capacity to pollute took a quantum leap, suddenly threatening the balance of the whole global eco-system. Individual psychic eco-systems had, too, been affected by manipulation and tampering for thousands of years, but it was not until arrival of mass society that these basic harmonies likewise found themselves threatened on a gigantic scale. Drugs, at this point, may fairly accurately be conceived of as detergents being added to oil slick in order to clean up the mess.

The central point about drugs is the most obvious: the fact that they do nothing except alter the chemical relationships in the brain. (The mescaline molecule, for instance, resembles adrenalin. When mescaline is introduced, this enzyme, mistaking the mescaline molecules for adrenalin, begins to destroy them. While its attention is focused on the mescaline, however, the adrenalin begins to accumulate elsewhere: the enzyme can't handle both.) Once the chemical environment has been altered, the brain begins to function differently. *It is still functioning.* But not in accordance with established frames of reference. Frequently, it begins to work overtime. Images, thoughts, impressions, always flashing about in the background, suddenly move to stage center. The brain is now functioning in a different continuum. Like an engine run at high speed, it gets "broken in," accustomed, that is, to operating at a different frequency, rate of speed, and along different perceptual avenues. It becomes, in many basic respects, more agile.

It is, as a result, more *prepared* to move in new evolutionary directions. The mind trains with drugs. It acquires new reflexes, a new kind of coordination. It exercises its muscles and gets itself ready to take the leap into the future. The drug phenomenon is not an end. It is the beginning of something which has never happened before. What will follow is now becoming apparent. Drugs, finally, are only another medium. In the context of technological society, acting synergistically in relation to rock music, mass media, urbanization, and a host of other factors, this major new medium carries the message of change, *real* change, as opposed to a mere change in flags, label, underwear, or oaths of loyalty.

# EIGHT WHAT THE GREENING IS

Drugs and rock music. Ecology. The Secondary Effect of mass media. A compensatory leap in relation to the loss of direct perception. The need for psychic equilibrium. The liberating effects of urbanization. Holism. Learning to pick up vibes. Simplification of communication. Homeostatic adjustments. Changes in rhythm. The rejection of operationalism. A self-structuring hierarchical leap.

In this discussion, we have been moving even deeper into the largely uncharted seas of the psyche. We find ourselves being pulled, in our search for the new world of consciousness, ever closer to the line etched in our minds by Western thought beyond which the universe is assumed to end, the line separating the cognitive world from the intuitive – a line not unlike the one appearing on ancient sea charts, indicating nothing about the regions beyond except that "Here be monsters." This is the one region never deeply penetrated or mapped by white adventurers and certainly never – until recently – "colonized." Here is a whole uncivilized continent, a primitive world. And it is into this world that the postwar generation is now advancing, tapping a whole new complex of resources, coming into contact with ancient wisdoms, and finally, setting up colonies of their own. Like their white ancestors, they are for the most part fleeing from tyranny and oppression – in this case the tyranny of a mode of consciousness. They come riding new currents of rhythm, many borne by very "high" winds indeed, propelled by LSD, pot, hashish, peyote, mescaline, others guided by astrological charts or the *I Ching* – if they make use of ancient maps it is only because the West has failed to provide them with new ones. Some of course will make it without either charts or chemicals, but, at this stage, only a few seem capable of finding their own way. Whatever the case, having arrived, having broken from the old world of consciousness, the settlers find themselves still being called upon to swear out oaths of loyalty to the old order, to pay taxes, serve in the army, salute, hoist flags. They are not free. A war of independence might yet be their only course.

We are close now to the taproot of the conflict in America and elsewhere throughout technological society.

"If a distinction is to be made between men and monkeys, it is largely measureable by *the quantity of the sub-conscious which a higher order of being makes conscious.* That man really lives who brings the greatest fraction of his daily experience into the realm of the conscious."[31] One moves on to higher levels of being by bringing out into the open more of the "buried" segments of one's consciousness. From the moment these freshly-unearthed portions of consciousness have been incorporated into the whole "aware" self, one begins to see more, experience more, comprehend more. It is as though a supercharger had been attached to the engine of perception. The interplay of the forces which determine one's degree of consciousness become more complex and sophisticated, exactly in proportion to the amount of hitherto buried "material" which has been brought to the surface. To the degree that previously merely "intuitive" capabilities are introduced into the regions wherein we are aware, our perception will be heightened.

That unexplored "continent" of intuitive faculty now being penetrated in droves by the young is the lost world wherein most of our potential lies hidden. The further they penetrate it, the closer they come to genius. Let us consider the enormous implications.

Aldous Huxley has written:

Perhaps the men of genius are the only true men. In all the history of the race there have been only a few thousand real men. And the rest of us – what are we? Teachable animals. Without the help of the real men, we should have found out almost nothing at all. Almost all the ideas with which we are familiar could never have occurred to minds like ours. Plant the seeds there and they will grow; but our minds could never have spontaneously generated them. There have been whole nations òf dogs ... whole epochs in which no Man was born. From the dull Egyptians the Greeks took crude experience and rules of thumb and made sciences. More than a thousand years passed before Archimedes had a comparable successor. There has been only one Buddha, one Jesus, only one Bach that we know of, one Michelangelo.[32]

Often enough we are told that ninety percent of all the scientists who ever lived are alive today. But the real meaning of what is happening in technological society today cannot be understood if we ascribe to that fact anything more than marginal importance. The phenomena of central importance for our time is the fact that *probably just as great a percentage of all the geniuses and saints who ever lived are also alive today.*

It is not that *all* youngsters – whether of the first, second or third stages of the emerging postwar consciousness, have drawn deeply upon their buried potential, thus coming to tremendously expand their consciousness, because, clearly, most – the majority – have *not*. But the ratio of genius to normalcy has shifted markedly. These "stages" of postwar consciousness to which I have been referring may be conceived of as being classes. The overall performance of the class is based on the average. The presence of one brilliant pupil will raise the class average, but not by much. The presence of two brilliant pupils – both scoring very high individual averages – will boost the class average more. The presence of three or four brilliant students will begin to make a substantial difference. In the stages of postwar consciousness, we see that at the first stage there were a few whose perception had jumped. At the second stage, the number increases dramatically. At the third stage, it will have increased by as large a factor again.

It does not matter whether all youngsters acquire the heightened awareness or not. Genius is still far from the norm and will possibly not be the norm for centuries but, in the past, generations have managed to leave large imprints on the wall of history by virtue of nothing much more than the presence of one genius, maybe two, possibly three. Think now of the imprint which could be made by a generation containing not a handful, but thousands, possibly tens of thousands or even *millions* of geniuses – that is, individuals who had realized even a few percentage points more of their unused potential, that very potential which, according to the dictates of the operational mode, had been written off as being "unreal" because instruments had not been devised which could measure it.

When, intuitively, we "sense" something, we are responding invariably to a *whole effect*, responding in that region of the mind which lies out of reach of the conscious. Cognitively, we must trudge from A to B to C in our search for an evaluation of any given situation. It is slow, laborious work, a kind of mental arithmetic. One and one is two, therefore ... The *conscious* computer in our minds can seldom work much faster than the rate at which words or symbols can be strung together. Having long ago chosen the cognitive course, we inevitably brought our thought processes down to the speed limits imposed by such an arrangement. The degree to which we are still in the grip of this mode of consciousness can easily be demonstrated: "thoughts," to us, are mainly *unarticulated words*. Below the level of cognition, however, the processes of our minds are not hitched to so cumbersome a vehicle as language. They move that much faster. The intuitive regions, unhampered, skip the arithmetic method and proceed with what is, in effect, *systems analysis*, just now emerging at the cognitive end as the most sophisticated of all approaches. The speed of the modern computer must now be measured in nanoseconds. (A nanosecond has the same relationship to a second that a second has to thirty years.) Yet our brains have been working at a speed which could only begin to be measured in terms of nanoseconds all along. Only in the realms of the conscious has that speed been reduced, drastically, to seconds. In real terms of speed and efficiency, the conscious portions of the mind are those where "thoughts" which might take a second to be completed in the unconscious take the equivalent of thirty years to unfold. The conscious mind bears the same relationship to the unconscious as Charles Babbage's steel counting drums to the latest planar diffusion computer.

The unconscious therefore shows itself to be a superior device, in terms of the velocities involved and the ability of the "system" to cope with incoming data.

All waves of creativity are the results of seismic activity in the intuitive deeps. We may study the waves, measure them, calculate their dimensions and the patterns they form; we may watch them roll up on the beach of accomplishment; but the deep disturbances which set these waves in motion remain hidden from our view. We know virtually nothing about the mechanisms of creativity. The first time anything is done, it involves an inspiration, a sudden shift, however slight, in the way that a given situation (or reality) is viewed. After that first time, however, men may memorize the technique and come to imitate it, requiring no similar ignition by the spark of inspiration themselves. Thus the most gigantic projects may be undertaken with often no inspiration at all involved. What is uninspired, however, always reveals itself by virtue of its flatness, *ordinariness*, its embodiment of nothing new. The *inspired* project has at least *something* that is new, fresh, original. Inspiration may be denied as the actualization of something new – the bringing-into-existence for the first time of an idea, method, expression, viewpoint, perspective or whatever which had not until then come into focus in the consciousness of any man. It involves, therefore, *an addition* to our collective pool of awareness. What is uninspired merely makes use of the material at hand, without adding anything. Creation is pure addition. Initially, it is adding something to nothing.

The great inspirations, the truly profound creative acts, add enormous gobs to the sum total of our consciousness (the Theory of Relativity, geometry, the discovery of fire). And even when a pure discovery is involved, at the very least a connection must be made. That is, there is no discovery if the discoverer does not connect what he finds to what he knows – in order for any discovery to have meaning it must be incorporated into the existing body of knowledge, *added*; otherwise it is not claimed (or reclaimed) and used. It acquires no value, has no effect, and thus may as well not have been stumbled-upon. The "discoverer" who does not find some way of connecting his discovery to what is already known in fact makes no discovery at all. The true "discoverer," therefore, is the man who is inspired to make the connection between the finding and what is known. He is the one who perceives something in a way that it has never been perceived before, whose experience of reality is to some degree (however slight, however great) deeper than anyone else's has ever been before. The extent to which he expands (or adds to) our over-all consciousness will depend entirely on how great his perceptual leap into the dark has been.

The key here is always what we call inspiration, creativity, genius, and it is a process which, no matter how much conscious information and perception it involves, is always triggered by some unconscious mechanism, an exercise of intuitive power. Our civilization, in this sense, has been built on insights engineered by that part of our consciousness which remains to this day beyond the reach of measurement. Today, almost our entire environment (concrete, real, factual, measureable) is fashioned from material retrieved originally by the working of intuition. Cognition has been but a chariot hitched to the winged stallion of the invisible parts of our mind.

Thus, what we see before us when we look at the way in which the post-war consciousness manifests itself is evidence of the passage of increasingly large numbers of those winged stallions. The consciousness projects itself along precisely those lines leading most directly into the deepest intuitive regions. Rock music, its rhythms emanating from some point far closer to the heart than any other Western musical idiom, loosens up the muscular responses, gets the body out of its straight-jacket, and comes thereby to influence one's mode of consciousness; for the psyche will acquire a rhythm derived from (or at least in harmony with) one's physical rhythm. The rhythm will be closer to the real center of the whole psycho-biological self, as opposed to the merely psychological self (so highly-developed in "literate" people) or the physiological self (developed in "illiterate" or "primitive" people). The rhythms of rock music achieve a fusion, slight in many, large in others, but still a welding-together of otherwise unintegrated parts. And, as the rhythm of consciousness is dragged downward, so to speak, it finds itself less and less constrained by purely cognitive, operationalistic processes. It may dip with ever-increasing ease and familiarity into the underground regions of the psyche, drawing upon the vast resources of the intuitive; resources not at the disposal of those whose consciousness still responds only to the slow, labored, mechanical rhythms of operationalism.

Similarly, drugs which scramble the inorganic and culturally pre-determined grid of consciousness have the effect of letting the subconscious play more freely in those territories of awareness where only consciousness had been allowed to move before. The word "flash" is uttered frequently among the young and among psychedelic drug-users. It is used because, under the influence of a drug, such as marijuana or LSD, images, ideas, thought, snatches of conversations, visions, impressions and so on move with tremendous speed through the user's mind, "flashing" past at a speed so great he "loses" almost all of it, or, on most occasions, *all* of it. The next day, or whenever he has "come down," he is liable to remember little of what he experienced. *Objective* events may remain fixed firmly in his consciousness. Unlike the alcohol consumer, the soft drug user will seldom have had his perception blotted out. He is far more liable to remember with considerable clarity what happened to him and around him. As for the internal experiences, most will undoubtedly be lost. We all know that dreams which seemed to take hours, sometimes days, to unravel while we were experiencing them, in fact took place within the span of a few seconds. Likewise, the drug-user's experience of time will be drastically altered, and a reverie which might have seemed to take hours will have passed within less than a minute. On other occasions, whole hours are likely to be compressed into the experience of little more than a handful of seconds or minutes.

Not bound to a single perception of time, the drug user may wander more freely among his impressions. He may experience them in different ways, perceiving aspects which – because of his "fixed" perceptual position before – had remained unnoticed. In effect, he may "shrink" in terms of consciousness to the point where he may deal with microscopic impressions as though they had been blown to gigantic proportions. Thus he may notice things about their texture, their shape, and so on, which he would not likely otherwise have noticed. In the same way, his consciousness may "swell" so that his perceptive is altered. Standing, in terms of consciousness, a mile high, he achieves a vantage point from which to look at a whole territory, rather like a man perched on a mountain. He "sees" things – the ways in which roads run together, the patterns formed by different plots of land, etc. – which he was not liable to see from down on the ground. Shrinking and growing in terms of perception like Alice in Wonderland (no accident that story is so beloved of drug-users) he is moved far more by the tides emerging from the unconscious. These tides, in fact, will flood the little towns of his operational consciousness, and when they drain away some debris from the deeps will remain. Much may be as useless as seaweed. But some treasures will have been disgorged as well. These will be the "flashes," the "connections," the "insights," the inspirations washed up by storms blowing from the subconscious. Stafford and Golightly say as much in *LSD. The Problem-Solving Psychedelic*:

But what is known of this extraordinary process that can produce the ingenious invention, the earth-shaking discovery which revolutionizes human thought and life? How does the suddenly "lighted mind" become illuminated? Are we all actually capable of being innovators?

Herbert Read, speaking of artists in the large sense, has said that all children are artists, as are some adults. As people grow older, they are thought to lose their creative ability, and such loss is widely accepted with unquestioning resignation. The readiness with which we accept this deprivation is puzzling, but the apathy, inhibitions, diminished faith and hope, weariness, and a "lack of time" that disfigure life – all these are certainly prominent culprits. Yet the significance of creativity to human beings is of untold depth and magnitude. The world as we know it is the result of the creative thoughts and discoveries of relatively few men; usually we recognize this by recognizing them.

Considering the number of people who have inhabited the earth, and do so now, the small body of invention and discovery is amazing. Why do we so easily fall victim to the forces which destroy creativity? Perhaps it is because the creative impulse is lodged in such a remote and inaccessible place:

It is a highly significant, though generally neglected fact that those creations of the human mind, which have borne pre-eminently the stamp of originality and greatness, have not come from within the region of consciousness. They have come from beyond consciousness, knocking at its door for admittance: they have flowed into it, sometimes slowly as if by seepage, but often with a burst of overwhelming power.[33]

LSD, they write, "calls forth unexpected intuitive material which may develop into an answer." And so, to a lesser but generally more controllable degree, do milder psychedelics such as marijuana and hashish.

It remains that drugs are but a vehicle which, when used and not merely mis-used, may liberate the creative intuitive faculty. They are not the "solution" or "answer" to the problem of liberating the greater consciousness: the "solution" is arrived at when the mind reaches the point where it liberates itself, when the process becomes natural or automatic, when the mind, in short, realizes its own potential itself, or actualizes itself. (Becomes itself its whole self.) Nevertheless, it remains that the "drug phenomenon" indicates a determined shift in the direction of liberation of the greater consciousness. Abruptly, millions of people are "making the jump," leaping into the dark of the subconscious, bringing their findings back into their everyday experience, adding large gobs of perception to their effective whole, seeing more than they were able to see before.

One last quote from Stafford and Golightly:

Current scientific research seems to be as varied and complex as are the countless forms of living organisms. The breakthroughs now being made strike awe in their observers, however different the areas of scientific inquiry may be. Today's exciting achievements no longer come mainly from the mechanistic, simplistic concepts of classical mathematics and physics, but are being made in biology and genetics, and in the study of the mind. In Washington and the Virgin Islands scientists are trying to communicate with dolphins. In California dozens of laboratories are working with electrical brain implantations, with "sensory deprivation" and with experiments to change genes. Throughout the country researchers are studying RNA, DNA, Cylert, acetamido-benzoate and a host of other chemicals with which they hope to probe the mysterious labyrinths of human mentality.

In all of these simultaneously conducted studies, we seem to stand on the threshold of discovering how to revolutionize life as it is now known. *A revision of man's total concepts, so drastic as to have no parallel in history, seems to be in the offing.* [My italics.] Much of this has been stimulated by the knowledge turned up through LSD, and more seems probable. This is because the simple ingestion of the chemical clearly demonstrates that other realities do indeed exist with their own boundaries, logic and laws.[34]

"A revision of man's total concepts, so drastic as to have no parallel in history" would seem, indeed, to be what is involved. All these manifestations of what is broadly called "youth culture" have in common a disregard for the old operationalistic mode of consciousness. These phenomena may be different from each other, but they are all different from the old mode in basically the same way – that is, they all draw upon the buried reservoirs of intuition. They stem from the regions on which Western logic long ago closed the door, building a civilization almost entirely within the walls provided by the concept of length. Those walls are being stormed and civilization itself, in the supremely technological form it has taken, is being changed as never before.

Protests against war are no incidental part of all this. For war is perhaps the most extreme fashion in which the operational consciousness expresses itself. Domination is pure operationalism. The air-tight logic of the Cold War is completely "rational" in terms of functionalism. No less so than pollution. The current attacks on war and pollution, and identically on poverty, are attacks which are directed finally against the very roots of Western civilization. War, pollution, and poverty are but obscene flowers blooming on the same warped stem. It does no good to snip off the flowers if the plant itself is not uprooted.

The conflict between the two basic modes of consciousness goes deep. Deeper, possibly, it could not go. For those who have had their boundaries of consciousness defined by the operational mode have long since come to accept their "reality" as being the *only* reality. They believe in their world, the world of manipulation, domination, power and role-playing. It is a functionalistic world, therefore measureable, therefore real. The new postwar consciousness operated at a deeper level, a level closer to that previously reserved for the rare individual, the man we would call genius. This new consciousness is most threatened by people who are aggressive and/or ignorant. And it is exactly those people who, for the most part, will have achieved positions of strength in the old cultural context. For one thing, the old order rewards aggressiveness with power. One must be aggressive indeed to "rise to the top," to fight one's way there, to retain power once it has been acquired. The unaggressive fall by the wayside or are trampled in the rush. Less directly, the old order likewise rewards ignorance. The ignorant are spared much agony. They need experience little conflict within themselves, need worry not at all about the consequences of given actions, need have no doubts or worries, simply because ignorance boards up the windows of perception through which one may view serious problems, dilemmas, crises. It is the ignorant in league with the aggressive who will yet trigger a thermonuclear war or poison the planet to death. The new consciousness, seeing this clearly, must (whether it likes it or not) finally opt to do battle with the old consciousness. It is a question, at this stage, of the survival of all of us.

Right at the onset of *One-Dimensional Man*, Herbert Marcuse described the situation perfectly:

Does not the threat of an atomic catastrophe which could wipe out the human race also serve to protect the very forces which perpetuate this danger? The efforts to prevent such a catastrophe overshadow the search for its potential causes in contemporary industrial society. These causes remain unidentified, unexposed, unattacked by the public because they recede before the all too obvious threat from without – to the West from the East, to the East from the West. Equally obvious is the need for being prepared, for living on the brink, for facing the challenge. We submit to the peaceful production of the means of destruction, to the perfection of waste, to being educated for a defense which deforms the defenders and that which they defend.

If we attempt to relate the causes of the danger to the way in which society is organized and organizes its members, we are immediately confronted with the fact that advanced industrial society becomes richer, bigger, and better as it perpetuates the danger. The defense structure makes life easier for a greater number of people and extends man's mastery of nature. Under these circumstances, our mass media have little difficulty in selling particular interests as those of all sensible men. The political needs and aspirations, their satisfaction promotes business and the commonweal, and the whole appears to be the very embodiment of Reason.

And yet this society is irrational as a whole. Its productivity is destructive of the free development of human needs and faculties, its peace maintained by the constant threat of war, its growth dependent on the repression of the real possibilities for pacifying the struggle for existence, individual, national, and international.[35]

It is "this society" *as a whole* which is the problem, and which must be transcended, not simply the particular forms in which its essential nature reveals itself. It is the realization of this fact that prompts so many of the young to call for a revolution. *Now*. With each passing year – each year in which the hand of the old consciousness can be seen to be tightening, not relinquishing, its grip on the levers of power – the situation grows more desperate.

We come now to the essential nature of the new consciousness. It is *holistic*. Holistic philosophies have always abounded, but against the karate blows of technological rationality they stood little chance. The superiority of the operational mode lent itself to easy measurement, could easily be demonstrated, and in any test of power was virtually bound to come off the winner. Thus the technological society came to inherit the world. Now, however, we see that operationalism has fatal flaws as a vehicle of survival. For the first time in history, the adoption of a holistic (as opposed to an exclusive, functionalistic) philosophy becomes a matter of necessity. We may not blow ourselves up for a while. But the continued preeminence of the logic of domination in terms of our dealing with our environment absolutely guarantees our destruction. The environmental collapse has long since begun, and while the slippage as yet has been relatively slight, it will not be long before it becomes an avalanche.

Problems relating to the environment go deeper than any that manifest themselves in the political and cultural spheres. While the new consciousness may find itself in opposition to the political and cultural manifestations of the operational mode to varying degrees, it finds itself in total opposition to the way in which the mode relates itself to the environment. In effect, on the issue of environment, the struggle gets right down to earth. By nature, the new holistic consciousness is basically an *ecological* consciousness. The less it is constrained by the narrow operational mode, the more it is capable of responding to the kind of "over-view" provided by ecology. The ecological consciousness, by itself, must lead us inevitably to a holistic philosophy, back to the pre-Socratic notion of everything being in a state of flux. This awareness is as alien to Western thought as Zen. Ecology involves, finally, the recognition of whole systems, instead of incomplete sub-systems. It teaches us to recognize gestalts, to understand synergy, to appreciate the extent to which we are only one facet of an environment. Already, it has opened the path leading to a theology of the earth, thus short-circuiting Christianity and pointing the way back toward the kind of unfragmented, harmonious mental space understood perfectly by the ancient Chinese and – more intuitively – by primitive peoples the world over. Ecological consciousness, in short, is the common denominator of the real revolution which is just now beginning inside the gates of the comfortable concentration camp fashioned by technique. It is the root whose growth will make the difference, in the future, between freedom and unfreedom, stagnation and flowering.

There is no need at this stage to argue that an environmental collapse is taking place and that we are collectively being forced to take steps – technical as well as psychological – to accommodate ourselves to the reality of our new situation.[36] *Fortune* magazine was able, in February, 1970, to point out that the bias in benefit-cost analysis had begun to shift in favor of environmental quality, on purely economic grounds. Studies had shown that in the long-range view, pollution abatement seemed likely to *increase* the real Gross National Product, once such factors as sickness and death benefits, training costs because of employee turnover, property values, medical services, corrosion and transportation problems associated with environmental deterioration had been taken into consideration. By reducing the "Gross National Effluent" – a statitistical basket for all those negative goods, effects and services produced in the process of production of positive goods and services – economists were able to show that there would actually be a net gain in the GNP. That discovery in itself, inauspicious as it might seem to many, had breached the real wall which capitalism had raised against pollution control; namely, that it reduced profits. Even for the greedy, it no longer made sense to go on indiscriminately plundering the planet. As for the politics of environmental quality, by 1970 it had become evident that a common ground had at last been found on which Students for a Democratic Society could stand shoulder-to-shoulder with the John Birch Society, Black Panthers could march with Republican businessmen, and even the AFL-CIO, the National Rifle Association, the National Audubon Society, the Sierra Club and the United Automobile Workers could come together in a front which defied all traditional political lines of tension. Acidheads and little old ladies in tennis shoes were suddenly in league – at least on this one issue. Breathers of the world, unite! The courts, too, had begun to respond to the new perspective. As James E. Krier, acting professor of law at UCLA, put it: "The promised surge of environmental litigation calls for re-thinking much of our substantive and procedural law. Much of that law was made during the prime of the old, proprietary lawsuit, which it suited well enough; it fits poorly, however, the frame of the new lawsuit brought to protect environmental (not economic) values in the public (not private) interest. The common-law concepts of nuisance and waste, for example, are not responsive to the needs of environmental litigation . . . they reflect a far too narrow and myopic view. . . . "

Those common-law concepts, narrow and myopic, were of course only a reflection of more general Western values. From the beginning, Western society was a ripoff culture (i.e. exploitative, extractive). The effect of the Industrial Revolution was to provide the pirates with bulldozers and cost sheets. The logic of the parasite had all along been the basis for the expansion of our civilization. Loren Eiseley gives us the following (accurate) perspective of ourselves, a perspective not limited to Western culture, but finding its most refined expression there: "It is with the coming of man that a vast hole seems to open in nature, a vast black whirlpool spinning faster and faster, consuming flesh, stones, soil, minerals, sucking down the lightning, wrenching power from the atom, until the ancient sounds of nature are drowned in the cacophony of something which is no longer nature, something instead which is loose and knocking at the world's heart, something demonic and no longer planned – escaped, it may be spewed out of nature, contending in a final giant's game against its master."[37]

It is precisely the "narrow" and "myopic" view, characteristic of Western culture, reflected in our common-law concepts concerning environment, which the ecological consciousness moves against. In short, the politics of ecology is not an interior decorating project (covering pastel plaster walls with paisley wallpaper); rather, it involves, finally, a tearing down of those walls – not necessarily literally, but, at the very least, psychologically. It is a fundamental assault, a storming not simply of the head offices of a polyglot corporation, but of the *head.* Attitudes, beliefs, values and cultural conditioning lie at the roots of our current environmental situation. Trimming the lawn at this stage is little more than an exercise in good sense. Beyond that, what is involved is a basic rearrangement of our psychic processes.

Ward Shepard comes close to putting his finger on it: "The ideological status of ecology is that of a resistance movement . . . [it] challenges the private or public right to pollute the environment, to systematically destroy predatory animals, to spread chemical pesticides indiscriminately, to meddle chemically with food and water, to appropriate without hindrance space and surface for technological and military ends; [it] opposes the uninhibited growth of human populations . . . the needless addition of radioactivity to the landscape, the extinction of species of plants and animals, the domestication of all wild places, large-scale manipulation of the atmosphere or the sea, and most other purely engineering solutions to problems of and intrusions into the organic world." [38] The organic world! We are getting close now to the real heart of the matter. But let us close in slowly ... A writer in the magazine *Manas*, reviewing Shepard's book, adds: "Ecology, then, is a profession by means of which its practitioners grow into the habit of having a care for the world. The dimensions of what they study insist upon nothing less. *Some primordial axiom of internal relations impresses itself upon men, who little by little, are led to see nature whole.* ... [My italics.] The ecologist sometimes sounds like a lay interpreter of ancient religions of nature. Himself a celebrant of the unity of life, he finds wonderful anticipations in the faiths of other times. He may, on occasion, declare his discovery that these people *knew*." [39] Which brings us to Shepard's key point: "It [the ecological consciousness] is manifest, for example, among pre-Classical Greeks, in Navajo religion and social orientation, in Romantic poetry of the 18th and 19th centuries, in Chinese landscape painting of the 11th century, in current Whiteheadian philosophy, in Zen Buddhism, in the world view of the Cretan Great Mother, in the ceremonials of Bushman hunters, and in the medieval Christian metaphysics of light. What is common among all of them is a deep sense of engagement with the landscape, with profound connections to surroundings and to natural processes central to all life." [40]

The ecological consciousness is not emerging strictly in cause-and-effect terms as a response to the threat of environmental collapse. So far as politicians, big unions, corporations and many a housewife are concerned, this may seem to be the only explanation. Yet is is no coincidence that, simultaneously, we see a tremendous surge in the popularity of astrology; the *I Ching* takes its place on Western bookshelves next to the Bible or in place of it. No coincidence, either, that "heads" are particularly responsive to the ecological message, along with people who have been involved in various kinds of group encounter experiences, particularly Gestalt therapy. The ecological consciousness is holistic, which explains the harmony it enjoys with these other seemingly unrelated contemporary phenomena.

"Turning on" is, in large measure, a process of acquiring a holistic view – that is, perceiving unity, harmony and interactions where, before, one perceived nothing but chaos. The "organic world" is that real world that lies buried beneath asphalt, obscured by political boundaries, latitudes and longitudes, sales charts and grids; it is the reality which the Western mind can perceive only partially through the filter of operationalism. The ecological *consciousness* is that which has penetrated the barrier of lineation and begun to perceive harmonies understood intuitively before the onset of the alphabet and geometry. There is nothing abstract about it at all.

As we are led – or rather, *forced* by the overwhelming evidence at hand of environmental deterioration – to take ecological factors into larger and larger account, we are, willy-nilly, being turned on. Our awareness of the environment is growing at the moment like a bruise: we are beginning to feel pain and becoming conscious of lacerations, deep self-inflicted wounds. Our lungs hurt. Our hearts betray symptoms of stress. Our nerves are shot. Each day we move closer to a realization that environmental disruptions produce corresponding disruptions in our own bodies; we are *not* isolated from our environment. If we blast tons of carbon monoxide into the atmosphere, the shockwaves penetrate deep into our own rib cages. And so, slowly, for the most part grudgingly, we are pulled down from our highrise temples. It turns out that we are not the masters of creation; like mice in a field being covered with asphalt, we are after all victims as well of our own aggression. When the technological whip is cracked, it is not simply the rocks and the trees and the rivers which suffer. We suffer too. There is a backlash. It gets harder every day to continue to assert our superiority over nature. We are forced to make concessions, and if these concessions are not made we will simply kill ourselves off.

These "concessions" – efforts to "control" environmental quality, to "manage" resources, to "balance" economic needs with biological needs, to "conserve" nature – amount finally to a tetanic admission that we are not so masterful after all. It is not just the natives who are restless, it is the earth herself. It seems there were some fine-print clauses in the real estate contract which gave us ownership of the planet. We, too, must pay rent – which is nothing less than homage to the need to maintain the integrity of the whole system. We cannot order it as we like. The brute cannot be made to go when we want it to go: we may ride it, but to try to steer it off the path it was following all along can only lead to its bucking us off into the ditch wherein the bones of all extinct species lie. Hey! Man, even technological man, is not the king after all! He is only one more servant – the high priest, if he so chooses. But if his intention is to be the assassin or nothing more than a pirate, he will be blotted out like a stain. For us to even approach this realization is no small matter of shuffling a few pieces of value-furniture. It represents a displacement from the center of the world stage as thorough-going as the displacement from the center of the universe wrought by Copernicus. Rather abruptly, we find ourselves knocked from our pedestals. We perceive, from our new perspective (on the ground) that there *is* a higher order to which we must pay much more than lip service. We must, at the very least, bend a knee. Yes, we are made more humble.

The point is not that we are making any great discovery through the agency of such sciences as ecology and cybernetics, but that we are re-discovering the essential requirement of harmony, a requirement well understood by less arrogant peoples, in less sophisticated times. Our own understanding will finally be more thorough, less tainted by superstition and fear. This, in the end, will be the gift of science; an understanding of natural processes which does not end with intuition, an understanding which perhaps will go no deeper (how much deeper can you go than to *know?*) but which will at least have been verified beyond all possible doubt, and which will not be helpless in the face of the logic of avarice; thus, better able to defend itself.

The ecological consciousness, therefore, represents nothing much more than the kind of comprehension of reality a child develops once he has learned he cannot always have his own way. It can be seen as a phase in our collective coming of age. It is, however, not an end. Only a beginning. Coming into contact with the organic world, learning to appreciate not only its beauty but its power (and retaliatory capability), heralds the beginning of the end of the period during which we thought of ourselves as beings somehow "apart" from nature. We are learning to know better. And so the door is open to a further understanding. We are not only tenants who must pay rent and abide by the house rules of nature; we are also her children. As we come closer to respecting natural functions, organic nature, the harmony of living things, a profound psychic uprooting takes place: we are no longer so dependent on the concept of length (which for a long time served as a weapon and a tool against which there seemed to be no real opposition). We are less inclined to dismiss those things which cannot be measured, less certain of our ability to relate everything to a set of operations. Doors in our minds once firmly sealed begin to open. Reflexively, many of us have begun to look with far less suspicion for *other* "higher" orders, other deeper harmonies, other dimensions of interaction and interdependence. Ecology demonstrates the existence of internal relationships to which we in the West were oblivious for centuries. "Primordial axioms" of subtle inter-linked mutual dependencies are no longer the subject of mystic speculation: they are established (and very empirical) facts. But those which *have* been established, and which furnish the basis for those so-far rather narrow anti-pollution campaigns surfacing everywhere, relate only to purely physical processes. We have begun to understand what the world "psycho-somatic" means: namely, that between biology and psychology there is no crystal-clear demarcation line. The psychic and the physical are no more fundamentally separated from one another than water and air. The *illusion* of separation remains fixed, but we have been taught by our physicists to distrust such illusions. (From the purely logical point of view, it has been argued that physical objects *per se* are a myth. Adolf Grunbaum notes that physical "things" are only physical events. Max Born observes that "often a measureable quantity is not a property of a thing, but a property of its relation to other things ....")[41] So, in short, the rationale (the operationalistic rationale) for rejecting outright the possibility of other more complex interrelationships and harmonies, has been dealt something very close to a death-blow. For every housewife who joins an anti-pollution group, one more human being has been added to the numbers of those who have had, or are about to have, some first-hand experience with the limitations of technological "rationality." It was faith in that "rational" order which initially turned her off to the possibility of regularities in nature which could not be quantified, categorized, and bottled by science. Now, as her faith in "rationality" crumbles under the impact of oil slick on beaches and poison in the air her children must breathe, she is that much less turned-off. The technologically rational way of doing things and perceiving things has its shortcomings.... Almost automatically, she finds herself being "turned on" to more organic processes. It is a small beginning, but it has tremendous reach. Once one's unqualified faith in the rationality of science has been shattered, one is no longer a true slave to the technological order. At least a small part of one's psyche has been liberated.

So, the hoisting of the green flag of ecology means that a lot of people, millions of otherwise perfectly "normal" people, are being turned-on to the realization that there *do* exist subtle harmonies and inter-relationships which they had been schooled to ignore, or whose existence had simply been dismissed. Now that there is DDT in the bodies of penguins, who can argue any longer that once a border has been drawn there is no more to be said? Who is to say any longer one is not affected by the behavior of men on the other side of the planet? Who is to say any longer that one's own behavior does not have an effect beyond those which are immediately observable? Who is to say that fences in reality are anything more than pieces of dead wood stuck in a regular fashion in the ground along a purely imaginary line in the earth? The ecological consciousness has tremendous political implications. The concept of "private property," its sacredness and validity, is not long for this world. And as the awareness of inter-dependency deepens, the arbitrary nature of political boundaries will become as commonly apparent as those of property lines. There is no small shaking up going on here. Few anti-pollution organizations as yet have faced (or even comprehended) the political and psychological consequences of their actions, and it really doesn't matter, since they are acting spontaneously. Once the pollution battles have been won, the green flag planted on the industrial equivalent of Iwo Jima, those people who have been involved in the battle will find themselves – to their surprise – looking around them with a very different set of perceptions. And it will be, inevitably, a very different world which they are perceiving, one where the central concern is for the forest first (the public domain) and the individual trees (the private) second. A basic reversal of priorities will have taken place.

If the new postwar consciousness finds itself in harmony with rock music, drugs, and so on, the degree of harmony is still small in comparison to the harmony it experiences with the purely ecological consciousness. In ecology we see the new consciousness finding its roots, just as the old consciousness found its resting-place in the embrace of technological society. The new consciousness therefore at last has a home, and it is hitched at this point to a powerful force working for rapid and fundamental change. So long as it could connect itself solely to such vehicles as mysticism or music or drugs there was not much chance it would make any serious penetrations into the power structure. Finding an outlet for expression through such vehicles as the anti-war movement, Black liberation struggles, student impatience, it took on considerable political weight – but still not enough, for the opposition was tremendous. Now, however, the consciousness begins to find expression through the potentially much more powerful medium of the environmental movement. The bullet has finally found its gun. Now it may be propelled far and fast, with explosive force.

And it is just at this moment, when the issue of the environment has come into focus, that the "third stage" of the postwar consciousness, the most potent stage yet, begins to roll in like a wave. It is a tidal wave.

# NINE THE FIRST THREE STAGES

The three stages of the holistic consciousness which has been developing in the postwar period may broadly be categorized as being:

At the first stage, cultural.

At the second, political.

At the third, environmental.

At each stage, the assault widens. Its sphere of action expands. Initially, expressed through the Beat Generation, it found itself in an attack upon the values, mores, concepts, and attitudes of the dominant culture. At the second stage, nothing has changed – the assault is against the same cultural bastions, but the new consciousness has begun to move on other fronts: the conflict spills over into the political arena. Now, as the third stage begins to congeal, we see that the conflict has expanded again. While it has shed nothing – it is still both cultural and political – it has achieved a far greater definition. Not only has the new consciousness at this stage transcended the cultural limitations of its incubator, not only has it outgrown the old political categories, but now, having passed through the "outer walls" of one-dimensional society, it finds itself at the innermost gate, confronted with the real beast astride the throne of the technological order: pure operationalism itself.

As the new consciousness attains its environmental perspective, it becomes an all but irresistible force. At this stage it cannot be rejected, as it was at earlier stages; the science of ecology becomes, in effect, the midwife of the new consciousness, delivering it from the womb of the youthful counter culture, depositing it on the doorstep of the dominant society, where it cannot fail to be adopted. Failure at this stage to adopt the holistic outlook will result, quite simply, in an environmental catastrophe. The realization that a reversal in priorities must come about – and soon – is dawning everywhere throughout technological society. Hardly anyone can deny any longer than technology is a dog that bites. In America, this is most evident. One may see the shift in attitudes that is taking place most clearly in California where in the lifetime of most of its citizens the state has gone from being a land of milk and honey to a land of junk piles and smog.

We are all aware that inventions, technological innovations, discoveries and theories do not come to be adopted until they are required, or at least until they can be harnessed – that is, connected to the given state of social development, incorporated into the existing body of knowledge. The same may be said of modes of consciousness. The operational mode seemed for a long time to serve all our needs; only recently have the fatal limitations of this mode become apparent. Now the need is for a more inclusive, greatly expanded, consciousness. The new holistic consciousness is exactly what is required. At its first two stages it could be rejected because none of the vehicles through which it expressed itself led directly into the existing body of social political knowledge. Rather, they went around, skirted, or generally avoided contact with the dominant social order. They were, at the very least, antagonistic. As the new consciousness comes into phase with ecology, however, it finds itself with a vehicle at its disposal which *does* connect it with society as a whole. Most of the citizens of technological society will reject outright the perceptions of the holistic consciousness; few, however, will reject quite so readily the perceptions offered through the medium of ecology. Thus, they are led to adopt the imperatives of holism. The new consciousness finally emerges from what is called the sub-culture and begins to be incorporated into the body of society.

The possibility of a relatively smooth transition from purely operationalistic to holistic consciousness now surfaces. Put nakedly, ecology will prove to be a bridge across the generation gap. Across this bridge the insights and perspectives of the new consciousness may flow. It matters little at this stage whether the old mode of consciousness willingly sheds its skin or not. The accumulating evidence of environmental collapse will force the adoption of radically different priorities, priorities much more in harmony with the vision of the new consciousness.

Thus we see that a wide avenue exists along which the new consciousness may pass into the social order, communicating its perceptions and coming to have them adopted. For the transformations – many of them just incidentally political and cultural – which will necessarily be involved if environmental deterioration is to be avoided will be in line with the perceptions of the holistic consciousness as opposed to the purely operational consciousness. The political and cultural resistance to change is too great for the transformation to take place in these other spheres. In the larger environmental sphere of awareness, however, the transformation can be seen to be essential and – more to the point – *functional*. The imperatives of the old mode of consciousness dictate that since environmental deterioration can be measured and related to a set of operations, it is *real*. Therefore it can and must be responded to. It makes no difference that the responses will inevitably lead to the adoption of the holistic consciousness (now understood, due to the fact that it has so far mainly manifested itself through rock music, drugs, mysticism, etc., to be antagonistic to the old order.) The old order will be transformed without really realizing the fundamental nature of the transformation.

It is important to realize, however, the new consciousness itself has, at each stage, been undergoing transformations. The first stage it pressed for a cultural revolution, at the second for a political revolution. Now, the incoming third stage shows every sign of having outgrown both these limitations. While a purely cultural revolution was seen by the second stage to be insufficient, thus pushing the conflict into the political stage, at the third stage it becomes apparent that even a political revolution will not suffice. At the environmental stage of development, the new consciousness proceeds *beyond* political categories.

Let us consider the organic nature of these "stages" in the development of the new consciousness. The rough categorizations are necessarily arbitrary. They are, moreover, based on the American experience. This was done because it is in America that the

new consciousness first appeared – *as a collective re-structuring.*
The basic, collective pattern has tended strongly to repeat itself in
other technological nations. To varying degrees it has been repressed, delayed, resisted, suffocated. But steadily, like a tide coming in, it has persisted. We see that in the Soviet Union the first
stage has hardly been able to come into focus. The Russians are
far from the second stage, although it is important to note that in
some ways the *third* stage is being allowed to manifest itself. This
illustrates the point made earlier: that ecology is the one medium
through which the new consciousness may express itself no matter
how rigid, dictatorial or hostile the dominant culture. The *organic*
nature of the restructuring may be more readily appreciated if we
peel back the labels "cultural," "political" and "environmental"
and look at what they mean in terms of personal growth.

Initially, what is involved is a purely "individual" matter. One's
relationship with oneself is altered. One begins to see oneself in a
new light. Assumptions about one's identity, role, the very nature
of one's perceptions, find themselves being challenged ("cognitive
dissonance"). The change begins in one's own head.

At the second stage, one begins to look around at one's society.
The doubts about one's self expand. Now one doubts the assumptions about one's society. It is the same process, but the connection between individual identity and the identity of the society
which produces the individual is made.

At the first stage, the cognitive dissonance may only be resolved
by a re-structuring of the individual by himself. In a collective
sense, this is a cultural change. At the second stage, re-structuring
can only be affected through political action.

At the third stage, however, one's doubts about oneself and
one's doubts about one's society expand again. Now the dissonance centers on even-deeper forces – namely, the basic nature of
one's relationship and one's society's relationship to the world
itself. The conflict becomes more fundamental than any merely
political conflict. What is involved is not simply a transfer of
power, but a transformation of the entire working relationship
with the natural world. At the environmental stage of development, the new consciousness has not only burst out of its cultural
and political frameworks, *it has transcended the entire edifice of
the man-made environment.* At both earlier stages, the new consciousness confronts basic problems which have been created by
men in the course of history. It is dealing strictly with synthetic

elements in existence, with the problems and tensions and mistakes which have been piling-up for centuries, burying us all in an avalanche of artifacts. The hangups have all been fashioned by human hands. The third stage begins to be *post-historic*. It does not merely confront social and political realities. It confronts the penultimate question of how man must order his existence in relation to his planet. It sees *over* the mountain-sized garbage heap and treasure pile of human history and begins to perceive the world again, its view no longer walled in by what has been wrought in the last few thousand years. Systems as much as toothbrushes are a part of our heritage and so long as one is only dealing with crises which are the product of that heritage, one is really only acting out an old family quarrel. One has not yet left the home or the social mansion. Domestic quarrels may be real, may be deadly, but they are essentially turned inward. In achieving the environmental stage of development, the new consciousness finally steps out of its home, its incubator, and goes out into the world. This is the moment of historic maturation.

A fourth stage is apparent. The collective experience of consciousness-expansion leads inevitably in this direction. The line of development is clear. But it cannot be the purpose of this book to even attempt to discuss the fourth stage, it is so bottomless. We will save any reference to it until the end of this book.

# TEN THE WITHERING AWAY OF THE REVOLUTION

As promised, no attempt has been made to examine *all* of the causes of the restructuring of consciousness which is taking place. Neither has any attempt been made to examine *all* the ways in which it manifests itself. Such an effort would have to range far beyond the rock phenomenon, the use of psychedelics, the effects of urbanization and mass media and those other few manifestations which have been touched upon here. The effort has been rather to approach a few of these phenomena and reach for the keys to their essential nature; to show, basically, how the doors of perception are being unlocked. We have not yet faced the central question: How can the new consciousness begin its real work of taking power out of the hands of those who are in the process of wrecking our world? There is a very specific deadline involved: the point, likely sometime in the next ten or twenty years, where the statistical probability of extinction will have become a certainty.

To speak of a self-structuring hierarchical jump is to speak of a revolution, a fundamental change in the way our affairs are conducted. Without such a change, the overwhelming likelihood is that we will kill ourselves off. No one suggests that men be put in charge of nuclear reactors who are only capable of "muddling through." Yet exactly such a suggestion is made when it comes to putting people in charge of the dynamic institutions which determine the course of society. The question is not whether a revolution is needed. The question is: How can it succeed? Where are the lines of least resistance? What are the weapons at the disposal of the new consciousness? Are these weapons being picked up? Is some sort of an apocalyptic bloodbath – the "shit storm" foreseen by Norman Mailer – inevitable?

In the past, in virtually every case, it was. Is there any good reason for believing that conditions have changed in some mysterious way? That a true revolution can now be effected without the streets being littered with bodies?

First, in order to get some sort of a perspective, let us consider the odds *against* a successful revolution. So long as we stick to the traditional definition of a revolution, the odds seem formidable, more formidable perhaps than they have ever been in the past. An impression of the sheer power of the existing power structure, particularly in America, might best be conveyed through the lens of personal experience:

PEACE, *NOW!*
PEACE, *NOW!*
PEACE, *NOW!*

It was as though the great buildings around us were hi-fi speakers in the land of the giants with the volume on full. The vibrations beat against the 162-ton Picasso sculpture, reverberating along the Cor-ten weatherproofed steel walls of the 31-storey Chicago Civic Plaza, a sound that had several dimensions: anger, frenzy, fun, frustration, fear, surprise. It was therapeutic, as raw as the first roar of a timid man who has discovered the heroic within his grasp. It was defiant and exultant because the sound was composed of ten thousand voices and each voice suggested the liberation of a ninety-pound weakling who has completed his Charles Atlas course and is now moving with a growl down onto the bully-inhabited beach. And then it was also pure rooting-for-the-home-team stuff, complete with cheerleaders:

*What do we want?*
PEACE!
*When do we want it?*
NOW!

And, finally, it was frightening. "PEACE, *NOW!* PEACE,

*NOW!*" The sound was blurred, like the noises of waves, and it was easy to close your eyes, let go of the mood for a moment, and hear them chanting, "SIEG *HEIL!* SIEG *HEIL!*" There was that hypnotic rhythm to it, a pace close to that of goose-stepping hordes.

This was October 15, 1969, the First Moratorium Day. The word was already out that the United States this day had lurched like an elephant slammed by a hand grenade under the impact of the biggest anti-war demonstration in history. And it was only a month since the Woodstock music festival had gone off like a land mine.

Now the speeches were done with, the Chicago six – looking pale and if not self-conscious, at least a bit uncertain – have been duly honored, every angle has been played except the last: time for a moment's silence for the dead in Vietnam. Heads were bowed. Even the traffic was stilled, the crowd having become so large the streets around the Civic Plaza were sealed off. The swelling silence engulfed the murmuring, and soon we were as quiet as ants, a colony of ants amid a warehouse display of fridge-like buildings and stacks of rusting canned goods; there was even an altar before us – the First Methodist Church, the world's tallest place of worship. The silence soon matched the height of the building. After a few seconds, hands started fluttering up, making the V-sign of peace, a gesture by now as religious as the Catholic sign of the cross. Soon almost all the hands were raised in the V-sign, except for those hands which were black, and all those black hands, thousands, were making the clenched-fist Black Power salute. I saw no black fingers making the peace sign. Something had happened . . . .

The demonstration was over. But the crowd was not quite prepared to dissolve. And now came the cry: OINK! OINK! It was the warning and battle-cry. It meant the riot cops were moving. Over the heads around me, bobbing like bubbles in a stirred-up bathtub, I could see a blue tide coming – a line of robin's egg riot helmets. The warning, almost a wave-action, had passed through me a second before, an impulse transmitted from nerve to nerve, body to body, thus flashing from one end of the plaza to the other, communicating to nearly ten thousand of us in seconds what would have taken several minutes to pass on by word of mouth – a flicker of tension, excitement and fear. Briefly, my sense of isolation, of self, of individuality, *cracked*. I was a small unit in a larger creature, one spark in the total field laid down by a brain composed of ten thousand such sparks. And the brain is stupid, composed of too few parts – it has not much more going for it than an insect. (No metaphor is intended here – a crowd is a gestalt, and its currents work like magnetism on the ciphers of our "identities," creating whirlpools and floodstreams where none existed before.)

OINK! OINK! screamed thousands of voices.

The effect of the cry was to cauterize some of the automatic fear which had been in the message of a few seconds before. Shout *cops* and the impulse, maybe nothing more than the Pavlovian reaction of children caught stealing apples, is nevertheless to run. Shout OINK! OINK! and the impulse is to press forward to the edge of the trough. Good mob psychology to change the object of terror into an object of contempt.

The movement of the crowd was like water toward a cliff. The robin's egg helmets might as well have been magnets attracting chips – but of course the police knew this, knew by now after years of riots and demonstrations all about the psychology of mobs. It is a psychology not so different from that of rats or very retarded children. Knowing it, the police had purpose in their movement. They were good cowboys. The round-up began. They were pulling us into a new position, the better to control us.

The round-up was underway. I tried to hang back close to the Picasso sculpture, rising like a giant steel bat over the plaza. Tried to hang back. It didn't work. The surge of the crowd was too strong, and too much of its deep herd impulse had gotten into my head – like a primordial gorilla hand groping for the controls. I did not fight as hard as I might to avoid being carried forward and, first thing I knew, I was right up against the police line.

Easy to imagine that these cops gave off no odor. They were, in fact, as odorless as astronauts or the hostesses at Disneyland and the Playboy Club. The cop in front of me, looking by chance into my eyes no more curiously than you would look into the eyes of a passing dog, seemed like a steel robot, a big one, wearing a rubber mask over a transistorized brain. His truncheon was at least two and a half feet long. When the walkie-talkie order hit that transistor of his, he would bash my face in as automatically as an electronic door opening to let customers into a supermarket.

Now I could see the purpose to the movement of the police.

They had taken up positions at one end of the glass-walled civic plaza, and the reaction of the crowd was not, after all, so unanimous. Only a fragment – the most hopped-up elements – had been drawn out, or, more precisely, *extracted*. So this was a dental operation. The police knew now where the trouble would come from. By their carefully-drilled movements, they had isolated the militants from their buffer of tax-paying citizens. These Chicago police were a good modern army. Beyond doubt their choreographer was sitting up in one of the skyscrapers, directing the performance like a man cutting a cake with sure strokes of his blue-edged knife.

And the crowd – the crowd was still a dull-witted gestalt. Part puppy-dog, part wolf. But in the end, manageable, more manageable than a baby. The police, having drawn the most dangerous part of it into position, (having snagged the fangs) now kept it on the line like a fisherman jerking his line to make sure the hook is in place. This was done simply by moving the police line a few dozen yards to the right, a few dozen to the left. The crowd followed. Meanwhile, as anticipated in somebody's calculations, the majority of the original ten thousand demonstrators had dissolved back into the rush-hour traffic, and soon there were fewer than one thousand left chanting and singing in front of the police line. After a while, they decided to head over to the federal building, where a few hundred others, many of them young blacks, and Black Panthers, had gathered to make speeches and throw insults (nothing more) up at the courtroom where the charade of the trial of the Chicago six was in progress. The police line followed the demonstrators. From the federal building, the movement was back toward of the plaza, then over to Lincoln Park. All along the way, police marched silently, shoulder-to-shoulder with the demonstrators. At last we arrived at the park. It was late afternoon, and the potent force of ten thousand had been whittled by the blue knife down to less than a hundred. The skill in that whittling was at least equal to the talent employed in the carving of totem poles. The police had a very effective machine going for them.

Yet there, in Chicago, I was watching the functioning of a police machine which was still only a primitive tool compared to the computerized technostructured operations now coming into existence. The difference between this Chicago police machine and those modern ones beginning to take shape everywhere is a matter of centuries compressed into decades. Compare a knife to a laser beam. You can at least see the knife coming. Against the laser beam you have no chance at all.*

Police machines, even the machines of Hitler and Stalin, were clumsy, forced to resort to terrorism and brute force. It has been shown that slave labor is poorly adapted to industrialization and adapted to post-industrialization not at all. The new machineries of police control are as far removed, in their most highly-developed forms, from Nazi Germany as helicopters from Icarus. The efficiency of the Chicago police on the occasion of the First Vietnam Moratorium revealed more about their state of development than did the police riot during the 1968 Democratic Convention. There, while the whole world was watching, the police broke their ranks and the machine sputtered to a halt. Under those circumstances, had the Chicago police been faced by well-armed, well-drilled opponents, they would have been cut to ribbons. As it was, they were chasing children, attacking journalists and bystanders, and so they seemed to have tremendous brute power. It was an illusion. In fact, at that particular moment, the Chicago police were at their weakest. If the Democratic Convention riots of 1968 had been the real measure of the effectiveness of the Chicago police, then the Black Panthers could be certain of victory. When the police become a mob, they are as helpless against precision attack as that crowd on Moratorium Day was against precision control. And yet the point here is that those chillingly-efficient Moratorium Day police tactics were relatively unsophisticated. The blue knife that worked so well was still not a laser beam. In the very near future, control of mobs of ten thousand will be child's play.

The mass media have communicated a false message to the younger generation: Look at the Democratic Convention! Look

---

* See my book, *The Enemies of Anarchy*, the section dealing with technostructures. A technostructure is a group decision-making apparatus, so far only successfully evolved in the industrial sector, accounting for the phenomenal effectiveness of the large modern corporation. However, the basic techniques grew out of the military logistical pressures of the Second World War, and technostructures are now as much a feature of militarism as advanced industrialism – at times, inseparable. This development stems in large part from the technical imperative of autonomy in order for technique to attain maximum efficiency. Technostructures are now emerging in the heart of government, from the federal to the municipal levels, in education, and, definitely, in police departments everywhere in the industrially-mature nations. See John Kenneth Galbraith's *The New Industrial State*; Jacques Ellul's *The Technological Society*; George M. Gavin's *Crisis Now.*

at Watts! Look at the cities that burned as funeral pyres in the wake of Martin Luther King's assassination! Remember the night when a tiny gadget near Niagara Falls broke down and all of New York was plunged into darkness? See how easy it is to throw a monkey wrench into the functionings of a modern industrial state? A bit of LSD in the water supply, a few snipers moving along the rooftops, a demonstration here, a reversal of a court decision concerning marijuana there . . . so easy, so easy.

Yet one has only to walk through Watts, or along West Madison, or through Harlem, to realize that probably fewer than a hundred miles of streets out of all the millions of miles of paved roadway in the United States actually were touched by flame the night after King died. And nothing has changed in New York because of the black-out, except that the hydro system is slightly more efficient now. LSD breaks down in water. As for snipers – they are killed, and have about as much chance of beating the existing system as a fly has of wresting power from the man with the fly-swatter. An overturned pot law can be planted back even more firmly on its feet a few weeks later. Guerrilla warfare? One might try reading *Quotations From Chairman Mao Tse-tung*, especially his ten principles of operation. In the context of modern America, it might well have been written by George Wallace. Point One: Attack dispersed, isolated enemy forces first; attack concentrated, strong enemy forces (*universities?*) later. Point Two: Take small and medium cities and extensive rural areas first; take big cities later. Etc.[42] It should be obvious to everyone that guerrillas can only operate if the population supports them, and there is no advanced industrial nation today where that basic condition exists. A mass base is completely lacking for a *putsch* or revolution in the old style of the French and Russian revolutions. And even if it weren't, in order to beat the technological and organizational opposition, the revolutionaries would have to forge a faster, more powerful machine. To fight a revolution in an advanced industrial nation today (on its own ground, in short) one would have to become even better at the game than those who currently wield the blue knife and the laser beam.

The argument against revolution in an advanced industrial nation, in the old sense of a violent overthrow of the existing power structure through the mechanism of an armed insurrection, proceeds along three lines:

A. It's hopeless.

B. It accomplishes nothing, except a changing of the guard.

C. It diverts us from the real struggle, which is to attain a higher level of consciousness, and to explore our potential (which is still unknown).

Let us deal with these in turn:

## A. *It's hopeless.*

The working class of late has not shown itself to be particularly responsive to the rhetoric of the New Left. The evidence would suggest that any insurrection at this stage in the affairs of the American state is more likely to come from the right. Movements such as Yippie!, the Black Panther Party, SDS, and so on have proven to be shorter-lived and far less tolerated than the Minutemen or the Ku Klux Klan. This is not simply because of the raw power of the police machine.

John Galbraith has pointed out that when capital was the key to economic success, social conflict was between the rich and the poor. But in recent times, education became the difference that divides. "Politics," he writes, "reflect the new division. In the United States suspicion or resentment is no longer directed to the capitalists or the merely rich. It is the intellectuals who are eyed with misgiving and alarm. This should surprise no one. Nor should it be a matter for surprise when semi-literate millionaires turn up leading or financing the ignorant in struggle against the intellectually privileged and content. This reflects the relevant class distinction of our time."[43] It is a distinction few intellectuals are willing to accept. Humanists and socialists alike would prefer to steer away from any position which might open them up to charges of elitism, yet everything points to a sharp (and widening) cleavage not only between the generations but between the new basic classes. Students can no longer appeal to the workers with much hope of being listened to (or, for that matter, of getting out of a union hall meeting without having their heads beaten in).

Add to that the fact that the very "masses" upon whom all organized revolutionaries pin their long range hopes are the people (in the highly industrialized states) who are the least likely to rise up against anybody except the revolutionaries themselves. Come the revolution, we will all be listening to Bob Hope. The problem in part is that only a minority of the population in any advanced industrialized nation is responsive to the new and accelerated pace of change. A few, among them many of the young and many of the intellectually privileged and content, are in tune with the new culture; that is, change is not something that frightens them. Mobility offers possibilities, not dread of being uprooted. The "broad masses," on the other hand, are still peeking out at the world from around the corner of their memories of the Depression and the Second World War.

Few will dispute that the guns and the tanks and the bombs and the advertising agencies and the mass media are in the hands of the established order. The target of any revolution cannot just be the White House, the Pentagon, and Fort Knox. It must be, let's say, "the hearts and minds of the people," whether Vietnamese or American. And these, at the moment, are largely under the control of the establishment press, the advertisers, and the politicians. So, already, the revolution must move against an enemy that commands the heights and is dug in everywhere, who, furthermore, has overwhelming firepower, with air and ground and naval support. And the odds are not yet through being added up. The establishment also has at its disposal a humming army of computers, an array of prototypal technostructures whose function is not only to anticipate trouble, pin-point likely danger spots, but, as a regular day-to-day operation, keep a closer eye on every individual citizen than could be done in any previous society. There is no one in America–or any advanced industrial state, for that matter–whose identity is not magnetically recorded on a tape somewhere. So, in addition to the overwhelming firepower of the enemy, the revolutionary faces the dangers of bugging, wiretapping, computerized surveillance, and so on.

So far, however, we have been ticking off the obvious. We have not really got the the *real* strength of the enemy, which is that, unlike a banana republic, the modern industrial state is not run by a strongman flanked by bullyboys, a division of armored jeeps, and financed by a clutch of businessmen with vested interests in keeping wages down. It may indeed stem from just such a basic structure, but in the process of its evolution it has become too complex, too bottomless, to be tackled as though it *remained* nothing more than that. The power of the industrial state is greater by several factors, and not just in terms of physical might.

Where we see progressiveness and openly liberal attitudes, we see the technological reality refining its methods of manipulation, organization, and, ultimately, control. It gets *better* at it all the

134

time, absorbing more, spreading out in ever-widening circles, and turning every attack to its own advantage, simply by accepting the attacker, swallowing him, and thus very nearly literally feeding on opposition.

Historically, it has been hard enough to get broad masses of people to bite the hand that *wouldn't* feed them; to hope, under conditions of affluence, to get those same broad masses to bite a hand that does feed them – and feeds them very well – is a thin hope indeed. Add this stark reality to the problems already mentioned, and one begins to see that it would have to be one hell of a super-revolution, the one which could smash the technological society.

Even if the odds weren't so bad, consider the state the troops are in. What happened to the crowd in the Chicago Civic Plaza on Moratorium Day demonstrated clearly where the real organizational muscle was. But there is more to it. Shortly before Moratorium Day, I was in Berkeley, at the University of California campus. Listen to one of the most radical students I talked to: "It's ready to blow, man. There's a revolution coming. It's overcrowded here. Construction everywhere. Bad food. Lousy accommodation. It's mean. Bad vibrations. Everybody's really uptight, only it's low-level uptightedness. People are bugged, I mean, really bugged ... the food prices, the shortage of rooms, the noise ... it's gonna *go*, man. Wow." So there is a revolution about to erupt. But follow the conversation further. It drifts. Soon, the student is talking about the intensity of the mescaline experience as compared to the hashish experience. A lot of quibbling gets going with other students present about the virtues of hash. And from there the conversation proceeds directly to the issue of the best places to go skiing. One place is generally conceded to be much better than the others, because "dampness from the ground soaks right up through your head and goes raining off in reverse right into the sky from your head, all those pores in your scalp, like they were sprinklers, man." This is, if you have been smoking hash. Somehow, no contradiction is seen between the desire to have a revolution and the desire to smoke hash and go skiing. The revolutionary fever was heavily seasoned with hedonism, which weakens it badly. And most conversations I got into on the campus seemed spiced in much the same way. A friend reports meeting two radicals at Berkeley, whose position is simple: Everything will have to be smashed from stem to stern; America has become that diseased. The conversation ends when they ask my friend if he would like to blow a joint. Okay. They go down the street and climb into a brand-new Thunderbird, property of the most talkative radical, and proceed to get stoned.

The story may be apocryphal, but not very.

Yet, through a process of nothing much more than elimination, we have arrived at a position where the vanguard of a revolution *must* be the "alienated" young. The working class has become reactionary (labor and management may quibble over the spoils, but none seeks to blow up the trough), the bourgeoisie middle class are more dominant than ever, the poor are already contained in ghettoes which are concentration camps lacking only barbed wire. Let us look, therefore, at the picture these alienated young presented as the 1960s drew to a close. Here is Barry Farrell's description of the last two nights of the Woodstock festival:

As night fell the scene became more dramatic still, disclosing a loud electric image of the future. From the fringes of the crowd, the stage looked like a pearl at the bottom of a pond, a circle of light fired down from towers as big as missile gantries. Just beyond it, helicopters fluttered in and out of an LZ ringed with Christmas lights, bringing in the rock groups, evacuating casualties and stars. Much music was lost under the beat of their blades – an annoyance until it was perceived as a higher music than rock alone – as rock-helicopter music, space music to accompany the sound-and-light vision of the American '70s.

The speaker's expert voice purred across the breadth of the farm, reading off lists of the injured and ill, urging respect for the fences. In the newspeak of our age, he praised the crowd for being groovy, cautioning them not to blow the cool thing they had going by breaking any of the rules. Then he would give way to another group, and the musicians would appear, tiny forms bathed in lurid light.

On the festival's last night, when the field had turned to slime and abandoned sleeping bags lay sprawled underfoot like corpses, my feelings for the event began to darken. Everyone around me was shivering under soaked coats and blankets. Their bonfires, fed with newspapers and milk cartons, cast up a stench that hung above the meadow in a yellow haze. On the dark roads, unseen faces whispered the names of drugs to passing strangers. Mescaline? Hash? At the central crossroads, anxious voices shouted the names of lost friends. Gloria! Donald!

The great stoned rock show had worked a countermiracle, trading on the freedom to get stoned, transforming it into a force that tamed the crowd and extracted its compliance. Not that anyone minded, of course – the freedom to get stoned was all the freedom they wanted. And, being stoned, everyone was content to sit in the mud and feed on a merchandised version of the culture they created. In the cold acid light, the spoiled field took on the aspect of an Orwellian concentration camp stocked with drugs and music and staffed with charming police. The speaker's coaxing voice only enriched the nightmare, which became complete when I asked a trembling blue-faced boy if he was feeling all right. "Groovy," he said, adding a frozen smile.

The Woodstock festival has already been recorded as a victory for music and peace, and that is as it should be. But it should also be remembered as a display of the authority of drugs over a whole generation – an authority already being merchandised, exploited, promoted. It was groovy, as the speaker kept saying, but I fear it will grow groovier in memory, when the market in madness leads on to shows we'd rather not see.[44]

As for *Hair*, one had only to glance at the faces in the lobby at intermission to see that these were not people about to take to the barricades. Flushed, excited faces, titillated. After all, hadn't they just had their jollies by becoming *involved* enough to cheer all the heavy anti-draft lines, the pro-pot lines, the ecstatic lyrics about beauty and truth? They got it out of them, all right. Now they will go home feeling liberated, some of them so liberated they will not even worry about how tired they're going to feel in the morning when it comes time to go back to work for The Machine.

*Hair* was only incidentally a piece of show biz. Its real significence lies in the fact that its arrival (along with the effective total collapse of censorship, the popularity of pot, the sudden militancy of every minority group, and the rediscovery of holism) signalled the beginning of a new stage in the affairs of the technological society. *Hair* was the death-knell of revolution, ringing joyously and ecstatically through the industrialized world. Then along came Woodstock, and as Barry Farrell wrote in *Life*, "no one there doubted that we were crossing a cultural Rubicon." The question is: How many realized that they had entered the gates of the comfortable concentration camp? The trap had begun to close. The barricades, like the guillotine, were suddenly relics of the past. As that small slice of humanity which represents the cutting edge of our evolution rushed forward to meet the dawn of the Age of Aquarius, they left their machineguns and ideologies and programs behind. Straitjackets were shedded like old skins. We had begun to give up. What every pessimistic modern philosopher from Huxley to Jacques Ellul had warned us against was finally happening. We were losing control of our destiny, losing our minds, throwing down our weapons and surrendering in droves. We had stopped fighting. Hegel's historical man, whose spirit was in "a mighty conflict with itself," who could advance to higher forms only by overcoming himself, was suddenly as obsolete and pathetic as the Priest King of Nemi, who could succeed to office only by slaying the incumbent, and having slain him, retained power only until he himself was slain, with the result that "year in year out, in summer and winter, in fair weather and in foul, he had to keep his lonely watch, (sword in hand, pacing around the tree that was his throne) and whenever he snatched a troubled slumber it was at the peril of his life."[45]

Revolution, whose death-convulsions had taken the form of student revolts in the fallopian tubes of the technological society, is finally finished as the vehicle of human advance. And since revolution really means cyclic recurrence, (a vicious circle) we do not have to bemoan, as Marcuse does, the "passing of historical forces" which seemed, at earlier stages, to represent the possibility of change. There is no political institution left on the face of the earth whose ideology is not basically technological, so all a revolution hitched to *realpolitik* can offer now is more of the same. Revolution is giving way to liberation and short-circuiting the vicious circle entirely. If *Hair* and Woodstock signal the triumph of the technological society, they also signal the end to futile and self-perpetuating conflict.

The *Hair* and Woodstock phenomena are complex, like the flight of Apollo 11; the question has to be asked: What is the effect? Do these phenomena liberate or do they add a deeper dimension, a new twist, to the elaborate and subtle mechanisms of aggregate control? The immediate problem with *Hair* is that its emergence – or the emergence of some immensely popular show employing exactly the same devices of protest, outrage, anger, obscenity and revolutionary rhetoric – was anticipated as far back as the 1950s by French philosopher Jacques Ellul, who argued that the more restrictive the social mechanism, the more exaggerated are the associated ecstatic phenomena. (Neither *Hair* nor Woodstock could be described as other than ecstatic.) "Technique," wrote Ellul, "encourages and enables the individual to express his ecstatic reactions in a way never before possible. He can express criticism of his culture, and even loathing. He is permitted to propose the maddest solutions. The great law here is that all things are necessary to make a society and even revolt is necessary to make a technical society."[46] *Hair*, which expresses plenty of loathing and not a few mad solutions, is tolerated (along with pornography, obscenity, and even, to an increasing degree, pot and homosexuality) not because there is more freedom than before, but because the expression of criticism allows people to let off steam. And having let off steam they are less likely to get serious about changing the social order.

Marcuse has a word for it: "repressive de-sublimation," which is the "release of sexuality in modes and forms which reduce and weaken erotic energy." (Erotic energy being the source of real rebellion as opposed to burlesques.) In tolerating a show like *Hair* or a happening like Woodstock, the technocratic order would be doing nothing less than moving into the realm of "pleasant forms of social control and cohesion." The thrust of the argument is that pleasant forms of control work more effectively than repression. Thus, there is the appearance of rebellion, but no substance. As Ellul puts it: "Technique defuses the revolt of the few and thus appeases the need of the millions for revolt."

*B. It accomplishes nothing, except a changing of the guard.*

Leonard Cohen remarked in 1968, when asked if there was a revolution going on: "Of course it's a revolution. But I want to see the *real* revolution. I don't want it siphoned off by the mobilization people. It's got to take place in every room. Revolutionaries, in their heart of hearts, are excited by the tyranny they wield. The lines are being drawn and people on both sides are beginning to terrorize each other. Somehow we have to break out of this process, which can only lead to both sides becoming *like* each other. I'm afraid that when the Pentagon is finally stormed and taken, it will be by guys wearing uniforms very much like those worn by the guys defending it."[47]

Many of us advance into our lives by little more than cause and effect. That is, we take a step for a variety of reasons and, having taken this small initial step, discover the consequences. We are then forced to deal with those consequences. and we do that by rationalizing the original act. Having rationalized it, one has then set up the crude framework of a behavioral pattern which can now be fleshed out by further actions – *proceeding in the same direction.* Each new action, so long as it continues to proceed in the same direction, becomes slightly easier than the one before. It's like learning to drive, acquiring reflexes. Once one is familiar with the gears it becomes largely automatic. Strong men, or men of action (such as revolutionaries must be), are therefore those whose behavior has been most effectively rationalized. They set themselves in motion automatically. Revolutionary heroes are therefore bound to a large degree to be behavioral automatons. Further, all revolutionaries are forced to accept a discipline which forbids them to freely explore interpretations other than those which serve as the basis for the revolution. Revolutionary zeal is one of the worst forms of tyranny, locking the individual into a position every bit as static as that of his opposite number, the reactionary. At the extremes, in terms of individual personality, the revolutionary and the reactionary merge. For both, the doors leading to personal growth and development of their own unrealized potential are closed.

The man of action requires an uncluttered setting with simple ground rules in order to function. Ideally: A setting as stark as a boxing ring. Only then can the Aristotelian proposition of either/ or be put to work. The object of the revolutionary (or reactionary) game is to reduce complex on-going processes to a fixed game board involving nothing more than two players; black vs. white, good vs. bad, freedom vs. slavery. If he is successful in reducing multi-ordinal reality to a simple game, the revolutionary has then "set the stage" for an uprising. Needless to say, in a complex highly-integrated modern industrial state, the initial task of the revolutionary is that much more difficult.

The point here is simply that the revolutionary stance is an *idée fixe,* monomania. Further, it is, on a grand scale, a kind of decadence – a rejection of the complex (and real) in favor of the simple (and less real). What the revolutionary offers us, finally, is one other idea about how things should be done. His goal is to ram that idea down our throats, and in order to be able to do that, he must first seize power.

Which brings us to the heart of the matter. Chairman Mao advises us that "the seizure of power by armed force, the settlement of the issue by war, is the central task and the highest form of revolution." It is a power struggle first and foremost. Exactly the sort of thing for which the Priest Kings of Nemi stand as the central metaphor. The revolutionary does not want change, he wants *one* change, the change which will bring him into power. And then . . . ? Why then his task is to fight off the next wave of revolutionaries who want another change. "Everybody wants to save the world," Henry Miller once noted, "but nobody wants to help his neighbor."

"The urge to manipulate others," writes George B. Leonard, "whether to 'solve' a 'problem' or build an empire, begins in the nursery . . . The drive for surplus power . . . is born of lack and nourished by deprivation. 'Power' – the word itself – appears only when there are unfulfilled needs. We would never have heard the term 'Black Power' if blacks had been treated fairly. 'Woman Power' is a statement of denial, a cry for justice. Ultimately, little will be gained if blacks, women, and others of the oppressed merely gain dominance, thus triggering yet another cycle of deprivation and desperation. . . . 'Power' is derived from an Old French word meaning, 'to be able.' When we return to this definition, the real question becomes, 'What do you want to be able to do or be, to feel or enjoy?' The past has taught us well: Playing power games and losing is a waste of time. Playing power games and getting exactly what you want is the ultimate despair."[48]

All political parties, whether revolutionary or established (along with their ideologies and systems) are built on a narrow base of power. Some specialize in humanism, others on exploitation, yet others on inevitable conflict. In all cases, the issue of power remains the locus of activity. All existing politicial organizations (again whether revolutionary or not) remain essentially anthropomorphic. The struggle is between people and groups of people, each locked into a monomaniacal opposing stance. Any disinclination to accept the whole ideological package is a sign of betrayal – one becomes a "revisionist" or a "Commie-lover" or something to that effect, depending on where and what you are. Revolutions are seen as mechanisms whereby our sickness might be cured: racism, greed, insanity, hate, fear, distrust, alienation, poverty, dictatorship. Revolution, at best, is seen as a kind of heart transplant; at worst, lobotomy. Always, of course, for the good of the patient, and always on the assumption that the operation will cure all ills. "Social change" is the vehicle, the means toward the higher end of more moral behavior, of greater brotherly love, of physical well-being, an end to hunger and deprivation.

And to affect these tremendous social changes, it remains absolutely necessary to seize power. Underdog must overthrow topdog. Underdog is then the new topdog and the old topdog now has a taste of being underdog. The guard has been changed. There is a new man in the saddle. Beyond that stage, what happens?

The operational mode of thinking remains the trigger of all practical change. Today, Marxism is the mirror image of capitalism, but basically no different. Because Communists and Socialists and Capitalists have all hitched their social wagons to the engine of technology, there can be no basic change. Exploitation of nature remains the key to wealth, whether equally distributed or not. And through the domination of nature, the men continue to dominate each other and be dominated.

Theodore Roszak puts in well:

> To immerse oneself in the old ideologies – with the notable exception of the anarchist tradition which flows from such figures as Kropotkin, Tolstoy, Thoreau – is to find oneself stifling in the stone and steel environment of unquestionable technological necessity. It is a literature of seriousness and grim resolve, tightly bounded by practicality, class discipline, the statistics of injustice, and the lust for retribution. To speak of the ecstasies of life in such a somber environment is to risk folly. Here where all men trudge, none may dance. Dancing is . . . for later. If the demise of the old ideologies begins anywhere, it begins with this delaying gesture. For to postpone until 'later' consideration of the humanly essential in the name of 'being realistic' is to practise the kind of deadly practicality which now stands our civilization in peril of annihilation. It is to deliver us into the hands of the dehumanized commissars, managers, and operational analysts – all of whom are professional experts at postponing the essential. These are the practitioners of what C. Wright Mills called 'crackpot realism.'[49]

Revolution is based in part on the proposition that institutions must be shuffled, and *then* the hearts of men and women can be affected. Control – through the institutional agencies – is the prerequisite for real change. It does not cross the revolutionary mind that institutions are the last extentions of man – that to begin attempting to cure human ills through the agencies of institutions is to start at the ass end. Institutions, laws, legislation and flags can be easily changed – what, we must ask, has that got to do with individuals? Such thinking misses completely the basic psychological insight that we cannot deliberately bring about changes in ourselves or in others. Any intention toward change will have the opposite effect. A "successful" revolution means simply that we are saddled with a new set of controllers. Meanwhile, in our hearts nothing has changed. The power games go on. Exploitation of nature continues. Man is still assumed to be, "realistically," the center of the universe. A king of flat-earth psychology continues to dominate our collective behavior.

Meanwhile, the earth continues to die.

*C. It diverts us from the real struggle, which is to attain a higher level of consciousness, and to explore our potential (which is still unknown.)*

Leon Trotsky once prophesied that the final revolution in the world would consist of a series of small and violent upheavels going on everywhere, lasting perhaps for generations. This sounds dead on, yet not even Trotsky could have envisioned how "small" and how "violent." The final revolution will be taking place in an arena no larger than my head and your head, and it will involve a psychic and emotional violence whose measure has not yet been taken. So long as we are concentrating our energies on power struggles, on toppling institutions only to replace them with others, we are channeling our energies outward; it is an exercise as futile as the trip to the moon, all part of an outward voyage whose aim is exploitation, whose method is manipulation, whose end is power and control. History is a stuck record, with human struggle caught in a single groove, the vicious circle of cyclic recurrence. Down goes one king, and up goes another. The day after a palace is stormed, the new bosses set up shop across the street. We have not yet escaped from collective childhood, in the sense that we still need leaders, and still do not trust our own senses. (Liberals, with their tremendous fear of being "judgmental," are among the worst offenders. It is the liberals who have come closest to building systems on a fusion of man and his works, yet they have not learned that their weakness – equivocality – is also their greatest potential source of strength.) Revolution is seen always as the means to an end which is human liberation, freedom not only from want, but from the tyranny of the emotions, racism, hatred, murder, crime, and exploitation. "Social change" will lead to a change in consciousness. Yet this is in reality a Rube Goldberg course. The possibility of moving directly from A to B, without having to climb to the top of the pyramid in order to get down to the bottom of it, has not even historically been considered; except, of course, by theologians and artists. The only way for the greater human being to come into existence is directly, giving birth to himself. No ideology is prepared to accept the idea that the *cure* might precede the revolutionary operation, that perhaps the operation might only make the patient sicker. Change – real change, as opposed to a change of political underwear – will only come after the fact of individual liberation. And since this is something that cannot be organized or led, that does not lend itself to political or ideological frames of reference, it is dismissed (by the operationalists) as being nothing at all. Yet we might with good cause demand: Revolutionary, heal thyself! The real revolution works in exactly the opposite fashion to what has always been assumed to be the case – changing the social institutions does no good, because the last link in the chain, the individual, is the farthest removed from the locus of power. When however, the individual is the *first* link to be affected, it turns out that the seats of power are themselves the last to be changed. Institutions and thrones are about as far removed from the ordinary citizen as anything in the social landscape. The aim of revolutionary types has been to organize the people to move against the thrones, to tear down the institutions. In the process, people submit to discipline and the need for violence, and thus become violent disciplinarians themselves. The fact that they may be crushing an entrenched set of violent disciplinarians at this point makes no real difference. How far have they progressed in the direction of realization of themselves? Nowhere. They may have succeeded in brutalizing themselves, in reverting to the logic of domination and can be certain of emerging from the bloodbath convinced that the operational point of view is the only point of view. Other than that, there is no progress in the critical direction – which is to explore unknown territory, to move upward, not downward, in terms of personal and collective evolution, to acquire a keener vision, a deepening of the senses, an enlargement of vision, to the point where we might perceive subtler harmonies, regularities which were not noticed before, and, finally, to bring our shattered selves back into a working whole. The task is to complete the human being, not turn him back into a barbarian.

The question arises: It's all very well to say that we must all "save ourselves," no one can do it for us, but what about the obvious inequalities of the present system? What about corruption? Police brutality? Militarism? Murder? What good does it do if you liberate yourself and achieve a state of "higher morality" or whatever, if, in the meantime, Vietnamese peasants continue to be bombed, Blacks are starving in ghettoes, Indians are processed and reprocessed through prisons, millions are dying of starvation, madmen have their fingers poised on the nuclear trigger, and the planet is being destroyed by parasitic corporations and governments? Isn't 'self-liberation" at this stage a luxury we can ill afford to indulge ourselves in? There is real work to be done, and done in a hurry if we are to survive.

The short answer lies in what Gestalt therapist Fritz Perls describes as the most important phenomenon in all pathology: "self-regulation versus external regulation. The anarchy which is usually feared by the controllers is not an anarchy which is without meaning. On the contrary, it means the organism is left alone to take care of itself, without being meddled with from outside. And I believe this is the great thing to understand: *that awareness per se – by and of itself – can be curative.* Because with full awareness you become aware of this organismic self-regulation, you can let the organism take over without interfering, without interrupting; we can rely on the wisdom of the organism."[50] In the sociological context, the message is clear enough: *awareness* is the starting point for action which is not pre-determined by ideological bias; without awareness, without having gotten to the "center" of our beings, as the Gestaltists call it, without having transcended the operational mode of thinking which reduces our actions to little more than acted-out equations, without having "cured" ourselves of our refusal to let the situation dictate our actions (rather than vice-versa), there is nothing we can do with certainty which will not simply amount to a subtler kind of power-game, a reversal of roles, or – and this is the unavoidable trap – which will not amount in the long run to a projection of our own disequilibriums. This is not to suggest a "moratorium" on political activity, which in itself can be therapeutic, but it is to say that the blind have no right to be leading the blind. Only when our own eyes are open can we presume to lead. Otherwise we may rest assured that whatever illusions we may have about "progress" are in reality nothing more than circular gropings in the dark, with pitfalls everywhere. The answers, once one's eyes are open, can be clearly perceived.

Before proceeding to look beyond the barricades (a garbage heap of antique social furniture) there is a point which needs to be cleared up, since much of what has been said so far about the futility of revolution can easily be misconstrued as a put-down of very real and just revolutions taking place not only in America, but in Canada and Vietnam and elsewhere. My argument is simply that revolution must take the shape of its container; it defines itself in relation to the system it seeks to defy or overthrow. But I am speaking of revolution in the context of the technological society, or one-dimensional society, or the affluent society, or whatever label one chooses to describe what is mainly a white man's modern world. Not everyone in North America lives in that world. The ghettoes – whether black ghettoes in Los Angeles or Chicago or Eskimo or Indian ghettoes in Canada and in the Arctic – are truly another country. And the struggles that go on within these territories are against colonialism, imperialism, and brutal oppression. They have much in common with the struggle of the Vietnamese. The "container" in these cases is quite different from the kind of container in which those of us who are predominantly white and living in suburbs and high-rise apartments find ourselves.

The Hudson Institute has calculated that within thirty years the first four post-industrial societies will have surfaced on the face of the planet. They will be, in this order, the United States, Canada, Japan, and Sweden. They will be characterized by the fact that *per capita* income will range from $4,000 to $20,000; most economic activity will have shifted from industrial production to the service industries, research institutes and non-profit organizations; private enterprise will no longer be a major source of scientific and technical development. Large-scale integration will be all but complete. We will be far down the path of convergence with the Communist world. At this point, the technological society will have clamped its iron arms around the world, bioelectronics will have succeeded in literally plugging us into world-wide hookups and a *de facto* police state will have emerged. It is in these areas (the post-industrialized regions) that the obsolescence of revolution will be most apparent.

This is not to say that, *outside* the affluent sphere, revolution will be obsolete. The "wretched of the earth" will still be with us, old-style police states based on brutality and oppression will still exist, colonialism in a variety of forms will likely still prevail. In these "outside regions," there is no reason to assume that armed insurrection, revolution, and violent overthrown of corrupt and brutal administrations is in any way unjustified or unnecessary.

To draw our models for revolutionary behavior from these other regions, however, is to refuse to recognize the qualitative differences between these societies. Within a single generation, there will be a difference between the most advanced societies and the ones trailing behind them which will not only be a matter of degree but of kind. Those of us in the most advanced regions will be living in a different world. A fundamental change is involved. For us to continue to assume that revolutionary programs applicable in China, India, most of South America and Africa (areas which have not even approached the industrialized stage) can somehow have any relevance in our own advanced industrial context, is, at best, an unsophisticated notion; at worst, plain stupidity. Within the comfortable concentration camp, inside a system which can absorb and contain and feed on all forms of protest and rebellion, a whole new set of tactics must be evolved, and *are* being evolved. Moreover, we have no choice in the matter, since old-style revolutionary activity simply will not work. We will be effectively blocked from indulging in the kind of uprising and overthrow which amounts to cyclic recurrence. We will have no Bastilles left to storm except those within our skulls, no oppressors left whom we can get our hands on except our egos. The struggles which were always directed outward – against tyrants and dictators – will have been effectively thwarted, and will be turned back on themselves. Inward will go the revolution, turning every man's head into a battlefield.

The "social bottle" of those regions on planet earth which are furthest into the future is different, unique; by the standards of other ages and other cultures, it is downright freaky. It has been molded into a new form – by the computer, by television, by changes in social character, by technoplanning, cybernetics, chemistry, psychology, technique. We all agree it is made from new materials: plastic, nuclear power, vinyl, electronic circuitry, data-points and programming. Yet how many of us are prepared to see that revolution, the counterpoint to all that is totalitarian and repressive (even when rationally totalitarian and repressive) must also change; it must, in fact, become as strange, as novel, as freaky as its container. And it is becoming all of that – so much so that most of us fail to recognize it as revolution. In drama we see, as Martin Esslin put it, "By all *traditional* standards of critical appreciation of the drama, these [modern absurd] dramas are not only abominably bad, they do not even deserve the name of drama."[51] Mark Gerzon goes on to say: "Many people have realized that nothing can be judged by traditional standards, for we do not live any longer in a traditional society. How many parents have said about modern music and painting that they do not even deserve the name? The arts have broken with tradition because they found the limitations on style and structure unnecessary and artificial . . ."[52] Similarly, "revolution" is in the process of breaking from traditional style and structure.

Before proceeding, it is necessary to clearly distinguish between this ultimate struggle and the penultimate struggles being waged by oppressed people living outside the perimeter of The Machine. Basically, these next-to-last struggles are efforts to break into the area already inhabited by those of us who are affluent. Although our own struggle is of a different nature, we cannot ignore those other struggles and neither can we afford to refuse to help. But first we must have some understanding of the *difference*. To this end, let me focus on the Black Panther Party, which is a real revolutionary force (in the old pre-technological style).

# ELEVEN THE OLD ANTI-NEANDERTHAL BATTLE

Simply, the blacks in America are trying to get where the whites are already. The same may be said of oppressed and poverty-stricken people everywhere. This is the difference between their revolution and ours. The affluent society, generally thought of as a cultural dead-end, is in reality the incubator of an historically new kind of man, one whose potential has only begun to be tapped. Our task is to develop that potential, to explore the vast territories excluded by the reductionist operational mode of thinking. The immediate task of the oppressed and deprived is to penetrate the incubator, to claim their right to take part in the journey which we – the privileged few – have only begun.

Eldridge Cleaver said as much in an interview with Nat Hentoff in *Playboy* Magazine when asked: What do blacks in America want? "I can only answer," Cleaver replied, "with what Malcolm X said. If you've had a knife in my back for four hundred years, am I supposed to thank you for pulling it out?

"Because that's all those [civil rights] laws and [Supreme Court] decisions have accomplished. The very least of your responsibility now is to compensate me, however inadequately, for centuries of degradation and disenfranchisement by granting peacefully – before I take them forcefully – the same rights and opportunities for a decent life that you've taken for granted as an American birthright. This isn't a request but a *demand*, and the ten points of that demand are set down with crystal clarity in the Black Panther

Party platform."[53]

One does not have to get very deeply into an objective American history to find, as Ronald Segal, author of *The Race War,* puts it, that "the traditional structure of American society, for all the neon signs of rewarded enterprise on its facade confines Negroes to the basement, and the commandments of free competition keep them there."[54]

It is assumed by many whites, usually liberals, that the Panthers represent some sort of aberration in the American black man's psyche, a recent and dangerous form of insanity. The non-violent civil rights movement (which was full of violence unleashed against the participants) is held to be the standard against which the morality of all forms of protest are measured. Yet the truth is that the civil rights movement failed in all its critical economic and social objectives. For every school officially integrated by the force of the movement, there are three today which are, in practice if not in theory, segregated. Martin Luther King warned what the consequences of such a failure would be. And the Panthers are but one of those consequences.

The black revolution in America began before the first twenty "negars" were brought by Dutch warship to Virginia in 1619 – many, on the way, had thrown themselves overboard or starved themselves to death. Since that time there has been no racial peace in America, only lulls between explosions. It was an unstable situation from the beginning. Countless slave conspiracies were mounted. In New York City in 1741, after a plot was uncovered, two blacks were burned alive at the stake by a white mob and twenty-nine others were executed. In Richmond, Va., in 1800, several thousand blacks were thwarted only by betrayal and a storm in their attempt to kill their masters. Twenty-two years later, Denmark Versey enlisted thousands in Charleston, S.C., but he too was defeated by betrayal. And of course in 1831 Nat Turner led an uprising in which sixty whites were killed. During the American civil war, slave uprisings flared in the South like bush fires and several key Confederacy installations were almost taken. One effect was to pin down many rebel troops, who had to guard against black revolt while others were up front fighting Yankees. The blacks were never anywhere near as contented with their lot as white mythology has made them out to be. In 1919 – the Red Summer, it was called, the predecessor of the long, hot summers of the 1960s – twenty-six serious race riots broke out, most in the North, and the worst in Chicago.

The beginnings of black self-assertion can be traced back to a gift of white bigotry – during the American Revolution, Baptists in Georgia and Virginia decided to organize Christianity among blacks by setting up separate churches, with jurisdiction controlled by whites. Finally, in 1816, the African Methodist Episcopal Church was set up, the first truly independent black church. "Black is beautiful" was probably first uttered in a 19th century all-black church. The pride which the church kindled in its congregations soon flowed out into the community.

One can trace the line of development leading to the moment Huey Newton decided to form the Black Panther Party back to the formation of the separate African Methodist Episcopal Church, or even further to the suicides commited by slaves being brought to America. But in a more political context, one might fairly trace it back to the formation of a group called The Boston Radicals in the 1880s. It was out of this group that William Edward Burghardt Du Bois emerged. Mainly, the radicals grew up in opposition to the "accomodation" policies of Booker T. Washington. In 1905, Du Bois, the leading Boston Radical, formed the Niagara Movement to fight racist laws in the courts. Lacking support, the Niagara Movement died, but it produced an heir, the National Negro Committee.

This committee, composed of black militants with the backing of liberal whites, became the National Association for the Advancement of Colored People (NAACP). Its publication, *Crisis*, edited by Du Bois, urged blacks to turn from "the blue-eyed white-skinned types which are set before us in school and literature" and concentrate on becoming "rich, brown and black men and women with glowing dark eyes and crinkling hair." The afro hair-styles and dashikis so stunningly worn by blacks in all large American cities today are simply the belated response to these imperatives.

Du Bois wrote – in 1917 – that "the dark world," meaning Japan, India, Africa, China, and the blacks in America, might someday wage war against the "white world." In 1930, he predicted an eventual alliance between American blacks and Asians and Africans, united in "a world movement of freedom for colored races." The early success of Japan against Russia in 1905 was not without its effect on blacks in America. At last, a non-white nation had stood up on its feet and knocked down a white power. This seemed to signal, in the minds of many black writers at the time, the beginning of the end of the period of white expansionism, which had lasted five centuries. This bond felt by many blacks for other colored races throughout the world was intensified by the emergence of black nations in Africa, by the rise of Japan and then China. It was in this period of swelling pride and expectations, coupled with frustrations on every front at home, that the Black Muslim movement, under W.D. Fard, really began to grow.

When Fard mysteriously vanished in 1933, his assistant, Robert Poole, now known as Elijah Muhammad, took over and membership rose to ten thousand with some fifty thousand believers. Mankind, the Muslims taught, began with the black race, which brought civilization to the earth, and the white race was nothing more than a degenerate offshoot whose purpose was to test the courage of the blacks. On the day of Judgement the white race would be destroyed. It was the Muslims who first called America "Babylon," a description the Panthers have adopted. And one of the converts picked up by the Muslims was Malcolm X, the man who more than any other was to inspire Huey Newton.

All through this century there has been a steady deepening of three critical attitudes which today find their sharpest expression in the attitudes of Black Panthers. First, the feeling that non-whites the world over must be united if they are to gain real equality with whites. Second, that direct action is the only means to substantial change in the present system of subjugation. And third, that the real barrier to racial equality is not white racism but the existing economic system which encourages exploitation and effectively bars all but a few blacks from the affluent society.

Now we can begin to comprehend the Panthers. They are opposed to capitalism. They align themselves with Chinese Communists, the Viet Cong, Arab guerrillas, Cuban revolutionaries, African nations, and in America with Mexican-Americans, Indians and Puerto-Ricans, all in accordance with the visions of Du Bois.

They are a logical advance on the Black Muslim movement, with its militancy carried one trigger-finger further – a few inches, in effect. However – and this is very important – they are growing in the direction indicated not by Elijah Muhammad, but by Malcolm X, who died opposed to "black racism." In one of his last speeches, Malcolm said:

"If you attack[a man] because he is white, you give him no out.

He can't stop being white. We've got to give the man a chance. He probably won't take it, the snake. But we've got to give him a chance." To this end, the Panthers have established the National Committee to Combat Fascism, so that "all ethnic groups can work together in a common direction."

Along with these three basic ingredients – solidarity, commitment to action, and anti-capitalism – is the even deeper-rooted black pride which was first nurtured by black churches in the South. And it is at this point, with these four factors now fixed into place, that the issue of guns arises.

It arose initially as far back as the time of slave uprisings in the south. But in is recent context it goes back to 1955 in Monroe, N.C. There, a Marine Corps veteran, Robert Williams, returned from service and tried to organize the black community with the aim, among other things, of gaining access for black children to the town's only pool. After some demonstrations developed, the Ku Klux Klan drove through the Monroe ghetto firing pistols and assaulting blacks. Police and civic officials rejected complaints on the grounds that the Klansmen were within their rights. The local chapter of NAACP decided, since appeals to the federal government for protection had also failed, to resort to the time-honored American tradition of arming themselves for defence. They bought a charter in – ironically! – the National Rifle Association.

The next time the Klan rode into the ghetto, it was greeted by gunfire. Klansmen quickly retreated. One aged member of the white community was later quoted as saying: "God damn, God damn, what has this god-damn country come to that the niggers has got guns, the niggers are armed and the police can't even arrest them."

The Second Amendment of the Constitution of the United States gives the right to bear arms. It is worth noting that this amendment was never challenged in California until the Panthers appeared on the scene. Since then, California law has been changed.

The point here is that if blacks in America have learned anything from their history it is that changes are not made to accommodate a docile minority. Nothing has been handed over to them on a platter. Each right had to be wrested from the existing power structure at a tremendous cost.

And after centuries of struggle, where, precisely, do blacks in America find themselves today? True, they have won substantial constitutional concessions – the total effect of which has been to bring them, in terms of "inalienable rights" to roughly the position whites were in at the end of the War of Independence.

In every other practical respect, they find themselves trapped.

In 1965, then assistant secretary of labor, Daniel Moynihan, reported that despite advances in civil rights and employment opportunities, the relative condition of the black in America was deteriorating rapidly. In terms of general prosperity, the average black family's income was slipping, the family itself was disintegrating (some 36 per cent of black children grow up in broken homes), and the handicap of poor education was taking a higher and higher toll as automation set in and the demands for sophisticated technological expertise rose. Karl E. Taeuber of the Population Research and Training Center at the University of Chicago, in an exhaustive study of 109 American cities, has shown that segregation in housing is becoming more pronounced all the time. It has been on the rise during most of the century. In *The Race War*, Ronald Segal concludes that "the growing violence of American thought, language, and action, the mounting acceptance of apocalyptic possibilities, are in significant measure the outcome of racial tension and turbulence within America itself.

"The racial struggle is a disease of the American system.... Certainly there can be no cure, no longer even much relief, in the patent medicines of civil rights laws and civic commissions. While America is economically two segregated races, it must be socially and politically so. And that is why America needs not another dose of reform, but a revolution....

"If there is any prospect at all of a lasting racial peace in the United States, it rests in the recognition by Negroes and an ever-growing number of whites, the more vigorous of them among the young, that American society needs reshaping at its roots."

It is to this end that the Black Panther Party is dedicated. It is not a racist anti-white organization. Nor is it, despite the pictures of Mao and sometimes Stalin which decorate its offices, even dogmatically Communist. And the critical thing which needs to be understood about Panthers is that they are *not* an aberration. There is nothing inherently violent in their program. They are opposed to senseless violence, spontaneous riots, blind outbursts of frustration and rage. There is considerable evidence that in several key areas where there was little burning or looting in the wake of Martin Luther King's death – such as south side

Chicago and Oakland – that the credit goes largely to the Panthers who were telling the brothers on the block to cool it.

The Panthers offer a measured response to brutality. In effect, they are balancing the scales, making oppression that much more difficult and so, in the long run, less likely to occur. And – here is the point – their emergence at this historic moment represents nothing more or less than the forward wave of a tide which has been coming in for a long time. The responses of the black masses to their society are inevitably shaped by the behavior and attitudes of the whites who control that society.

In his 1965 report, Moynihan noted that "the present generation of Negro youth growing up in the urban ghetto has probably had less personal contact with the white world than any generation in the history of the American Negro." He might have added: Except for personal contact with white police, recruited for the most part from the conservative and racist white working class.

The Panthers say simply that white America is the mother country, and the ghettoes are colonies ruled by occupation troops, the police. This is not simply rhetoric. As the Moynihan Report indicates, to most young blacks in the ghettoes, white America *is* as far removed as an imperial mother country. Black Panther "rhetoric" and the reality of ghetto experience are frighteningly (to many) close. It must be remembered that the Black Panther Party is composed for the most part of ghetto youth. The aim of the party is to move "the brother on the block." The Panthers do not address themselves to white or black liberals or the middle class, they address themselves to the reality of the ghetto kid. They speak his language.

Many people deplore violence. It is, in fact, a cliché to deplore violence. Violence breeds violence. Certainly – the violence of white cops in black ghettoes has bred precisely that. The assumption which seems to underline most criticism of the Panthers is that the violence *they* threaten (in self-defence) can only lead to violence on the part of the police. And the killing of young men like Fred Hampton is pointed to as proof of the proposition. Yet the violence committed by the police against blacks in the ghettoes was there all along. The Panthers have not created it or even substantially increased it. They have, if anything, become lightning rods attracting the bolts which were crashing blindly before. And now, since the lightning bolts of violence are converging on that one highly visible rod, we begin to see it. The cries of "Stop the killing!" grow stronger every day. The cowardly lion of the white liberal community is finally being aroused by the storm. Before the Panthers had surfaced, the white liberal community chose not to hear or see, simply because police violence flashed in the back lanes and alleys or inside tenements. The Panthers do not breed violence, they were bred by it – and it is their refusal to be shot at without shooting back that has made the violence visible to us all and made it that much less easy for us to pretend it doesn't exist.

"The tensions in the American psyche had torn a fissure in the racial Maginot Line," wrote Cleaver in *Soul on Ice*, "and through this fissure . . . the black masses, who had been silent and somnolent since the '20s and '30s, were now making a break toward the dimly seen light that beckoned them through the fissure."[55]

Many put their shoulders to the gigantic battering ram of the civil rights movement under the leadership of Martin Luther King. But when King fell, the battering ram, already slowing, finally lost its momentum. Like some cumbersome machine of social war, it shuddered and lurched, axles screaming, huge wheels spinning uselessly; it had finally bogged down in the swamps of Bureaucracy Land. About this time, shots were heard echoing from the West Coast, signalling the beginning of a new stage in the assault. Huey P. Newton had stood up – as Cleaver puts it – "in front of the deadliest tentacle of the white racist power structure," and had defied that tentacle with an M-1 rifle. A gear shifted somewhere. Young blacks – most just in spirit and mood, but many in reality – began to pull away from the heaving battering ram. They started reaching for guns. Whether they actually picked loaded weapons up or not was mostly beside the point. They had come to terms with something in themselves. For every one which did not actually pick up a gun, there were perhaps five, perhaps ten, perhaps twenty, maybe even a hundred or a thousand who accepted, for the first time, the idea that they might *have* to. And so the struggle for racial equality had reached its penultimate stage. Now the black masses would either make it through the fissure in the racial Maginot Line or the long-feared race war would be upon America. The Black Panthers have moved into the final staging area of a conflict which has been brewing since the very day the Declaration of Independence was signed in the presence of black slaves who wondered why its terms did not apply to them. Consider the absurdity of two-and-a-half million white Americans shouting "Liberty or death!" while three-quarters of a million black Americans were in chains. The nation was founded on just such a contradiction, and in the centuries since the contradiction has festered, reaching the point where it is now a devouring tumor requiring drastic surgery at the roots.

The ghetto is a concentration camp – economically, sociologically, and racially. Blacks in America for the most part are the victims of oppression, brutality, and exploitation. They can be murdered with relative impunity. The situation is not much different so far as native Indians throughout North America are concerned. Exploitation by the white power structure extends its hold right up into the Arctic Circle, where Eskimoes too are forced to live in ghettoes and denied any share of the profits which accrue from the plundering of their land. Frantz Fanon has pointed out, in *The Wretched of the Earth*, that a psychological transformation takes place in the minds of a subjected people beginning to struggle for their freedom. A collective impulse to violence develops, which usually works itself out in slayings and fighting among the oppressed, who shrink from confronting the overwhelming might of the oppressors. Fanon, a psychiatrist, has managed to legitimize the revolutionary impulse to violence. As Cleaver sums it up: "[Fanon] teaches colonial subjects that it is perfectly normal for them to want to rise up and cut the heads off of the slavemasters, that it is a way to achieve their manhood, and that they must oppose the oppressor in order to experience themselves as men."[56]

The whole history of blacks in America, and their present state of mind, their general acceptance of the need for violence, the crime-rates experiences in the ghettoes – all would tend to bear Fanon's findings out. The Cuban Revolution, the Russian Revolution, the First French Revolution, the Chinese Revolution: all have more or less followed the same pattern, whether the staging area is Kenya, Algeria, Angola, Vietnam, Los Angeles, Quebec, or Chicago.

It is not surprising that the Panthers should dismiss what they term a "cultural revolution" among whites as being abstract. Nor is it surprising, or even inaccurate (in the context of the black ghetto) that intelligent and perceptive young men should be reduced to thinking of *all* policemen as racist-facist pigs. The Panthers represent the oppressed and the exploited. And their revolution contains the psychological justification so accurately pin-pointed by Fanon.

However – and this is crucial – while talking about colonial sub-jects, oppressed and subjugated peoples, and the victims of overt brutality, we are referring to those large areas of the world where the "technocracy" has *not* taken hold, where repressive de-subli-mation is not yet the main vehicle of containment, where tech-nique does not apply, where "pleasant forms of social control and cohesion" have not been brought into play, and where organized and administrated mimesis has not yet replaced introjection. The rate of change in the world is not as even as thinkers like Ellul and Marcuse would seem to suggest. In those areas, such as ghettoes and Latin American and African and Asian nations, where the technological society is still a vision of the future, it makes no sense to worry about the problems that plague a "rationally totali-tarian society"; in *those* areas, poverty, hunger, brutal repression, and torture remain the reality.

The points made earlier about the futility of revolution are intended to apply only to those few areas of the world where the technological society has taken root. *Our* struggle is of a different order. And it is this qualitative difference which needs to be recog-nized if we are not to waste our energy by adopting revolutionary models which – no matter how applicable they may be elsewhere – simply *will not work* in the modern context. Those of us who are not colonial subjects, who are not subjugated people, who do not need to seek our manhood through cutting off the heads of the oppressors, are facing an enemy far more elusive and efficient than those who are still fighting an ancient war. For us to model ourselves after them is to take a backward step.

A large part of our responsibility remains, as Cleaver puts it, to help compensate for centuries of degradation and disenfranchi-sement, to assist as concretely as possible those who remain op-pressed. But if we make the mistake of believing our whole strug-gle lies in that one engagement, we may emerge triumphant, with the formerly oppressed poeple standing beside us on an equal footing, only to find then that *all* of us have been snared in another kind of trap. We have another responsibility at the mo-ment – to ourselves. And another opportunity. In part, it is a chance to bore from within against whatever oppressive power structures these others may be fighting from without; but there is more to it. We cannot simply mark time while trying to haul others up to our level. For one thing, the oppressed need to triumph by virtue of their own efforts in order for their victory to be truly liberating. As for us, we have the right (while still lending a hand, when and if it is required or asked for) and at the same time to undertake the final assault, which involves not just the storming of the external citadels of power, but the internal fortresses of the mind. Blacks in America today are still pinned down battling Neanderthals. So too are oppressed people everywhere.

# TWELVE A BRIDGE OF GREEN

We have seen that a wide clear avenue exists along which the new consciousness may pass in its journey to succession over the old perceptual mode. That avenue is the demonstrable need for the adoption of ecologically-sound methods of human organization. Even the most hopelessly bound operationalistic mind can perceive the need for such an adjustment. Further, as the pressures generated by environmental collapse continue to increase, the rate at which these essential changes will be made will be forced to accelerate. It may take a thousand or ten thousand oil spills before the awareness that the earth is dying penetrates the last sealed door along the corridors of power, but it will likely only take one air inversion disaster or two. We value our own lives more highly than those of seagulls and fishes. The detonation of two atomic bombs was enough to stay the finger on the nuclear button for a whole generation. There is no reason to suppose that an environmental disaster of similar proportions will not have at least as strong an effect.

It is the trans-political nature of the environmental crisis which makes it potentially such a force in human affairs. Racists, capitalists, communists, etc., are all locked into positions from which they cannot budge without surrendering their own basic natures, so it is conceivable that they would plunge the world into a suicidal war long before they would consider giving in. Yet in terms of environment, positions are not so fixed. Everyone agrees that breathing is a good thing. Thus, once it becomes apparent to everyone that this particular "good thing" is being lost, they can easily unite to hold onto it.

The new consciousness, at its third stage of development, therefore runs into nothing like the opposition it was confronted with at earlier stages. Yet while the opposition has a vested interest in adopting the insights fundamental to the new consciousness in this one vast area, it still retains its interests in the other political and cultural realms. Those who have acquired the new perceptions, likewise, cannot let go of their own quite different insights. So while the environmental issue opens the possibility of a *rapprochement* between the two modes of consciousness – holistic and operationalistic – leading, sooner or later, to the permanent adoption of the newer mode, on these other critical scores no such possibility exists.

Before we may consider the significance of this, there is a point which needs to be dealt with. It concerns the argument that the adoption of the holistic consciousness by the dominant culture is somehow "inevitable." Many will dispute this. It may seem that the environmental crisis can be dealt with operationalistically, that a disasterous "collapse" can be avoided by the rigorous application of technological methods. Yet it has been shown that the single largest factor in the equation of environmental deterioration is not one particular form of pollution or another (carbon monoxide, say, or rising radiation levels) but rather *attitudes*. Legislation of its own cannot solve the problem – for if companies large and small, communities and individuals fail to change their attitudes, and thus their deeply-ingrained habits, pollution will continue on a large-enough scale to bring on major ecological disruptions. The attitudes in need of change are *those which reflect the operationalistic consciousness*. Without at least some altering of that consciousness and the perception it involves – an alteration in the direction of holism – the attitudes will not likely be changed enough to make any significant difference. It is true, as the writer in *Manas* magazine was quoted as saying earlier on, that ecology "is a profession by means of which its practitioners grow into the habit of having a care for the world... Some primordial axiom of internal relations impresses itself upon men, who little by little, are led to see nature whole..." It is just as true that people who become aware of ecological relationships likewise are led to see nature whole. Thus, since it is attitudes and habits – of not caring for the world, of not seeing nature whole – that must be changed, by force or otherwise, and will be changed (assuming we are to survive), it is the fragmented, exclusive operationalistic consciousness which will of necessity have to be re-shaped. And re-shaped into the holistic mode, which is the only mode of consciousness perfectly in harmony with the new information being unearthed by ecology – and perfectly in harmony, let us add, with the developing *needs* of technological society.

Western society springs from a primitive culture which understood itself to have been banished from Eden. It found itself in an environment which was, at bottom, viewed as a place of punishment. It had been banished. Other cultures – those the West was eventually to overwhelm – considered themselves to be living in Eden still. The "inherent" aggressiveness which was to give the West such power over other cultures can be traced to just such a root conception of self. The West began as an outlaw. Native American, Eastern and African societies remained at peace with their world. The notion of "conquering nature" never crossed their minds, and so they were able to build what they needed, create only those tools and weapons they needed to survive, without being driven on like men possessed. The West, corrupted from its beginnings by its alienation from its environment and by notions of power stemming from the belligerent stance adopted in relation that that "hostile" environment, went on to build more than was needed to survive. Today, as the environment begins to topple like a tree (a tree containing his home and family) Western man is forced to abandon his basic aggressive posture. Once this *fundamental* shift has taken place, a "softening" of his position in relation to other peoples and individuals will begin to take place. Western man will begin to recover his primary balance. With the emergence of the holistic postwar consciousness we see the beginnings of that convalescence.

There is another reason for the inevitability of the adoption of the holistic mode. No technological society can do without well-educated citizens. Edward F. Denison, in his famous report, showed clearly that the most important factor in American industrial expansion has been education. The lesson has not entirely been lost on the rest of the world. Students thus come to be enormously important to the well-being of industry. They cannot be denied access to control of industry and eventually government because their expertise is absolutely required. And it is students, mainly representing the affluent middle class, who have been most directly affected by the processes which flushed the new holistic consciousness into existence in the first place.

Present-day university students, as a whole, are not the ones in whom the new consciousness has most deeply taken root. The ones most *deeply* affected, as a group, are those who have dropped out. Not because they were unwilling to make use of the universities, but because they are the ones whose consciousness was most in conflict with the operational mode. Their perceptions had leapt so far they simply could not fit themselves into the compartmentalized, fragmented spaces insisted upon by the universities, which embody the logic of the old mode of consciousness. These youngsters could no more survive psychically in the university environment than an oxygen-breather could survive naked on the moon. However, these people *can* be denied access to industry and the machine of government. Industry and government, in fact, have no need of them. They may be ignored or, if necessary, locked in prisons or shot.

Students, as a group, come a relatively poor second in terms of development of the holistic consciousness. Yet they are still deeply enough affected to guarantee that they will bring the new perceptions and attitudes (to a considerably less complete degree) with them into boardrooms and public offices. Technological society, at this point, will find itself being run by people whose consciousness has shifted from the old mode to the new, and thus the directives coming down the top will be of a qualitatively different nature.

This will take time. Perhaps not much. If, as most of the best-informed ecologists are saying, the 1970s will be the decade in which the basic reversal must take place if an environmental collapse is to be avoided, then we expect that the sheer pressure for change will mount so quickly that the new perspectives and consciousness will have to be rushed into office; literally, *dragged* in by an old order which understands itself to be in a tarpit from which it cannot escape without help. However – and this is critical – the very individuals upon whom the old order will be calling for help will be those whose perceptions do not allow them to operate on the same narrow perceptual basis which provides the rationale for the present behavior of the dominant culture. Just as human beings are said to be what they eat, so governments and industries are what they contain. Composed (as they are at present) of individuals whose consciousness is firmly in the grip of operationalism, they will behave accordingly. Once these same governments and industries have "ingested" enough individuals who embody the new consciousness, their behavior will *change* accordingly. The smaller the organization involved, it goes without saying, the more quickly the changes may be affected. One editor on a newspaper who has himself made the perceptual leap may move the whole paper quickly. But the more people there are involved, the more divisions, departments, branches, etc., the greater the inertia. National governments today represent the organizations where, because of their sheer complexity, the inertia is bound to be greatest. Since, in large measure, the new consciousness actualizes itself by drawing upon intuitive resources not previously drawn upon, since it involves the realization of a greater percentage of one's potential, it follows that those organizations which most quickly "ingest" the new consciousness will be those which subsequently show the greatest creativity, the most inspiration.

From these points we may observe that:

The consciousness, precisely because it *is* holistic, cannot truly be adopted in part; it involves an essential adjustment in methods of perception which must lead to equally essential adjustments in behavior.

The holistic consciousness involves a reversal of the priorities generated by the logic of domination which lie at the root of almost all present discriminatory, imperialistic, belligerent Western political positions.

But the essential point is this: *the new consciousness is an end in itself.* It is the very end envisioned by all sincere revolutionaries.

Whether anarchists, Marxists, New Leftists or idealistic Communists, their aim is to liberate all men from the prisons in which they find themselves locked, to free them from the grip of the lies and distortions which have been forced into their minds. Then, once all men have free minds, racism, hatred, poverty, injustice and wars will end. Men will not tolerate racism for they will no longer be nourishing notions of superiority. They will not tolerate poverty because they will understand that it exists only because too much wealth is being hoarded elsewhere. They will have developed a reverence for life. They will experience each other, regardless of race or language, or status, as human beings like themselves – as brothers. They will come to relate to others as they would members of their own family. They will love one another. There will likely always be anger, but hate, produced by feelings of impotence, will cease to exist as a force in human affairs – for all people will be free to realize their own potency. None will any longer deny them that. If the state will not wither completely away, it will at least slip into the background, becoming a thing taken for granted, as useful and welcome as a home, and no more obstrusive. All men being equal, each will be able to be himself without having to measure up to the standards anyone else would impose.

These, at their diamond-hard center, are the aims of genuine revolutionaries. Frauds, of course, abound. The false revolution-aries – there are many – are those whose real goal is to seize power for themselves so that they may avenge themselves on those who previously had power over them and so that they may come to control others, to be bosses. It may be that almost every revolu-tion in human history was sooner or later betrayed by frauds. That does not mean that the essential vision has been lacking, or that – no matter how blurred the image – it has not moved men by the millions, no matter how badly led or misguided they might have been. As for those that were no doubt led by true revolution-aries who were to lose sight of the vision once they had been corrupted by the perverse experience of power, theirs is the great-est tragedy.

Still, the vision remains. Driven by something that would seem to be close to the force of the impulses which guide animals in their sure search for a place to nest, we move clumsily, but as doggedly as salmon, in the direction of just such a vision. Human history has been a convulsive thrashing toward this goal. What has been dismissed as "idealism" has, in fact, been the stirrings of a great *impulse*. It is not an abstract, cooked-up theory. Nor has it been a fantasy. Whenever this vision moves men, it moves them from the deepest level of their being. It is a search for bal-ance, for a harmonious environment; it is a search such as the spider conducts as she readies herself to build a web – to do what her nature demands she do; it is a search for a stable relation-ship between oneself and one's world such as wild animals achieve in an undisrupted eco-system. This vision of brotherhood and harmony has been with us all along. Everything in nature seeks balance so that it may function according to the genetic in-structions which guided it into being. Human beings are no less fundamentally impelled to seek the stable relationship essential to natural functioning. Human consciousness, however, is so much more complex than other forms of consciousness that there are far more pitfalls into which it may stumble in its search for harmony. Further, man alters his environment all the time. He is in the position of a pheasant trying to build a nest in a field being turned one day into a pasture, the next day a garden, the next a park, then, in rapid succession, a parking lot, a runway, a building, and finally a basement within a larger building. Man is a creature who, because he ceaselessly alters his environment, is never able to work out a stable relationship with it. Clearly, in earlier, slower times, when change was almost imperceptible, relatively stable relationships could be worked out. These are the mark of primitive cultures. As the pace of change accelerates, as the man-altered environment begins to re-arrange itself more and more frequently, the stability of the relationship disintegrates. One has no sooner begun to be achieved than the environment shifts again. Through the last few centuries, we see the pace of change accelerating rapidly, shifting into a higher gear every few decades. At this point, technological man has about as much chance of achieving the required equilibrium in relation to the world he inhabits as a bird has of building a nest in a cyclotron. The vision of the true revolutionary would therefore seem every passing year to have grown more unrealizable.

Yet in fact the reverse is true. As the pressure mounts, as the imperative to find balance grows from a murmured occasional reminder to – as it is today – a constant high-pitched scream, like the howling of a siren, the drive toward balance becomes that much more powerful and urgent.

And as the drive reaches its extreme point – embracing, at last, all major levels of relationships, it brings the revolutionary vision ever more clearly into focus. For the "vision" is in reality the instinctual picture we all carry deep in our beings of what is required in order for us to function fully, to actualize ourselves, to fulfil our potential. It is a picture as clear as the one carried in the being of a pheasant which tells him to keep moving until he finds a setting "matching" that picture. Human beings are no less compelled to "keep moving" until we find the right setting. That *setting* is what is vaguely referred to as Utopia – variously known in its many guises as the classless society, the people's state, the free society, the just society, the great society, paradise on earth, the Marxist state, call it what you will. It is to this aim that genuine revolutions direct themselves.

What is being sought, through the medium of a violent over-thrown of a system which obviously does not provide this equilibrium, is what has been described here as the new consciousness. *That* is the *goal*. Wherever we see evidence of that consciousness, we see that the real revolution has already taken place, In effect, the *end* is being achieved before the *means*. The emergence of the postwar consciousness tells us that the objective of the revolution has been achieved before the revolution itself could take place.

One of the first men to understand clearly what the real revolution was all about was Gestalt therapist Fritz Perls. *"We cannot,"* he said, *"deliberately bring about changes in ourselves or in others.* This is a decisive point: Many people dedicate their lives to actualize a concept of what they *should* be like, rather than trying to actualize *themselves*. This difference between *self*-actualizing and *self-image* actualizing is very important."[57] Here is the deep trench into which most revolutionaries stumble, missing the understanding that *awareness per se – by and of itself – can be curative.* One who is "aware" is one for whom the revolution has already been won.

Led by no figure more heroic than its own internal need for psychic equilibrium, the postwar generation has begun to win that revolution. The critical "assault" was the compensatory perceptual leap. It was an assault won the moment the new consciousness emerged, even at its first stage of development. For had that consciousness not emerged, if no perceptual leap had been taken, then the gloom of thinkers like Jacques Ellul would have been justified. America today would be a land whose younger generation was the most robot-like in all human history. The fact that America's young are the most *un*-robot-like in history tells us much – it tells us, mainly, that we need not fear the comfortable concentration camp. Technology could fashion a beautiful prison which might easily hold minds responding to the dictates of the old operational order, but has shown itself to be incapable of constructing a prison – beautiful or not – large enough and air-tight-enough to contain the new consciousness. The beautiful prison may still come into existence. Technique might still appear to be taken over human affairs completely. Repressive desublimination may indeed appear to be working. But in fact the new holistic consciousness which is technology's real gift to humanity has long since escaped the trap. Young minds today are going on voyages to places where no machine can follow.

In a very real sense, the child-parent relationship has been reversed. For the parent – technological man, still under the influence of the First Effect of his own genius – is *still* mesmerized by the "toy" of technology. His child – who has grown to the point of acquiring the holistic consciousness – is not mesmerized at all. The child finds the toy boring, except where it becomes dangerous.

The parent, under its spell, finds it fascinating, and understands its dangers only vaguely.

The reversals brought on by the emergence of the new consciousness are so basic that the "child" is now in the position of having to take the loaded gun away from the "adult." The "adult" cannot be entrusted with it.

In few countries does the unwillingness of the "adult" to let go of the gun, go so deep as in America.

# THIRTEEN **THE AMERICAN TRAGEDY**

The "real revolution" is an individual event. As Ken Kesey put it, "We've got to keep it on a one-to-one basis, that's why I'm opposed to an organized movement." It is taking place, *has* been taking place before our eyes during the whole of the postwar period. And there is nothing inevitable about an Armageddon-like clash between the new and the old modes of consciousness, since there are wide bridges, fashioned of mutual need, between the two. The metamorphosis taking place within the cocoon of technological society has been far more rapid than has been assumed to be the case. While the rate of technological change has been telescoping, so that each "growth period" has been shorter than its precedent, each containing part of its successor, so too has the rate of psychic adjustment – always in response to the need for equilibrium – been telescoping. One more extension of the "telescope" may bring us to the point where the holistic consciousness will have become the dominant mode, thus restabilizing the relationship between man and his environment which has been deteriorating steadily since the initial adoption of the functionalistic concept of rationality. In effect, we will have arrived back at the Neolithic village, but with all our technological baggage and equipment, rather like the *enfant terrible* returning to the fold.

This is the *possibility* inherent in our present situation. Technological society is changing its citizens from within, and the fact that many of them are responding to the challenge renders the alarm of the technological pessimists meaningless. Arnold Toynbee reminds us that it is in response to the challenge of the environment that races make their great formative leaps. Ease, he suggests, is inimical to civilization – "the stimulus toward civilization grows positively stronger in proportion as the environment grows more difficult." Harsh environments, new ground, blows, pressures and penalties all tend to force a response at least equal to the challenge. The same, we see, can be said of consciousness. We are witnessing nothing less than the creation of a new civilization in response to the tremendous pressures generated by the old. It is a sink or swim proposition. And the young have learned – many of them – to swim.

In those areas of technological society where resistance to the holistic consciousness is least, we may therefore expect to see a Renaissance within a very short period, one which will undoubtably eclipse any yet experienced in the course of human history.

In those areas where resistance is greatest, however, the new consciousness will not be able to realize itself. There will be at least a relative slowdown in terms of growth. (*Industrial* growth may proceed – the self-augmenting nature of technique all but guarantees this. But Gross National Products do not a Renaissance make. In terms of human development, the realizing of potential, industrial growth more likely *impedes* such growth. Certainly, it would not seem to be in harmony with it.)

The resistance will be greatest where the stakes are largest – where interests are most deeply vested in the old order.

In America, the interests of those in power could not be much more deeply-sunk in the old mechanisms of consciousness. America's greatest liability at this stage is her sheer power. When environments undergo reversals, great strength in the passing context becomes a great liability in the new. The other arm of the scale falls.

America today indeed has great responsibilities. What these responsibilities entail, at bottom, is the maintenance of the status quo. Power is derived from given sets of relationships. Alter the relationships, and power is derived from given sets of relationships. Alter the relationships, and power is inevitably affected. It changes exactly as much as the relationships change, no more, no less. (Power itself may remain, but its shape will have been altered, it will have been redefined, just as water redefines its shape in relation to its container. It may no longer be recognizable as long as one sticks to the old definition.) Power must seek to maintain the set of relationships upon which it is based. Power, by its very nature, therefore demands of those who wield it that they become conservative. They can serve themselves, and the power they command, only by seeking to stabilize the relations from which their power derives. As the degree of power rises on a curve, so too does the degree of conservatism.

Power affects relationships in two distinct ways. First, when it is being sought, existing sets of relationships must be altered, disrupted, broken. And when it has been attained, power then attempts to stabilize the new relationships. The Establishment represents power attained, and revolutionaries represent power being sought. Each converts into its opposite once the reversal of positions has taken place. Much of the admiration the young in the West today feel for Mao Tse-tung stems from his unleashing of the Great Cultural Revolution; for here, it appeared, was a revolutionary who had somehow managed to resist the law of conversion. Much of the appeal of Che Guevara may be traced similarly. Rather than trying to stabilize the new relationships achieved by the revolution, he went on to attempt to disrupt other established relationships. The wide-spread youthful antagonism toward the "Establishment" similarly flows from an intuitive comprehension of the nature of power and how it works. For the new consciousness is very much in the power-being-sought stage. Operationalistic consciousness is power-attained.

American rhetoric was calcified in the days prior to the War of Independence, when the country was at the power-being-sought stage. So, too, was current Soviet rhetoric. Accordingly, both countries are traditionally sympathetic to others now at the preattainment stage of power. In reality, the law of conversion has gone to work in both nations. Both represent power-attained. Their basic guiding impulse is therefore maintenance of established relationships. Both, of course, seek to alter *some* relationships. (Russia, relationships in the Mid East. America, relationships in Indochina.) Yet the nature of these alterations are such that achievement of the goal would only *improve* the existing relationships in terms of the degree of power they confer on both countries. Power is a house. Power-being-sought is a builder, who must usually call in the demolition experts before getting to work. Power-attained is a repairman, who must also serve as a guard.

The relationships – political, cultural and otherwise – which have been forged by technology are based on the degree to which the operationalistic mode of conscious has been adopted. The two most powerful nations are those which have most successfully accomodated themselves to its imperatives. (The rewards of domination, after all, are an increased Gross National Product. The logic of domination, whether industrial or military, has paid tangible dividends.) Coming up behind them are the nations which are getting better at it. Those nations which have not yet fully abandoned their more ancient (and more holistic) modes of perception are those which, in the contemporary operational-derived relationship, are those which find themselves in the weakest positions of power.

The farther up the scale of power a nation is, the more antagonistic it must be to holism, which the dominant culture cannot help but equate with "powerlessness." The U.S. is at the top of the scale. For that reason, the holistic consciousness may be expected to be resisted there more fiercely than anywhere else. And it *is* being resisted.

These are perhaps the two main reasons why the U.S. is the most hostile environment into which the seeds of the new consciousness could be dropped. Its basic impulse is conservative, even when the incumbent administration proclaims itself "liberal." And its power derives from a set of relationships based on the operational mode, precisely the mode of consciousness it must stabilize in order to retain that power.

There are other, less basic but more visible, reasons.

Although the possibility exists that the third stage of the new consciousness can achieve a *rapprochement* with the old order on the basis of the environmental crisis, it cannot surrender the characteristics acquired at the first and second stages, any more than the outermost layer of an onion can be peeled off and somehow no longer be onion. If the young in America are increasingly aligned with the oppressed blacks, it is because, having taken the great compensatory perceptual leap, they can no longer accept the self-deceits which formerly served to rationalize discrimination. They are unable to avoid seeing clearly that the oppressed *are* oppressed. Where there are oppressed, there are oppressors. The real world of power and exploitation is masked by skilful manipulation in the mass media. That manipulation only works on those whose sense of "real" and "unreal" has been diluted by the First

Effect. The perceptions of the young penetrate this level of manipulation; the reality of power and exploitation is not glimpsed
through a screen: it is perceived directly. They thus find themselves living in a real world which does not correspond to the
"real" world of the previous, and still dominant, generation. The
great battering-ram of the civil rights movement was powered in
large part by the fact that it moved through the real world which
the young saw all around them, and moved *against* the deceits
which those in the grip of the old mode of consciousness had long
since accepted as being truths. The new consciousness was able to
hitch its perceptions to the battering-ram. The conflict in Vietnam, on the other hand, was built entirely on the imperatives of
domination, rationalized right from the beginning by the old order of "truths" which the young had come to perceive as deceits,
and was dictated at every turn by the impulses of power-attained.
The civil rights movement became for a time the most perfect
vehicle through which the new consciousness could express itself.
Vietnam at the same time became an equally-perfect expression of
the impulses of the old. The polarization was almost magnetically
flawless. In Vietnam we saw the "rationality" of pure operationalism at work; in the civil rights movements, the greater rationality
of holism. It did not take long for the civil rights and anti-war
movements to make common cause. Nor did it take long for pro-
war and anti-black sentiment to coalesce. Power-attained came
into direct conflict with power-being-sought.

The struggle for black liberation had become the cutting edge of
the struggle for liberation of the new consciousness. As young
blacks, the Panthers in particular, took over positions in the front
lines, however, young whites found their main vehicle of expression riding off on its own. Increasingly, they put their energies
into their other vehicle, the war in Vietnam.

As the third stage of the new consciousness surfaces, we see that
the young now have at their disposal a vehicle greater than the
other two combined: the environmental crisis. For the gates are
not locked and bolted against the approach of this vehicle as they
are against black liberation and ending of the war.

But the new consciousness is not – by its very nature – capable
of riding the environmental issue through the gates without bringing black liberation and the end of the war with it. That is, the
young in America will not be able to hitch their sensibilities to
environmental programs alone. They will not be able to work with

the old order on this one score, closing their eyes to what is going on elsewhere. The trick of refusing to see is the trademark of the old perceptual method, not the new.

The civil rights and anti-war movements came into phase with one another because they addressed themselves to the same realities. The environmental movement no less addresses itself to those realities. And its embrace is so much larger that many who would otherwise have managed to maintain their neutrality are being dragged into the conflict – on the side of those in opposition to the established system.

The vigor with which the new consciousness expresses itself has been increasing, snowball-fashion. At the second stage, working its way to the surface through the black liberation and anti-war movements, it acquired a ferocity sufficient to bring America to the outer edges of civil war. At the environmental stage, this consciousness is even better-defined. Its power – as yet barely tapped – is of almost limitless dimensions.

The distance between the *experience* of a black in America and a young middle class white is impossible to measure precisely, but this much may be said about it: it is a fundamentally different experience. Consider relations with police. Police behave differently toward those who have no power over them than they do toward those who are suspected of at least having access to such power. The citizen will have recourse to sympathetic courts and judges and juries. He will have lawyers at his disposal, possibly he will have personal friends in high office, or at least he will likely know someone who does. More to the point, he can count on support from society because he belongs to society, and is representative of others who can identify with him and who will therefore protect him as they would protect themselves. He *is* his society, a part of its body. Police, no less a part, understand this. Their individual understanding will not necessarily be clear, but they will sense the limitations of their power over a given citizen – the limitations being the retaliatory capability of that citizen. Laws aimed at protecting the individual attempt to arrive at a *detente*. Constitutionally, the individual citizen is armed. He can "shoot back" at the police through the courts, through political machines, and, mainly, he may count on massive support from the "troops." This will not always manifest itself – but the understanding exists that there is such a balance between the powers of the police and the powers of the individual citizen.

The police will therefore treat the citizen as a power to be reckoned with. The average tax-paying, law-abiding white citizen in the United States thus may view the cop as being a peer. So long as he remains within the law, the citizen carries a shield off which the lances of the police glance harmlessly. Regardless of how many times this ideal situation fails to be realized, it remains that this is the basic relationship which the individual understands himself to have with the police. It is the psychic reality of his world.

The reality for blacks – and likewise for other minorities – is something else. They are not part of the social body, they cannot count on automatic support from the community at large manifesting itself through the legal and political systems. While constitutionally they may be as well-armed as any white citizen, their legal sidearms have too frequently proven to be without ammunition for them to have any automatic assurance about their ability to defend themselves. They may not be certain that a judge or jury will be sympathetic. Experience has taught them that the opposite is more likely to be true. Unlike the white citizen, the black goes into the street with no certainty that his constitutional shield will deflect the lances of the cops. And the cops, understanding that the black does not have the same ammunition available for his constitutional weapons, tends to treat him as though he were, in fact, unarmed. It goes without saying that exceptions to this rule are so numerous as to be, in some areas, the rule itself. But those areas will be exceptions. For the most part, the simple reality is that police are not as inhibited in the exercise of their power with blacks as they are with whites. Nor are they as inhibited in dealing with other minorities, whether Puerto Ricans, Indians, hippies or youngsters generally. Power loosens inhibitions as surely as booze. People possessing power over others are always at least slightly impaired in their relationships with these others and, all too frequently, they are completely zonked. Power is not just in any metaphorical sense an opiate. It is, in psychological fact, the most powerful and stimulating intoxicant known to man.

Young whites may bring their experience of relations with the police into line with that of blacks by challenging police or by adopting attire which cuts them from the herd, leaving them without assurance of support manifesting itself through the legal or political systems. They pit themselves, inevitably, not only against the police but against the whole cultural definition of the society which those police represent. Police *are* soldiers – mercenaries, if you like, enforcing the will of their bosses. Except that unlike mercenaries they will be *like* their bosses. They are, after all, citizens themselves, "brothers" in the social family. Minorities, those who have not truly been accepted into the family, remain outsiders, and are treated as such. And when these outsiders challenge the family, challenge its authority, challenge its father (whether president, prime minister, or pope), the family reacts. The solution, obviously, is to bring everyone into the "family."

Yet, just as obviously, the "family" in America is fairly exclusively defined as being white and straight. Young whites must therefore *make an effort* to break out of the assumptions they have inherited about their relationship with police – if, that is, they are to comprehend the attitudes of those outside the family circle. Many will stumble on this comprehension inadvertently. That is, having adopted a mode of attire which does not correspond with the family image, they will find that police are treating them as outsiders. Others will be driven to this comprehension less directly. Seeing other young whites, whom they understand to be their peers, being treated like minorities, they cannot help but perceive that the understandings which serve to shield the typical white citizen do not – despite what they've been told – extend themselves throughout society. Whether affected directly or not, these young whites thus find themselves much closer in terms of experience to minorities which might remain physically very distant. These youngsters, like their parents, would seldom, if ever, actually witness the abuse of police power in ghettoes, and so they would never quite believe it. The rhetoric about justice and equality would still exercise too much influence in their minds. So long as the rhetoric is not visibly contradicted, it retains its power. However, whenever these youngsters witness their own peers being subjected to harassment and abuse from police, just such a contradiction registers. The roving eye of the television camera, zeroing in on further scenes of violence and differentiated use of power, heightens the contradiction. It is not so much that the young thus come to be "radicalized" rather, their accepted picture of their society – a "free," "just," and "equal" society – is shattered by the evidence before their eyes, their own experience, the experience of their peers, and finally the experience of "outside" minorities which they can now comprehend.

Still the young white must extract himself from his given social and cultural context in order to arrive at this juncture. And this is important – any time that the pressure gets too great, any time his own fear of the powers arrayed against him becomes too unbearable, unless he has become too visibly associated with the "enemy," he may shear off his hair, throw away his peace button and flared pants, and retreat safely into the anonymous womb of the dominant white culture. He has a way out.

So it remains that few young whites can draw upon the same desperate ferocity as young blacks may command in their struggle against the police and, through the police, the dominant culture. It is the difference between troops who may retreat through a pass and troops which are trapped in a position from which they cannot possibly escape. The former know that when their losses become too great they may pull back; the latter will fight, because they have no choice, to the death – they will inevitably be tougher troops to deal with. They will appear to be more heroic – evoking the admiration of the less-steadfast troops. Yet the heroism of the troops, which do not retreat even when they could, is somewhat greater. Young whites must call upon more reserves of strength if they are too match the determination of the young blacks.

Most, of course, cannot. And if they cannot as readily bring themselves to shoot a "pig" – or if it is harder for them to reach the point where they might want to – it is because their real experience of being maltreated by police is not as concrete as that of bona fide outside minorities. Or at least there is a restraining dichotomy, a conflict in their actual experiences. For at one time, all young whites lived within the protective embrace of the dominant cultural family.

Yet the vigor with which the second stage of the holistic consciousness applied itself to the civil rights and anti-war movements demonstrates clearly how many whites were capable to taking the giant step out of their inherited cultural estate. The security they gave up was monumental. Having broken so far out of the selective perceptual pattern dictated by the blueprint upon which their cultural identities were based, they may not easily revert to "form." They may know that they can *appear* to revert to the necessary form – that is, they can, if the battle goes too badly, flee back into the warren and disguise themselves, but at this stage it can only be a cover. Their experience of being persecuted, of being harassed and perhaps brutalized, cannot, once it has taken place, be wiped lightly from the mind. The student (or youth) who is hassled in the street, who has guns and bayonets aimed at him in a demonstration, who is perhaps bashed on the head by a nightstick, does become in a part of his consciousness a "nigger." He experiences nigger-hood, however lightly.

The civil rights and anti-war movements thus had a startling and far-reaching effect. They changed the population ratios in America. The millions of whites who took part in these movements were converted by the treatment they received into niggers. Suddenly, the "nigger" population in America swelled enormously. And as the demonstrations go on and grow in size, there is a steady and even more rapid rate of conversion from "citizen" into "outsider." If the Black Panthers suddenly seem to be commanding far more support from young whites than might "reasonably" be expected, it is because they are waging a struggle for liberation which encompasses all "niggers," and in the ranks of "niggers" we may include all who have experienced police (or military) power as it is used in relation to people who are not part of the dominant cultural "family." In effect, it is as though tens of millions of foreigners had abruptly arrived in the United States. Couple this factor with the essentially "alien" nature of the developing holistic consciousness (in the context of the old consciousness) and one begins to perceive the depths of the conflict. It is no passing phase.

The basic conflict – between the old and the new modes of consciousness – is now inextricably bound up in the black liberation and anti-war struggles. If it was not so completely bound up in these other struggles (if racial equality had in fact been achieved and if an imperialistic war was not being waged) the new consciousness could reach the third stage of development and pass relatively calmly on into the main body of society. We see that in the United States this is not possible. Violence, as Dr. Frederick Perls reminds us, is *always* the result of impotence. "Niggerhood" refers to a state of social, cultural, political, and economic impotence; the Negro slave is the symbol of such impotence. And as more and more young people in the United States are driven into positions where they discover their essential "niggerness," that is, their inability to change the direction of their society, their sense of impotence grows even more acute. As the sense of impotence increases, the impulse toward violence likewise increases. The "old revolution" – the revolution of the dispossessed and oppressed against their "masters" – thus becomes the struggle of those who have acquired the new consciousness, meaning most of the young in America. The impulse toward violence which develops in such people now becomes the impulse developing in these young whites. They number themselves among the wretched of the earth. At the same time, as their own tendency toward violence increases, they stimulate ever more furious reprisals. The old order, boxed lightly on the ear, might restrain itself. Kicked in the groin, it will not. The dominant culture now realizes it is being threatened to its core, that this is no game its children are playing. It becomes frightened and lashes back with the fury which fear invariably commands, the effect of which is to make the young feel even greater identification with the outcasts, and even more impotent and outlawed themselves. The "old" revolution in the United States thereby comes to be the crucible into which the main energies from all critical quarters are flowing.

Technology has worked upon us in many ways. Most visibly it has created a new kind of totalitarianism, a comfortable concentration camp, which in time will make revolution impossible just as all-out war has been rendered all but impossible. No one argues that the obsolescent of war is a bad thing, but many will still argue that the obsolescence of revolution is, definitely, a bad thing. Yet revolution means cyclic recurrence, and in terms of the rate at which awareness is developing in technological society, cyclic recurrence slows us down in our evolution. It does *not* speed things up. Revolution is an institution peculiarly adapted to the needs of other times and places. The new vehicle of growth is auto-evolution. Revolution interferes with this process. While the "new totalitarianism" (rational totalitarianism) has been observed at work, what has *not* been observed has been the true nature of the new mode of consciousness which transcends all previous political and social categories, which brings us into a new universe of perception and response. Revolution in the "old context" is still valid, but in the "new context" it is not. The new context does away with the need for it, since liberation can be achieved directly, short-circuiting the revolutionary process. However, the longer the new consciousness remains bottled up in America, the greater the chance that it will be forced to express itself through the only available channel, that is: the channel of revolution. And since an "old context" still exists in America, that may be the "leak" through which the new consciousness will be forced to blow.

# FOURTEEN A PSYCHO-REVOLUTION

Where war and racism are not so manifest in the behavior of the old order as they are in the United States, the environmental crisis promises to become the main vehicle for expression of the new consciousness. In the U.S., however, it shows every sign of simply deepening the current conflict. Vastly greater numbers of people will be dragged into opposition to the present system. If they find themselves unable to "move" society, to check the rapid deterioration of the environment, they too will begin to experience that deadly sense of impotence. The level of violence will rise. And the level of retaliation. Millions more will find themselves experiencing niggerhood. The advance of the new consciousness will be checked. It, too, will become a part of the "old" revolution.

Relatively few whites find themselves willing or able to shoot a "pig," mainly because – so long as the individual remains white and appears to represent the dominant culture – he is seldom confronted by a 'pig'. Rather, he is confronted by a peer. The relationship may seldom be that ideal, but the cop is at least the guardian of the straight white's society, and so that white does not have an automatic and fundamental disagreement with the cop. He may have a specific and incidental disagreement over the details of a traffic charge or something to that effect. Whatever, most whites do not themselves experience police as the soldiers of a conquering nation. Even when he has come to experience them as such, the individual white does not have generations of grievances accumulated inside him and so the violence he might direct at these authorities lacks something of the violence unleashed by persecuted minorities. Whites would not put the knife into their own society quite so deeply or quite so willingly as blacks would.

Yet as the environmental crisis deepens, this qualitative difference between white and black revolutionary actions dissolves. For here the white is threatened, affected, endangered every bit as much as the black. At its third stage of development, the new consciousness can be expected to commit itself to the environmental issue even more passionately than it did, at its second stage, to the civil rights movement. At the second stage, involved as they were in black liberation, young whites still had an avenue of retreat open to them. Many of them took it. Yet others, aware that in a crunch they *would* take it, distrusted themselves and did not enter the struggle, fearing that they would not have the strength to resist the urge to retreat when things got bad enough. These extra few ergs of strength which were required to keep whites in the forefront of the civil rights movement made a crucial difference – there were tens of thousands, possibly millions, who were almost there but could not commit themselves because their strength was not quite equal to the task. In the environmental crisis, however, there is no avenue of retreat available. This shifts the configuration, bestowing upon whites the same desperation that drives the Panthers so far beyond themselves. And requiring, incidentally, that much less moral strength. This is not to say that such strength is not present, but it is to say that the fact that it is not absolutely necessary makes the environmental movement accessible to many who could not step into the civil rights or anti-war movements.

The environmental crisis threatens everyone's life. So all whites suddenly have a vital stake in its outcome. But particularly the young, who are beginning to understand that unless major cultural, economic, social, and political reversals take place, and soon, they will not get to live out their lives. And also, since the consciousness which they have acquired is holistic, they are that much more able to see the ways in which they are threatened. Ecosystems they can understand. Ecology they dig. For most of their parents, whose minds are still very much in the grip of the operationalistic mode, these are little more than words – more or less meaningless scientific terms.

The speed with which the environmental issue has come into focus has dazzled many. It should not have. The telescoping process is at work. The first stage of the developing holistic consciousness lasted roughly from the late Forties to the early Sixties, when, hooked solidly into the civil rights movement, it began to refocus itself. It was not until the Berkeley uprisings that it moved decisively into its second stage. The third stage was already coming into focus by late 1969, and by early 1970 – with the celebration of Earth Day – it established itself. We may look for parallels with the civil rights movement. It took from 1954 until 1966 for the movement to give birth to the Black Panthers. It was only when it had become apparent that the movement had failed in its main objectives that the Panther approach began to make real sense. We may expect to see the environmental movement run its course in a far shorter time. If, within a very short time, the rate of environmental deterioration is not at least slowed, the non-violent stage will pass, as it passed in the civil rights struggle, and into the forefront will move the Green Panthers or their equivalent. Such organizations already exist.

Earlier, I suggested that an old-style revolution could not succeed in the context of a modern industrial society, that it was hopeless, that it accomplished nothing, and that it diverted us from the real struggle, which is to actualize ourselves as full human beings. These points applied, however, only where standards of living had passed beyond a certain minimum level as they have in the affluent sectors of technological society; where such sophisticated operations as repressive desublimation had begun to be adopted in place of the old tactics of repression; where the comfortable concentration camp had at last begun to take shape. The new consciousness is a revolutionary end in itself, and its emergence means that this most modern of all revolutions – the struggle to liberate the mind from its too-narrow and restrictive operationalistic mode – is being waged. That struggle, whether those in command realize it or not, is being won. The environmental crisis guarantees that such a mode of consciousness will have to be adopted. It is, at this stage in our history, a prerequisite to survival. A distinction exists between this post-industrial struggle for liberation of the mind and the struggles being waged by oppressed people for the basic standards of living and liberty already enjoyed by those who are a part of the dominant culture in technological societies.

ʿThe United States is the most technological of societies. The post-industrial struggle for liberation of the mind has proceeded further there than anywhere else. The odds against an old-style revolution are at least as overwhelming there as anywhere else. And, certainly, the environmental crisis is deeper there than anywhere else. By rights, the real internal revolution should proceed more quickly – and, in fact, it is so proceeding. However, because the black struggle for liberation has been denied, because the war in Vietnam continues, because the old consciousness has tightened, rather than loosened, its grip on the reins of power, those who should by rights be in a position to concentrate on the real revolutionary task of liberating their own consciousness find themselves pinned down fighting old, unfinished battles. Their struggle has become deeply committed to these other, more ancient struggles. American youth find themselves unable to proceed with their own evolution simply because the old battles have not been won.

What we see in America is a struggle which takes on more and more of the character of an old-style revolution, as increasing numbers of young people, possessed of the new consciousness, find themselves being converted into "niggers." And not just young people, it goes without saying, but all who have acquired a more holistic consciousness.

Yet the revolution would seem to be hopeless. Are these people then doomed to containment, repression, extermination?

Just as a distinction was drawn between anti-imperial and post-industrial revolutions, so too must a distinction be drawn between *pre- and post-environmental* revolutionary struggles. In the *present context* of America, an old-style revolution would indeed seem to be out of the question, for no mass base exists which is sympathetic to the goals of such groups as the Black Panthers, SDS, or the Weathermen. However, the context is changing. The rate of environmental deterioration is so great that within as few as ten years we may expect to see major air-inversion disasters, critical water shortages, epidemics of cancer and emphysema.

While a mass base does not exist at the moment which would support radical political and social changes, no one may guarantee that once the environment has deteriorated enough, a mass base will not then exist which *would* be sympathetic to such changes, so long as they are related to a problem apparent to everyone.

"Green Panthers" would be supported by vast sections of the population who would not touch a *Black* Panther with a ten-foot pole. The cries of Black Power, Student Power – any minority protest – may be rejected by the majority at present. But these cries emerge only because minorities continue to find themselves in intolerable situations. Environmental deterioration promises to spread the misery around, regardless of whether the wealth is spread around or not. More and more people will find themselves living in "environmental ghettoes." They will experience the sense of deprivation which now goads minorities into violence. The Black Panthers moved into the front lines only after the non-violent civil rights movement had spent itself in a futile struggle. The environmental movement is now at the opening stages of its non-violent period. It will likely not take as long as the civil rights movement to give birth to a violent successor. And while the cries of Black Power fall on deaf ears, the cries of Green Power will not. The black revolution and the peace movements may never crack the walls raised against them, but the green revolution has the potential to smash those walls. Exactly the same forces at work in these other struggles will be at work, supplying the same kind of energy and desperation, channelling the same kind of consciousness. Only on a vastly larger scale.

The peace movement derived in large measure from the civil rights movement. The environmental movement derives from both. These force America into a trap. If the struggle is defeated, America will have had to drive into hiding, lock up, or kill the very people who are most capable of guiding her through the new world her technology is creating. If the revolution succeeds, those very people will have had to take a giant step backwards in terms of their own evolution in order to fight such a battle. About the Panthers it may be said: What a *waste* that such perceptive, sensitive, and complex people should have to expend their talents and energies fighting for standards of living the technology of the country was quite capable of giving them automatically. How much more might they have learned and passed on, discovered, created, and unearthed had they not been forced to fight an old war? About young Americans in general, committed as their consciousness is to this ancient struggle, the same may be said. Within another generation, America could have been Utopia. As it is, about that time America will likely just be convalescing.

# FIFTEEN INSIDE THE STEEL WOMB

Eldridge Cleaver remarked in an interview in Algeria: *"I believe that consciousness has been expanded in the United States of America beyond the consciousness possessed by any other people on the face of the planet Earth."* Certainly it is manifesting itself there more quickly than anywhere else. If it stems in large part from a compensatory perceptual leap taken in response to psychic disequilibriums induced by the intrusions of mass media, then it would *follow* that the new consciousness would come into existence in America first. This is precisely the problem. The real crisis in American can be traced to the fact that this country has become the first battleground between the old and the new modes of consciousness.

Given ten or even only five years, the over-all psychic atmosphere could have been softened enough by the hammer-blows of the crumbling environment for the necessary adaptations (to a holistic mode) to be made by the dominant order. But the environmental crisis is not yet apparent enough to everyone. Concessions have not truly begun to be made. Faith in The Machine runs so deep that the operational mode is still assumed to be capable of making the necessary adjustments.

The new consciousness in America, brought into being by technological Caesarian section, has left the womb before the mother is ready to deliver. While American youth are indeed the vanguard of the new consciousness, they find themselves in a container as yet completely unwilling to re-shape itself. The container of American society is therefore being pressed against from within more forcibly than any other on the planet.

Elsewhere, the new consciousness is not so advanced and so it does not press so forcibly. It is not so inextricably bound to other, older struggles. Nor is the resistance so great, because the power being threatened does not have quite so much at stake. By the time the consciousness attains the definition it has in America, the "environmental vehicle" will be available – is already available – and through this medium the consciousness will be able to express itself without having to "haul through the gates" the other more violently opposed vehicles of its expression. The "backward" step into old-style revolution, which inevitably forces the victors as well as the vanquished into relationships based on power, will not necessarily have to be taken. The new consciousness, unimpeded, may therefore develop. It is a utopian end in itself, since it represents the individual attainment of psychic equilibrium – the instinctive goal of all revolutions.

If the young are vague about the goals of their revolution it is only because they have reached the point of development where they realize they are, in fact, seeking nothing more than just such a natural equilibrium: a "setting" in which they can function in their uniquely human way, just as an animal requires a certain environmental equilibrium in which to function properly. The "vaguer" the objectives of the revolution the better, for rules imposed at one stage of development quickly become restrictive at the next stage. (It is fine to tell children "not to play with fire," but if that ruling were to remain in force once they had become adults, who would stoke the furnace?) All revolutionary programs, once implemented, become barriers on the road to further progress. To set up a program is to put limitations on growth, to deny evolution. To do away with programs and timetables is to leave the door wide open to further growth. In seeking nothing more than an end to exploitation, racism, domination, etc., those possessed of the new consciousness show a crystal understanding of the defects built into all revolutionary schemes. Elimination of the destructive elements in the environment is *all* that a revolution need seek. To attempt to do more, to define the nature of the post-revolutionary world, is to freeze it at a given level of development.

The "idealistic" impulse toward nothing more fixed than brotherhood, love, and freedom seeks nothing more than a clearing away of the garbage from the landscape. It is a matter of weeding the garden, plowing the soil. No one may determine what grows in that garden in advance. Ideologies, of course, attempt to do just this. They are biased in favor of single-crop gardens. About such ideological gardens there is nothing natural at all. Where no ideology except the impulse toward a balanced environment is involved, plants of all species may grow. We see today that countries where the revolution has succeeded are as repressive and totalitarian as any on earth, their "crop" having been decided upon even before they came into being. These societies can experience further real growth only through the medium of another revolution which, in its turn, will impose yet another straitjacket. Only the completely open-ended revolution, which demands that limitations on human development be removed, can escape this trap.

At the third stage of the development of the postwar consciousness, this is the revolution being sought. Where the second or third stages have not yet succeeded in realizing themselves, however, the third cannot proceed.

This consciousness, let us make sure we understand, is fundamentally new only in the context of literate Western society. Otherwise it is a very ancient means of perception, one which has acquired the extra dimension offered by the insights of operationalism. So long as the operationalistic mode is only one fact of a consciousness which is otherwise holistic, it is a powerful, useful tool. The West developed magnificent tools, but instead of *making use* of the tools, came to *adapt* itself to the use of these tools; the yardstick became the master and Western man began to model himself after the yardstick. The new consciousness does not represent a simple regression to an ancient perceptual mode, but rather the repossession of the wider, older mode – without letting go of the yardstick. It is something more than retribalization. The yardstick (which has become a totem) is displaced from the center of the village and understood again as being a yardstick, nothing more, nothing less. The new consciousness therefore comes to transcend all previous modes of perception. It represents a fusion of East and West, the coming together of the deep sense of harmony still known in the East and the practical talents of the West. But the twain is not just meeting, it is producing a new sensibility combining the deepest instincts of both root cultures and synergistically producing something more.

"Thinking" and "perceiving" are organically linked. Our cognitive processes are shaped by our perceptual processes. Nothing is in the intellect which was not previously in the senses. "The components of intuitive thought processes interact within a continuous field," writes Rudolf Arnheim. "Those of intellectual processes follow each other in linear succession."[58] The young, drawing ever more heavily upon intuitive forms of cognition, tend to see things in terms of whole systems, or, if not whole systems, at least larger systems than those whose perception is still limited by the imperatives of operationalism. Because they perceive differently, they think differently. Their thinking follows the contours of their perceptions as forests follow the contours of the land. As their perception expands, becoming more holistic, they can see that Vietnam is not somehow separate and apart from the phenomenon of ghettoes in the midst of affluence. They may see that automobiles and lung cancer go hand in hand. The older generation, accustomed to thinking in sequential "chains," will not make these connections unless every link in the chain of causality between the lung and the internal combustion engine is made clear to them. The young need not have the links clearly established because they can "see" relationships which are part of a whole pattern. Their vision is that much more powerful. Their thinking is thus closer to reality which is itself a continuum, a continuous interrelated whole.

Where this new consciousness is not so violently opposed it may realize itself without having to step back and assume a violent revolutionary stance.

Where the old revolutionary option is out we may be spared another cyclic recurrence, forced back on ourselves. This is the "real revolution," which has been taking place all along. The storming of the mind has gone far, and has already accomplished its essential mission – to jog us out of the fragmented, exclusive spaces which lead to conflict and struggle, to break the idea of conquest, to force us away from notions of domination and hostility, to open us up to the possibilities of growth in awareness virtually unlimited. The "door" has been opened. Previously, our consciousness refused to acknowledge even its existence; thus we were trapped. Now, we are free. We may take hold of the tools of technology without being their slaves. The "comfortable concentration camp" may come into existence, but it does not matter because our minds will have been freed from the tyranny of operationalism. We may accept the gifts of technology just as "primitives" accepted the gifts of nature. All revolutions aimed at liberating us. Now, we are being liberated anyway – without going through the vicious circle of a revolution. However, the "old" revolutions have not 'yet run their course and must succeed. In those countries (such as the U.S.) where not even those old revolutions have run their course, conflict is inevitable. The new consciousness will flow most freely where there is least conflict.

# SIXTEEN THE DEMANDS OF POST-INDUSTRIALISM

In the meantime, what about basic problems of deprivation, inequality, injustice, poverty, misery? How are these to be dealt with? Can responsibility to others be abdicated in the name of evolutionary growth? In putting forth the suggestion that there is a qualitative difference between the new revolution in consciousness and old, unresolved anti-colonial conflicts, does one not run the risk of aiding and abetting the entrenched powers? (Divide and rule.) As the reader will see shortly, this is hardly my intention. A strategy will be presented which, I believe, will prove in the long run to be far more effective against the Powers That Be than any yet fashioned by revolutionaries whose models have been drawn from the past. It is, moreover, a "strategy" which has been simultaneously grasped by thousands of individuals already at work, a fifth column which is busy subverting the old order of consciousness at every turn.

Before turning to this strategy, we must linger over the question of priorities. There are problems – misery, hunger, deprivation – which must be dealt with immediately. These problems *are* being dealt with, clumsily, perhaps, but – in historic terms – relatively rapidly. A direct armed confrontation is not the fastest or most effective way to deal with technological society. For technological society, even left to its own devices, is in the process of turning itself inside out. It is converting itself into something very much like its opposite. So long as one remains insistent on the idea that any given system – particularly capitalism – is absolutely fixed or rigid, one can easily arrive at a position where the only course open (if real change is to be affected) seems to be direct, frontal assault. In the modern industrial society this is not the case. The system itself is its own worst "enemy." For, faster than almost any other force in existence, it is transforming itself. An "invisible revolution" is taking place, and has been taking place for ten decades. It is only now building up to a critical point. This invisible revolution is far more real, in terms of long-range effects, than virtually *all* the highly visible – but less substantial – revolutions now being carried out in the industrialized world. It is as though the "invisible hand" so much counted upon by capitalists to steer the market was, in fact, the hand of the ghost of Marx. For the world it is creating is more "communistic" than anything which has yet been achieved by even the most leftward government. Consider these points:

In the spreading environmental ghetto, we are faced not with *problems*, but with what Michel Chevalier has called "meta-problems."

In an address to the Town Planning Institute of Canada Conference at Minaki, Ontario, in June, 1968, Prof. Eric Trist noted:

[Chevalier's] central point is that not only have the problems themselves developed far wider ramifications through the increased connectedness in the casual texture of the environment but that this quality of diffuse extension is also becoming more widely perceived. This is the equivalent to saying that it has become "existential," and that this existential dimension represents a new factor which must be taken into account. In his view, "society has come more and more to perceive and articulate a new kind of problem. It is not only a matter of putting related problems together; new knowledge and expectations have caused a fusion, an interrelation or problems into a class of meta-problems. And society, once having perceived a meta-problem, begins also to perceive that courses of action to relieve it are as inter-related. . . ."[59]

Meta-problems cannot be coped with in the old "problem" frame of reference. Yet it can be seen that most decision-makers cling to whatever part of the problem lies within the jurisdiction of their departments, simply because our whole institutional structure, geared to the conditions of industrialism, have been built this way. The difference between "problems" and "meta-problems" is identical to the difference between "planning" and "technoplanning." Technoplanning emerged in the military and industrial spheres during or immediately after the Second World War, in response to new logistic demands, and also, as Chevalier would have it, "the increased connectedness in the casual texture of the environment." High on the list of meta-problems right now are poverty, depletion of natural resources, environmental pollution, racial and cultural conflicts, and, of course, war. The holistic postwar consciousness, with its essentially existential character, is ideally suited to the perception of meta-problems. This kind of perception is precisely what we need in order to survive. At this moment in our history, the perceptions and consciousness of the counter culture clearly have the highest survival value. Old operationalistic orientations are no longer able to cope with the situation. Meta-problems elude the grasp of the technological problem-solver. It is the counter culture which most clearly perceives the nature of the meta-problems. They are as real to the people who make up the counter culture as they are *unreal* to those in the dominant culture; and conversely, the "problems" of the dominant culture ("the threat of communism," maintenance of present levels of affluence, etc.) appear completely unreal to those who have evolved to the point of perceiving meta-problems.

A container awaits the growth of the counter culture, one well suited to the kind of perception involved. That container is the post-industrial society. It is important to realize that the structure of post-industrial society is already present, that *given enough time* it will evolve to the point where the critical social balance will have shifted in favor of the holistic mode. Eric Trist has made this abundantly clear.

We must prepare ourselves, he states, "to assist the emergence of a society radically different from the industrial societies which have evolved in the last two hundred years – whether these remain substantially capitalistic or have taken on a socialistic complexion ... An irreversible change process is proceeding in the world, at an accelerating rate but with extreme unevenness, both within and between countries. ... " He refers to this as the "drift" toward the post-industrial society. He notes that the contemporary environment has taken on the quality of a turbulent field. "This turbulence arises from the increased complexity and size of the total environment, together with the increased interdependence of the parts and the unpredictable connections which arise between them as a result of the accelerating but uneven change rate. . . . "

In the most advanced countries, the post-industrial society is already structurally present; it has already "occurred." It has, in fact, been building up for quite a while and in its outline form we may detect it in our midst. "What, by contrast, has not yet occurred, and is not building up at the pace required, is any corresponding change in our cultural values, organizational philosophies or ecological strategies. . . . " (In saying this, of course, Trist has failed to look closely at the values, philosophies, and strategies which are common to the counter culture, which correspond to those *required* by the structure of post-industrialism. In fact, these too have been building up for quite a while and are now developing at an accelerated pace. The juncture we must look for is the point at which the skin of industrial society is shed, revealing a society which is predominantly post-industrial. For, when this juncture is reached, what is now simply the counter culture will have found its home. It will have become the dominant culture. The problem now facing all advanced industrial nations, America in particular, is one of timing. The post-industrial social mansion is being built and its future inhabitants are ready to move in.

With the added insight of understanding the essential nature of the counter culture, we may follow Trist's description of the emerging post-industrial society and see how aptly suited it is to the postwar consciousness.

The "power base" of change has, in the last thirty-odd years, shifted decisively in the United States. In 1935, the type of scientific knowledge, for instance, which was salient was "empirical." By 1965, salient scientific knowledge had become theoretical. Energy was the main type of technology. Today it is knowledge. The politically most influential establishment was made up of financiers and industrialists. Today it is knowledge. The politically most influential establishment was made up of financiers and industrialists. Today it is composed of scientists and professionals, "though the former group is still there and is likely to continue as a power and needed 'Third Force'." Governments, are, however, now themselves the wealthiest capitalists and control the markets for the most advanced industries. The resources they need are more than ever those provided by the knowledge-makers and the knowledge-appliers, and these compose interdependent fraternities, who still own the means of their own production – which are in their heads. . . ."

The character of the economy, too, has undergone major changes in the last thirty years. Service-related services and person-related services now account for more than half of the Gross National Product, for more than half of total employment, and for most of the gains in numbers employed. If the activities of all other non-profit organizations are included along with those of government, they now contribute more than a half of what the market sector contributes; but if a value is added for households (non-paid personnel, capital, productivity gain, and volunteers) *the total non-market sector begins to exceed the market sector.* "The relevance of pooling all components of the non-market sector in this way is that it releases us from being controlled by the industrial 'image' which assumes that somehow the market sector alone counts in producing the wealth of a society." Leading private enterprises, mainly domestic in 1935, had become, by 1965, mainly international. And the costs of bringing into being and maintaining the total environment (which includes urban and social aspects) by 1965 had begun to approach the cost of producing the commodities themselves. Social costs had begun to become more salient than marketing costs. Thus;

> Post-industrial society may already be seen as a service society in which the market, though remaining highly important, is nevertheless becoming sub-dominant. Economically, it will be a more international society, though one in which "nationalism" and "sub-nationalism" will continue to assert themselves. Though remaining a mass-consumption society, with social costs beginning to overtake market costs, it will tend to become, to use Daniel Bell's term, a more "communial" society in which the individualistic values of industrialism will be less pronounced. Not that these values, any more than the other industrial features listed, are likely to diminish beyond a certain limit. Rather the question is one of a change of emphasis. This different emphasis does, however, imply a change of structure. A new type of social balance must somehow be struck if the new order of complexity is to be regulated.[60]

In terms of occupational structure and education, massive shifts and displacements have likewise taken place since the 1930s. The work force, then mainly blue collar, had changed by the 1960s to white collar. The average educational level had jumped the hurdle of high school. The work force came to be matched, in fact, surpassed, by the "learning force." And single careers had become serial. "The large mass of jobs depending on unskilled, semi-skilled or even skilled labor when this is manipulative, is being automated and computerized out of existence. The jobs that remain, or are being created, *involve perceptual and conceptual skills on the one hand and interpersonal skills on the other.*"(My italics.) And finally, the ratio of working hours to leisure hours is shifting decisively in favor of leisure.

Michael Harrington has referred to what he calls "the social-industrial complex," rising in the wake of the military-industrial complex. The first is a response to the urban crisis just as the second was a response to nuclear and international political crises. In the environmental context, we see that since the 1930s the degree of salience has shifted from large single organizations to inter-organizational clusters, from single metropolitan areas to inter-metropolitan clusters, from quasi-autonomy in rural areas to either urban-linked or dissociated rural areas, and we see that pollution, considered "within safety limits" thirty years ago is now surging past the safety limits. Natural resources, treated then as inexhaustible, are now feared as exhaustible. "To sum up," says Trist, "the structural presence of the post-industrial society discloses that we have reached or will soon reach a number of limits critical to our survival. Unless we can learn new methods of social regulation, the chances are small of our being able to realize the immense possibilities that now exist for improving the quality of life."

Coming to his key point, Trist notes that "new values [which] can be regarded as appropriate" to post-industrial society "are discernible," but "nearer to the horizon than the main sky." (In 1968, from the remote vantage point of a professorship, this may have seemed to be the case. In 1971, this is much less so the case.) What post-industrial society demands, he notes, is "values which enhance our capability to cope with the increased levels of complexity. . . . A greater pooling of resources . . . more sharing, more trust, more co-operation. . . . The inference may be drawn that appropriate emergent values will tend to be communal rather than individualistic. Their direction will be opposite to that which value-formation has taken in industrial societies, moulded as these have been by the Protestant Ethic. One may, therefore expect resistance to their establishment and diffusion. . . ."

In discussing the "cultural absence of the post-industrial society," Trist argues that while *structurally* such a society exists in the midst of the advanced industrial nations, cultural, philosophic, and ecological values have not been permitted to develop which are ideally adapted to it. In the following table, he compares those which are adapted to industrial society with those who will be required to suit the frame of post-industrialism:

## CHANGES IN EMPHASIS OF SOCIAL PATTERNS IN THE TRANSITION TO POST-INDUSTRIALISM

| Type | From | Towards |
|---|---|---|
| Cultural values | achievement | self-actualization |
| | self-control | self-expression |
| | independence | inter-dependence |
| | endurance of distress | capacity for joy |
| Organizational philosophies | mechanistic forms | organic forms |
| | competitive relations | collaborative relations |
| | separate objectives | linked objectives |
| | own resources regarded as owned absolutely | own resources regarded also as society's |
| Ecological strategies | responsive to crisis | acticipative of crisis |
| | specific measures | comprehensive measures |
| | requiring consent | requiring participation |
| | short planning horizon | long planning horizon |
| | capping conflict | confronting conflict |
| | detailed central control | generalized central control |
| | small local government units | enlarged local government units |
| | standardized administration | innovative administration |
| | separate services | co-ordinated services[61] |

Column One summarizes classical organizational theory and prevailing management practises. Column Two summarizes attitudes and values which are "beginning to take hold." Trist notes that *"the appropriateness of the strategies through which ecological as distinct from organizational systems are regulated becomes . . . a decisive feature in determining the adaptive effectiveness of the cul-*

*ture of post-industrialism.*" [My italics.] In short, the adoption of ecological strategies by the existing (industrial) order is indeed the bridge along which the holistic consciousness may pass in its journey to dominance in the post-industrial scheme of things. This is the critical means to diffusion of the new value system.

The structure of advanced industrial society is changing in such a way that adoption of the values, perceptions, and consciousness of what is now simply the counter culture is inevitable. We can survive no other way. The counter culture embodies the values and philosophies which will clearly be the central characteristics of post-industrialism. It similarly adopts the essential ecological strategies. The balance had been shifting steadily toward this new kind of equilibrium, and it cannot at this stage be checked, particularly in view of the environmental crisis. Just as the military-industrial complex came into being in response to one crisis, and a social-industrial complex is coming into existence in response to a new crisis, so something very much like an "environmental-social-industrial complex" is likewise beginning to take shape.

One recurring criticism of many who make up the counter culture is that they "don't *do* anything." Exactly. Perhaps it is apparent now that we are moving into an economy in which there will not be enough things for people to "do," in the industrial sense of contributing to production of goods. Automation and computerization will largely be "doing" that. Greater and greater numbers of individuals, whole strata of society, will find themselves with nothing particular to "do." The new kind of work which will be left for them to involve themselves in will center around experience more than it will around production. Already, many of the young measure themselves in relation to each other not by the quality of what they produce, but by the quality of their *experience.* The experience of oneself has never had any particular industrial value. In the post-industrial period, it will. Artists and mystics have traditionally been the only ones to involve themselves in this kind of "work," and as the balance tilts from industrial to post-industrial patterns, we see that fifty million Americans are already involved in amateur art courses, that group and other kinds of existential therapy ("journeys to the center of the self") attract more and more people. So, too, do the consciousness-altering drugs. All these are better adapted to the post-industrial framework, wherein the most important product will be *oneself.* It counts less and less, as we move toward post-industrialism, what one does as what one *is*. Already, what is in demand in the advanced industrial sphere, is perceptual and conceptual skill, and interpersonal skills. Neither craftmanship nor technical skills are the critical criterion, but rather personality. As we drift further and further into the developing situation, it becomes apparent that what we need most are cooperative, sharing, trusting, communal individuals. Individuals who are "producing" nothing at all except a personality suited to these demands are, in fact, "producing" in the most critical sense. That particular product can be a life's work. It is a full-time job, and it can only be done on a one-to-one basis. A pothead or a mystic or a just plain "beautiful person" has no place in the industrial scheme of things, but in the post-industrial scheme will contribute to society in the most direct and important means possible. The real work of the time will be the creation of something which has never fully been realized: A civilization composed of non-competitive, non-violent people oriented to a further exploration of their own capabilities, rather than acquisition, extraction, aggression, and imperialism.

We see that the structure of the post-industrial society has already emerged in the advanced industrial nations. We see that the type of perception, consciousness, and values which are ideally suited to it have likewise come into existence, and are now being opposed by the prevailing industrial mode of consciousness. We see that in the United States this conflict has come most quickly into focus and that as the counter culture achieves a greater degree of self-definition, it is forced to press ever more forcibly against the old order. The old order, increasingly aware of its impending obsolescence, begins to fight back.

In *The Pursuit of Loneliness, American Culture at The Breaking Point*, Philip E. Slater has gone (although overlooking one critical point) to the heart of the situation:

> There are an almost infinite number of ways to differentiate between the old and new cultures. The old culture, when forced to choose, tends to give preference to property rights over personal rights, technological requirements over human needs, competition over cooperation, violence over sexuality, concentration over distribution, the producer over the consumer, means over ends, secrecy over openness, social reforms over personal expression, striving over gratification, Oedipal love over communal love, and so on. The new counter culture tends to reverse all of these priorities.

It is important to recognize that these differences cannot be resolved simply by some sort of "compromise" or "golden mean" position. A cultural system is a dynamic whole, resting on processes that must be accelerative to be self-sustaining. Change must therefore affect the motivational roots of a society or it is not change at all ...

There is a limit to the amount of change a system can absorb ... In any case there is no such thing as "compromise": we are either strong enough to lever the train onto a new track or it stays on the old one or it is derailed.

Thus it becomes important to discern the core motivational logic behind the old and the new cultures. Knowing this would make rational change possible – would unlock the door that leads most directly from the old to the new. A prolonged, unplanned collision will nullify both cultures, like bright pigments combining into gray. The transition must be as deft as possible if we are to minimize the destructive chaos that inevitably accompanies significant cultural transformations. (This of course makes the assumption that some kind of drastic change is either desirable or inevitable. I do not believe our society can long continue on its old premises without destroying itself and everything else. Nor do I believe it can contain or resist the gathering forces of change without committing suicide in the process.)[62]

Although Slater does not acknowledge it here, it is apparent that the "Silent Majority" is determined to contain or resist the gathering forces of change, even though as he is aware (and they are not) that they cannot do so without committing suicide in the process. The "prolonged, unplanned collision" has been going on for two decades now, becoming an exhausting, debilitating struggle in the last ten years, with more energy, more creativity, and more will being squandered with every passing month. In the other advanced industrial nations, we see that not nearly so much energy, will, and creativity are being used up. Increasingly, in all advanced nations, that same energy is being funneled into the struggles to prevent an environmental collapse. The point is, in the United States, that the very people who are turning their energies into the environmental struggle are those who have become most closely associated with (and identified as being associated with) the other, older revolutionary struggles. Thus it is possible for a member of the Daughters of the American Revolution to announce, on Earth Day, that "subversive elements are trying to force our children to live in an environment that is good for them." A joke? No. What it reflects is the fact that the identity of the dominant culture in the United States is hitched so obsessively to industrial achievement that it cannot deal rationally with the requirement to reverse those priorities. America rode to its present position of industrial and military preeminence on the back of industrial excellence. More so than any other nation, it derives its power from the concepts of rugged individualism and industrial imperialism, precisely the two concepts which are most dangerous in the environmental sense. In cultural terms, as well as economic and military, its vested interest could not be greater.

Nations (such as Canada) which have never been able to keep up to the United States in this kind of achievement will not have such an investment at stake. Nowhere near as successful as the Americans in the channeling of their energies into industrialism, these peoples have tended to stress other national traits. It was a question of cultural survival. When one has so obviously been surpassed by one's neighbour in one kind of activity, one must rely, in order to maintain any sense of personal worth or identity, on other abilities. ("Diplomatic skills," for instance, or the quality of one's art, or more generally, the quality of one's life.) It will be easier for nations which have never prided themselves primarily on rugged individualism, industrial aggression, and expansion, to abandon these styles in favor of more passive, cooperative behavior patterns than it will be for Americans. This is one reason for expecting post-industrial society to emerge more swiftly, with less damage inflicted in the process, in advanced industrial nations other than America. Another reason is the one already submitted: Where the holistic consciousness does not find itself forced to fight old social revolutions at the same time that it is fighting its own post-technological revolution, it will be able to impregnate the dominant culture without having, in effect, to forcibly rape it. It will be less hysterically resisted.

Finally there is this point. As Slater notes:

> The most glaring split in the new culture is that which separates militant activism from the traits we generally associate with the hippie movement. The first strand stresses political confrontation, revolutionary action, radical commitment to the process of changing the basic structure of modern indus-

trial society. The second involves a renunciation of that society in favor of the cultivation of inner experience and pleasing internal feeling-states. Heightening of sensory receptivity, commitment to the immediate present, and tranquil acceptance of the physical environment are sought in contradistinction to old-culture ways, in which the larger part of one's immediate experience is overlooked or grayed out by the preoccupation with utility, future goals and external mastery. Since, in the old culture, experience is classified before it is felt, conceptualization tends here to be forsworn altogether. There is also much emphasis on esthetic expression and an overarching belief in the power of love.

This division is a crude one, and there are, of course, many areas of overlap. Both value systems share an antipathy to the old culture, both share beliefs in sexual freedom and personal autonomy. Some groups, the Yippies in particular, have tried with some success to bridge the gap in a variety of interesting ways. But there is nonetheless an inherent contradiction between them. *Militant activism is task-oriented, and hence partakes of certain old-culture traits such as postponement of gratification, pre-occupation with power, and so on. To be a competent revolutionary one must possess a certain tolerance for the Protestant Ethnic virtues, and the activists' moral code is a stern one indeed. The hippie ethic, on the other hand, is a "salvation now" approach. It is thus more radical, since it remains relatively uncontaminated with old-culture values. It is also far less realistic, since it ignores the fact that the existing culture provides a totally antagonistic milieu in which the hippie movement must try to survive in a state of highly vulnerable parasitic dependence.* [My italics.] The activists can reasonably say that the flower people are absurd to pretend that the revolution has already occurred, for such pretense leads only to severe victimization by the old culture. The flower people can reasonably retort that a revolution based to so great a degree on old-culture premises is lost before it is begun, for even if the militants are victorious they will have been corrupted by the process of winning.[63]

What these insights bring out is a glaring split which has developed in most "social" literature. On the one hand, we have environmentalists pointing out that the whole base of life is being destroyed. The need for radical and immediate changes in economic, political, social, cultural, and individual priorities is underlined repeatedly. Clearly, we cannot continue on the course we are on now without wiping ourselves out within roughly the time it is expected to take for post-industrialized society to emerge. What this means, simply, is that the changes which are already taking place will be forced to take place at an accelerated rate, thus increasing drastically the tension and conflicts "normally" experienced in periods of cultural transformation. On the other hand, we have observers who – however accurately they may pin-point the areas of conflict, and the nature of the conflict – nevertheless continue to measure the contemporary situation against those of the past. The assumption in this kind of analysis is that the stage of human conflict, the world, is not itself tipping over on its side.

The "totally antagonistic milieu" in which the counter culture finds itself is assumed to be inflexible. Yet, even in the United States, it is apparent that a fundamental reexamination of values is being forced by the evidence of environmental deterioration. It is more bitter and divisive there almost anywhere else. Yet even there, certain commonly agreed upon goals are emerging. (Despite the fierce opposition to anything that smacks of "communism" or state intervention or whatever.) Elsewhere, however, the milieu is not necessarily so "totally antagonistic." As the dimensions of the environmental crisis unfold, as the nature of the solutions becomes more apparent, the ability to differentiate between the values of the counter culture and the values of the dominant culture (as they are bent, step by step, to meet the requirements of ecological soundness) will be greatly impaired. The "differences" between the new and the old cultures will dissolve bit by bit until, finally, at the post-industrial stage, they will merge, or at least the new will displace the old.

This is not to suggest that violent conflict between the two modes of consciousness can be avoided in the other advanced industrial nations. There, too, the struggle has already begun, even though, in its present form, it got started later, and even though it is not necessarily hitched to so many old unresolved struggles. But the stage is not fixed, as it has been through history. To expect the present conflict to follow the pattern established in roughly similar situations in the past is to ignore the overwhelming fact that it is not just a new culture which is pressing against the old, it is, in a real sense, the earth itself. The very foundations upon which the old industrial culture was built are caving in – and the old culture is not entirely blind to the fact. As the collapse becomes more pronounced the old culture can be expected to make some desperate efforts to save itself. No matter how proud a man may be of his expensive clothing, he will rip it off once he finds himself drowning and unable to swim because the material is clinging to his limbs. In large measure, the survival tactics which the advanced industrial nations will be forced to adopt are those very cultural, perceptual, and cognitive strategies which have already been arrived at by the counter culture in the process of its own, so far largely separate, growth. The new culture has Earth on its side.

Political analyst Samuel Lubell has pointed out that the "hidden crisis" in American politics stems from the apparent fact that the point of irreversible polarization between the old and new cultures has been passed. On the basis of an examination of electoral trends in some ten thousand precincts across the U.S., he concludes that most whites in the South are "still not reconciled to much more than token desegregation" and that throughout the nation "sizable majorities" want to repeal open housing and end school busing. He expects to see racial conflict continue unabated. It is but one of the meta-problems which have emerged to divide Americans among themselves. Looking at the meta-problems, he concludes: "It is our inability to reconcile these conflicts that divide us that I see as the hidden crisis in American politics today."

What other advanced industrial nations have passed the point of irreversible polarization? Canada, for one, would seem not to have – not yet. The process of fusing the old and the new cultures through adoption of environmental strategies – and concentration of the energies of both cultures in this common arena – would seem still to have a chance in this country.

In the period of our history during which industrialism was the key to the quality of life, America became supreme. She adapted as quickly as any other nation to the changes wrought by the Industrial Revolution, and she adapted more enthusiastically and successfully. Her present position among nations flows from the flexibility displayed at that time, the willingness and capability of the nation as a whole to adopt the new strategies offered by industrialism. Now, however, as we move rapidly into the post-industrial period, America as a whole is showing no such flexibility, willingness, or capability. In the industrial period, now coming to an end, the American standard of living was judged to be highest. In the post-industrial period, new standards will have emerged, based on the quality of one's experience of life, not on any merely quantitative criterion. Already, the standard of living in America has plunged. Only in terms of per capita income would America still seem to be ahead of other regions. In real terms, allowing environmental factors, including security and sensory deprivation (especially in the urban areas) no one can fail to see that America's standard of living has sunk well below that of less crowded, less technologized, less polluted, less socially turbulent nations. Those nations which show themselves to be capable of adapting to post-industrialism as successfully as America adapted to industrialism will be the ones which will be rated highest according to the emerging standards.

The structural presence of the post-industrialized society within the existing framework of advanced industrial nations tells us, among other things, that "the revolution" against old capitalistic (and otherwise) exploitive social forms is proceeding rapidly without the assistance of peoples' armies of liberation, without any barricades being mounted, and without a single shot so far being fired. The post-industrial society, with its emphasis on the very values subscribed to by most modern revolutionaries, represents the fulfillment of the revolutionary impulse without the prerequisite bloodbath all along assumed to be essential. The more radical style of those who have chosen to carry the revolution on within themselves thus emerges, in view of this development, as not only being more contradistinct from the old culture, and less contaminated by it, but in the long view *more realistic* than the style of those who have chosen the route of a power struggle. It is a kind of realism, however, which is not, at this stage, applicable in America – where the meta-problems which have emerged are the more-or-less direct result of the application of the old industrial patterns. The meta-problems are too immediate. They affect too directly the lives of too many individuals. The pressure has mounted in such a short period that there has not been time for the differences between the old culture and the new to be dissolved through the adaptation of the old culture to new environmental realities. Moreover, at its environmental stage the postwar consciousness cannot afford to lose its momentum. Nor is it likely to do so. It will hurl itself with increased vigor against the old industrial society – forced to by its perception of the rate of environmental deterioration. Simultaneously, the old order will be trying to right itself in relation to the same problem, but because it has come to identify the attitudes and values which it needs to embrace in order to assure its own survival with the same groups which are opposing racism and militarism, the old culture is bound to be slowed in its own rate of adaptation; many will realize that they cannot have clean air without having a black man for a neighbor and without at least tacitly agreeing to let the Communists run where they will. As Philip Slater has noted, in this situation there is no such thing as compromise. The dynamic whole of the cultural system which springs from the postwar consciousness rests, definitely, on processes that are accelerative. The New Left in America has tended to recognize this. So has the Right. Only the liberals have continued to hope that it could be otherwise. And what is now the case in America could not help but be the case soon in other advanced industrial nations – if it were not for the fact that the rate of environmental deterioration is forcing adaptive social and economic measures, giving birth, even faster than would otherwise be the case, to the post-industrial society. The slower development of the postwar consciousness in the other advanced industrial nations, coupled with the faster adoption of the cultural norms of post-industrialism may allow these other nations to cross the line without having to make a fight to the death about it.

Anti-Americanism had undergone a profound change in the last few years. Not long ago it was embarassingly obvious that it was based for the most part on the raw, bucolic envy that people in hand-me-downs feel for obscenely rich relatives. Today, it is based to a far greater degree on fear.

The critical difference is that envy will not scare us off. Whether we admit it or not, we go on imitating. Although secretly outraged by Rich Cousin's wealth, we are not likely to refuse a ride in his Corvette. Fear, on the other hand, gets right into the webbing of our nervous system. Once we start to feel that Rich Cousin is driving as though bent on suicide, we want out at the next red light – assuming he is still sane enough to stop for it. This is but one of the reasons why the U.S. today finds so many of her allies deserting her. We are watching the speedometer twitching way over the speed limit. We feel the impact of the American Dream hitting too hard on the bumps.

Just a few years ago we were smugly contemptuous about American materialism. Our tone was one of moral and cultural superiority. It came out in conversations: talk about Yankee status seekers, the Land of the Boob Tube, Hollywood the Vulgar. Today the conversations are different. Listen carefully – to yourself as well – at parties. Who here talks about American materialism now? The talk touches a deeper, more sensitive chord. Often it seems as though we are a bunch of Lilliputian psychologists perched nervously atop a mad Gulliver who is thrashing in his straitjacket, his mouth full of foam, his lips in tatters. He howls with rage and pain. Any moment he may turn over and crush us.

This change in the essential nature of anti-American sentiment reflects a dawning awareness: that America might not make it through the impasse.

# SEVENTEEN THE LOSS OF IMMORTALITY

It all depends, finally, on the vigor and awareness of America's artists.

For in the modern, post-colonial context of technological society, it is the artist who is the true guerilla fighter. It is the artist who is trained in the use of the most potent weapons around. If no revolution ever succeeded in producing a truly just people, if no democracy has succeeded, and no dictatorship has succeeded, it is because people were only made to memorize new sets of social rules and drilled to obey those rules, *without having their consciousness itself altered.* Yet, as phenomenologists since Edmund Husserl have repeatedly shown, whatever human beings know, become aware of, think or feel, happens in their consciousness. Consciousness is the absolute ground of all reality for human beings, whether we are aware of it or not. Thought may develop elaborate structures, even moral codes, ethics, philosophical and political positions, without any reference to its roots in consciousness – but consciousness remains the prior reality in which all of these transactions take place. If this itself is not changed – if it remains, for instance, basically operationalistic – the same patterns of behavior will dominate whether one is an avowed Communist or an American hard hat. In any collective sense, unchanged consciousness means unchanged behavior. The logic of domination retains its position, regardless of the look of the flag it hoists. Without reference to its roots in consciousness, even the most carefully-designed edifice of social conceptions is lacking in a fundamental means of self-correction.[64]

Consciousness, finally, is the interlocked picture of the world, the pre-existing filter or structure through which all perceptions must pass. If this is not changed in some way, then human beings may be moved like pawns by organized forces outside themselves, they may be pushed in different directions, but they remain powerless to really *move themselves* since they are locked into a fixed way of viewing the world. Their background, their culture, their training, their education – all continue to exert tremendous control over individual behavior. The ghosts of our parents live on in our minds, holding us at least partially within the cultural and perceptual context which was *their* experience. *Their* conditioned reflexes become *our* conditioned reflexes. As a result, whether an October Revolution comes to pass or not, the Russian people remain Russians. Their distinctive group characteristics continue to dominate their behavior. A switch at the top, from a Czarist regime to a Communist regime, may effect changes, no doubt about it. But, within a handful of years, the new political skin has adapted itself to fit the shape of the old cultural body.

We see a perfect parallel in the technique of "rolfing." Rolfing, or "structural integration," involves radical manipulation of connective tissue, muscles, tendons, and ligaments. The entire body is forcibly untangled from its collected knots. (The equivalent of a successful political revolution.) Deep emotional discharge and change accompany the process. In the end, the individual is liberated from a physical posture which has been holding his emotions and thoughts in cramped, locked-up postures themselves.[65] Yet follow-up studies have shown that unless some sort of psychotherapeutic experience is had in conjunction with rolfing, the individual soon reverts to his old physical posture. The posture is largely dictated by conditioned reflexes, habit, attitude, and psychological orientations. If the individual's consciousness or reticular system is not changed in some way, the fact that his mind remains fixed will eventually re-impress itself on his muscular system and he will change back – physically – into his "old self," simply because the change has not been complete. If his consciousness has not been changed, any changes in his body are doomed to failure.

A political revolution may be compared to the experience of rolfing. It is "social rolfing." And if no change in consciousness takes place in a collective sense, it too is doomed to failure. This failure has claimed every revolution to date in human history. Even the largest, in Russia and China, have not succeeded in creating a truly "new .man," one who has transcended culturally fixed and limited points of view. In the end, nationalism – the self-assertive tendency – reasserts itself over internationalism, the integrative tendency.

Groups like the Black Panthers dismiss a "cultural revolution" as being nothing at all, because they themselves are aiming at an overthrow of a regime which relates to them as a colonial power. Yet a cultural revolution, a revolution in consciousness, goes far deeper and is far more profound and far-reaching than any anti-colonial revolution could ever be, except in terms of the immediate life situation of the oppressed at the moment they liberate themselves.

With the emergence of a new consciousness, we see the really critical revolution has begun to take place. It was not led or organized. Cadres have not been rushing into the schools propagandizing to the students. Certainly books and underground newspapers have been circulating, but – and this is a point completely missed by the authorities – these have not tended to *lead*, but to *follow* the course of the change in consciousness. Underground newspapers are a reflection in the community of the change in consciousness. They have themselves done virtually nothing to flush it into existence. In this respect, they are no more powerful or inspired than the Establishment Press which does the same thing on a larger scale, reflecting the values and limitations of the community at large. As a weapon in the struggle to transform human consciousness, the Underground Press is a fifteen-cent pocket knife. The real underground newspapers at this moment are LPs, just as the closest things to political leaders of the new consciousness are musicians. Jerry Rubin's "authority" in comparison to Bob Dylan's is marginal, limited strictly to militant political elements of the new consciousness which have not yet found any way, in terms of strategies and tactics, to transcend the political stage of development. It is no coincidence that Yippie! ended up on trial with a Panther, while a rock star banged Abbie Hoffman over the head with a guitar at Woodstock. In America, the new consciousness cannot help but find itself having to assist an old unresolved anti-colonial struggle, but at the same time its growth is in a direction that transcends the political arena. It is vaulting over the walls and impressing itself directly on the population, one person at a time.

New, post-political strategies are being adopted. These are strategies based, directly or indirectly, on the phenomenological insight that consciousness is the absolute fortress which must finally be assaulted. All other changes are re-arrangements of the furniture and the seating order. More people may be made comfortable, but if, afterwards, a conservative black middle class joins the conservative white middle class in suburbia, what has been accomplished? If the Indian peasant gets to buy a car, a toaster, a refrigerator and a color TV, are we any further from Armageddon – nuclear, environmental, or otherwise? These kinds of "changes," in fact, only worsen the overall situation if no fundamental change in priorities takes place, if the quality of life is not placed well ahead of the "quantity" of life-stuffs. And if the self-assertive tendency of groups to place their own welfare ahead of the collective welfare of all groups is not reversed, the fingers remain poised on the atomic button. All that happens is that more fingers move into position. The odds against survival get worse.

Before proceeding to look at the new strategies, we must consider the essential nature of the pressures which are flushing the new consciousness into existence. These are *biological* pressures. They cannot be turned off. The points made earlier in the section dealing with self-structuring hierarchical growth dealt only with facets, not the main engine of change itself.

Having described the change in those terms, we have not necessarily said much about it. Self-structuring hierarchical growth might be an accurate description of the process, the mechanism of change itself, but the theory really says very little about the forces at work triggering the restructuring which is taking place. In order to approach the magnitude of the change, we must understand that the new consciousness is being flushed into existence under extreme pressure.

A change in this order of magnitude would require a tremendous amount of pressure behind it, for what is happening is a shift in the course of evolution. Evolution acquires its own forms of "inertia." It has, after all, been proceeding for a long time, moving as a rule more slowly than mountains. The last great evolutionary change wrought in man was accomplished in birth contractions which could be measured in ten thousand year units. This one is being effected, in its broadcast outlines, in a mere matter of centuries – and at the moment of sudden, hierarchical convulsion, the new version of man is being *spat out* (like a balloon bursting). The pressure needed to make evolution change gears so abruptly would have to be greater than all the "inertia" acquired in the last few million years. It would have to be a fundamental, pervasive pressure applying everywhere. Can such a pressure have come into existence without our even noticing it?

It has. That pressure is a collectivized fear of death.

We all know we are poised on the brink. If an individual *were to be able to see* that within minutes he would be dead if he didn't do something drastic, and yet did nothing at all, we could only assume he had become frozen with fear or, as suggested earlier, insane. Right now, the human race shows signs of being both insane and frozen with fear. But with a healthy human being, even most "mad" ones, the fear, after intially paralyzing the body, gives in to the greater instinct of self-preservation and the body begins to *move. Fast.* The human race appears sick, certainly, but it has displayed too many signs of excellent health – in its art, its various cultures, its religions, its love – to be yet judged incurably ill. And if it *is*, in fact, this sick – it will indeed remain frozen by its fear, its madness, and it will perish.

What is true for an individual member of the species, in terms of basic survival reflexes, will be true for the species at large; we may generalize that much, because we are speaking in purely biological terms. The reflexes of a monkey, electronically tested, reveal "monkey-type" traits. The basic *instinctual* reflexes of a man will no less be "man-like." We may say that monkeys as a species are roughly "like" any given monkey, and therefore we may reason that humankind is at least roughly "like" a given man, even an average man, who *will* – if he is able to see it coming – jump out of the path of death. (*Humanity* is no doubt "manlike.")

The race, as a whole, for the first time, is threatened with extinction. That has never happened so far. Or, even if it did happen on a smaller scale at some now forgotten point in time (say, during the Middle Pleistocene, when the last great evolutionary burst came), it has never happened at a time when a global communication network existed, thus allowing everyone similtaneous-ly to see what was happening. Since Hiroshima, the race has been looking its own death in the face. The postwar generation is the first to be raised with the knowledge of its own impending doom.

In this generation, the reflex *to jump out of the way* has begun to take control, wresting the body out of the grip of paralysis. The new consciousness is the embodiment of that reflex, the "expres-sion in the muscular system" of the collective reaction. It is a collectivized reflex, identical to the collectivized reflex which sends legions of young lemmings into the sea when their senses suddenly hold up the picture of their own extermination, due to overpop-ulation of their territory. The young lemmings, less conditioned into fixed behavior patterns, abruptly respond – collectively – and search for a new survival strategy. Their range is so limited, their adaptive powers are so harshly constrained, that the only strategy they can adopt is a sudden throwing of themselves into a void. They are using all their resources. Their brains are already being used fully. So the only unexplored void into which they can plunge is a river in which they drown. Human beings, however, are equipped with a brain which, neurologically, has hardly been used. Only two or three per cent of its potential has yet been activated. A collective leap into the void in search of new survival strategies on the part of our young need not so certainly end in disaster. We may relatively easily attain a new, higher level of integration, a new, higher level of awareness. The evidence is clear; our potential lies overwhelmingly ahead of us. Lemmings have nowhere to go, in terms of their available equipment. This is the point at which any comparison immediately breaks down.

Deep-rooted biological forces are here at work. These are forces about which we know very little. Only in recent years, thanks to tremendous strides made in zoology and anthropology, have we begun – however dimly – to perceive tremendous regulatory pow-ers at work in the biological world, which includes human beings, no matter how violently our minds might struggle against the tides moving through our deeper biological and psycho-biological beings. The discovery of "biological clocks" within us a few years ago marked a large step forward in terms of understanding this essential dimension of our nature.

A collectivized awareness of impending death triggers a "mass" movement among the young in a lemming colony. To deny that such a force is now at work in the human "colony" of the industrialized nations is to refuse to look around at the evidence.

Constant post-McLuhan references to "global communications systems" should not be allowed to confuse us on this point. The "global communications system" daily reaches into the lives and minds of only a relative handful of the human beings on this planet: the inhabitants of technological society, the millions who live in the industrially-advanced nations. Billions of others live outside that network. For them, the "news" about impending doom barely penetrates the outer boundaries of their day-to-day experience. There are few television sets in the living-rooms of the Indian countryside, the Chinese hills or basins, the Upper Amazon. Fighting against crop failures and disease, deeply entangled in a closely fought struggle with the land, these peoples have neither the time nor the means at their disposal right now to confront a threat looming *out there*. The inhabitants of technological society, engaged in no such way in desperate day-to-day survival, get up in the morning with the crack of doom and go to bed with it. It pervades our lives. It soaks into our subconscious. It appears in our dreams.

Robert Jay Lifton has pointed out that our sense of the continuity of life is profoundly threatened. There is a strong undercurrent of imagery of death and technological annihilation in our thoughts, our art, our work, and it becomes increasingly difficult for us to give significant form to our ideas, our actions, and to ourselves. Lifton has shown that the awareness of impending doom pervades our dream-life, it saturates our subconscious minds.

He points out that our collective sense of immortality has been lost. Throughout history, individuals have clung to that sense. Freud noted that "in the unconscious every one of us is convinced of his own immortality." The reason is simple: unlike any other creature on earth, man is equipped with a neocortex which enables him to know that he will die. We have never really adjusted ourselves to this absolute bad news. In our art, in our religions, our cultures, our moral codes, our institutions, our architecture and design, we have found ways to let ourselves live on beyond the moment of our own individual extinction. "One can ... see the historical process as a continuing collective effort to maintain, under constantly changing conditions, symbols for transcending death. ... But the young have grown up with an inner knowledge that their world has always been capable of exterminating itself."[66] Otto Rank stressed man's perpetual quest for an assurance of eternal survival. He suggested the man creates culture in order to maintain his spiritual self. The "unsolicited gift" of the last great evolutionary leap, as Arthur Koestler has remarked, was the new brain which "discovered death." From there on, the human race proceeded to try to avoid facing that new piece of information. There were "psychological outs." By choosing to believe in a life after death, one successfully avoids coming to terms with death. By believing in social or political or cultural or racial systems which would outlast one's own ego, a *part* of one's identity could be understood to carry on. All these were strategies of avoidance, of secondary ego survival.

Today, even the "psychological outs" are gone – at least for the young in the industrialized nations who have grown up with the knowledge that their whole world is on the verge of extinction. The full knowledge of likely extermination presses daily against their senses. The pressure exerted by the awareness of death in the past was sufficient to forge pyramids and empires, to raise the Taj Mahal and the Thousand Year Reich. Each of these acts was, in its way, an effort to transcend mortality. Today, the effort is both collective and spontaneous. And it is even more thorough-going than the efforts of the past, because not only must the individual find some way to transcend his own mortality, it is the *race* which must act. Under these conditions, the idea that a collective response (a search for new strategies) might come into being is neither far-fetched nor illogical.

With this kind of pressure at work in our society, the only "surprise" would be if the young were *not* changing radically. If this were the case, we could only conclude that the human race had somehow lost, or successfully eliminated, its adaptive capabilities. In view of the neurological evidence that we have just barely scratched the surface of our mental potential, this would make no sense.

More – much more – could be said on this subject. There is evidence that the pathological streak running through human history is directly attributable to a basic flaw in the construction of our brain, that the neocortex was superimposed on top of the older mammalian and reptilian brains but has not yet had a chance to wrest complete control from these older regions of the brain, that we are – in our "normal" human state – *biological freaks.* The reader who would go further into this subject is advised to read the latest works of Arthur Koestler, particularly *The Ghost in The Machine.* As Koestler suggests: "To become hypnotized by the specific pathology of the twentieth century narrows one's vision and blinds one to the much older, much more fundamental problem of the chronic savagery of human civilizations, ancient and modern."[67]

But a deeper examination of the inherent "schizophysiology" of human nature, which finds its highest expression in the adoption of a purely operationalistic mode of consciousness (completing the split between mind and body), cannot be our purpose here. Rather, let us reach for whatever conclusions we may about the avenues remaining open to the new consciousness in its search for new survival strategies, new ways to carry a revolution in a technological environment wherein all the old strategies have been exhausted.

# EIGHTEEN MINDBOMBS –THE IVORY CONTROL TOWER

The strategy which is emerging comes *on top* of all the pressures referred to so far. While, to date, the new consciousness has been coming spontaneously into existence as a form of self-structuring hierarchical growth in response to the new ground rules of our life experience (urbanization, automation, etc.); and while it is being further stimulated by rock music; by drugs; by a ever-heightening awareness of ecological interactions; by the need to compensate for the psychic disequilibriums induced by mass media; and finally, by the awareness of impending racial death itself; *the new consciousness is now involved in a deliberate attack not only upon the political and institutional bastions of the old order of awareness, but upon that the awareness that shapes that order itself.* The new consciousness is starting to engineer a change in the very minds of the "enemy." It is, probably, the greatest engineering project ever undertaken.

This is the revolution which takes place beyond the barricades, when the barricades have become obsolete.

Often enough we have been told that sooner or later man would have to begin to assume control of the evolutionary process. Biologists and geneticists having been saying for years that the power to do this will soon be within our reach. It has been assumed that the task would fall to scientists, that the burden of responsibility would be entirely theirs, and that the job would have to be carried out in the laboratory. At this point, Aldous Huxley's nightmare of a Brave New World begins. For if the old consciousness were, in fact, to be in control of the engineered change, it would inevitably implant its own perceptions and imperatives into the new creature. The man-made man of the future might be an improvement on the Neil Armstrong model, but it would certainly not be different. It would, clearly, be capable of serving the old order. Nothing truly new would emerge.

The engineering task now being undertaken by the new consciousness proceeds along lines quite different from those anticipated by the technicians. It starts from an awareness that technological society is fundamentally different from all earlier types of society. In the past, there were no mass media. No transistor radios. No movie houses. Few art galleries. Few theatres. In the past, the true revolutionary who wanted to make man more humane, more sensitive, who wanted to free him from bondage, had only a few weapons in his arsenal. Pitchforks, swords, muskets, sub-machine guns, Molotov cocktails, grenades. The only medium through which a revolution could communicate itself was armed struggle. The only way the revolutionaries could proceed to liberate men was to attack the forces which kept them unfree, for men had to be released first from the grip of the powers that dominated their existence. The same holds true today. The difference is that a mass communications system exists. What this mass communications system provides is a "delivery system" for whatever "mindbombs" the new consciousness chooses to manufacture.

The objective is to change the consciousness of the "enemy," meaning those still in the grip of the old suicidal modes of consciousness. In the past, a person who choose to remain loyal to the king or czar had to be dealt with in exactly the same way as his ruler. The revolutionary had no means at his disposal except *reasoned argument* to affect a conversion in the loyalist. If that failed, the revolutionary had to turn to his sword or his gun. He had to kill his enemy.

Today, he may do something else: he may "bomb" the enemy's *mind*. What the new consciousness amounts to, finally, is simply a more "open," less inhibited, less rigidly structured and therefore more existential and phenomenological means of perception and cognition. A person whose consciousness has thus been liberated "sees too much" for him to be able to keep on believing in the old, operationalistic order with its emphasis on domination and control. The liberated consciousness does not willingly put a dog collar back around the neck of its awareness. And whether the means of control used by the dominant order are openly totalitarian (as in the Soviet Union) or more reliant on repressive desublimation, the end is always inhibition of individual growth. These kinds of social order are based on the assumed need to force people to agree to put "brakes" on their own development, to freeze their growth at a level agreed upon by other people (namely, those who stand to gain the greatest advantage by maintaining the given status quo). A leader-follower relationship must be worked out, and such a relationship can only continue to exist as long as some people – the vast majority – agree to follow. They must surrender the right to be their own masters, and even to explore or attempt to develop their own potential. Virtually all social systems imply an end to evolution. None has yet been devised which is open-ended.

The strategy of the new consciousness must be to break down the perceptual inhibitions which keep the old consciousness blind, deaf, and dumb to its own potential for growth, for evolution. In order to do this, the new consciousness must begin to steer the evolutionary process, to begin reshaping the old consciousness, prying it loose from its cement foundations, so that it may flow more freely. Awareness is curative. Once freed from its cage, the old consciousness becomes "new." A conversion takes place.

When geneticists talk about reaching for the evolutionary control panel, they fail to acknowledge the phenomenological insight that consciousness is the absolute ground of all reality for human beings. A man need not be rebuilt from his DNA to his optical nerves in order for this absolute ground to be restructured. His consciousness may be worked upon more directly. As we have seen, even operating mindlessly and at random, mass media have helped to reshape human consciousness. That initial period of "accidental" effects is passing. We see that the media are now being deliberately brought to bear in an effort to stimulate further changes in consciousness. This is the "third effect." For, behind the cameras now are not the old consciousness technicians, but the new ones.

If the pen was a hundred or a thousand times mightier than the sword, we can only estimate that television is at least a million times more powerful. Not only can it be used across immense distances (in fact, distance makes no difference now), but it can be targeted with complete accuracy to strike at a point precisely two inches behind the victim's eyes. No bullet flies so fast, so far, with such unerring accuracy. Not even a hydrogen bomb can affect so many people at once.

Consider the first landing on the moon. Far more historic than the landing itself was the fact that for several moments, perhaps as many as one-quarter of all the human beings alive were simultaneously involved in the same perceptual experience. In those moments, Teilhard's "Noosphere" existed. A mindbomb of sorts had gone off in hundreds of millions of individual human brains simultaneously. In some slight way our collective consciousness was altered. It may take years or even decades for the effects of that single experience to be measured, but once the instruments are precise enough, measured it will be.

The point about television is that it launches an unending stream of mindbombs into our homes, day and night, and while none of these can in itself change anybody, the cumulative effect is, definitely, a change in consciousness. Apart from what McLuhan has been saying, this was acknowledged by Dr. Norman Zinberg of the Harvard Medical School, who noted that prolonged exposure to TV changes our concepts of psychological boundaries. In effect, it diffuses the boundaries between the inside of the mind and the outside, thus bringing a quality of "one-ness" into the world. This, precisely enough, describes the holistic consciousness.

In television, even commercials amount to mindbombs. Anybody who supposes that the change in consciousness can be effectively blocked through continued suppression of psychedelic drugs has failed utterly to realize that "visual hallucinogens" and "audial hallucinogens" are just as potent and just as real in terms of their effects as purely chemical hallucinogens. The only difference is that while the chemicals may take effect in minutes or hours, the visuals and audials may take months or even years to take effect. In terms of their effects on society as a whole, this makes little difference. The six-year-old child of today might be "protected" from psychedelic drugs, completely insulated from any contact with them whatsoever, and yet by the time he is seventeen he will likely be in possession of the holistic consciousness. For, during that period, he will have been exposed to some 23,000 hours of television. The psychological boundaries (established by his cultural frame of reference) will have been dissolved as though by acid. More specifically, within the context of this general experience, the child is increasingly exposed to programs which are deliberately designed to have a psychedelic effect. Children's cartoons are almost all visual hallucinogens. Commercials have been converted similarly. Their "message" is shoved further and further into the background, buried in a torrent of eye-catching (and small, but definitely mind-altering) visual hallucinogens.

Rock music is an audial hallucinogen. The effects of rock described in this book were all primary effects, hammerblows applied against the kind of physical rigidity which was the expression of the old consciousness. We may now compare it, as we compared political revolution, to the technique of "rolfing." It was a process of forcibly untangling the body from its knots. In the wake of that initial therapeutic experience, we see that rock music has already evolved into something else. Acid rock, in particular, takes the listener out on a trip. Music such as that produced by the Moog Synthesizer goes even further. It is "music beyond music, music that is not about man." Stereophonic music is now being designed with the explicit goal of altering consciousness. In the weapons arsenal of the new consciousness, stereo headphones rank about as high as the ICBM does in the old consciousness arsenal.

For instance, a stereo recording called Environments Disc I appeared in early 1970. An analog computer was used to interface one hundred different recordings of the sound of waves coming up on a beach. The result was called The Psychologically Ultimate Seashore. The second side of the LP featured something called The Ultimate Aviary – bird sounds, similarly interfaced by computer to produce a consciousness-altering experience. Only a few months before, a recording Songs of The Humpback Whale, became available. Listened to on stereo headphones, this too had a hallucinogenic effect. Electronic symphonies (such as Terry Riley's *A Rainbow in Curved Air*) or the productions of the Moog Synthesizer are all aimed at producing the same "charge." Groups like the Moody Blues, Santana, Led Zeppelin, and stars like the late Jimi Hendrix, likewise worked directly upon the structure of consciousness. At the same time, movies like *Easy Rider* and *Woodstock* are fired like heavy-gauge cannons right into the solar plexus of mass society.

Coming up in the wake of these large and small mindbombs are such devices as David Rosenboom's brainwave modifying techniques, wherein, using Arp synthesizers and electroencephalographs, one may "project" one's brain waves into recognizable sound patterns, thus learning to differentiate between different patterns. Alpha waves are associated with sensitive, intensely creative mental states; delta waves are lower frequency, usually associated with deep sleep; theta waves operate at higher frequencies, producing stillness and "wakeful dreaminess"; beta waves are the furthest-out, having to do with abstract thinking, intuition, and in some cases getting into those mysterious psychic regions out of which both genius and insanity flow. In time, these techniques will be refined into a means of "instant turn-on." One will be able to alter one's state of consciousness at will. We are probably less than a decade, possibly only a few years, away from electronically-engineered states of *satori*. Already, as these references to music, stereo "sound environments," and visual hallucinogens show, the day of the technological turn-on has arrived. And at the same time, against this backdrop, more and more group techniques are coming into being, ranging from Abraham Maslow's methods to those of gestaltist Fritz Perls, to induce "peak experiences."

The "peak experience," whether induced by group psychotherapeutic techniques, LSD, stereo, or by use of a brain-wave modifier, amounts to a major mindbomb. The person hit by it will likely never be quite the same. He will, to greater or lesser degrees, have acquired the new consciousness. He will acquire it, too, if he is much exposed to modern art or theater. For, since pop art, the artists have been moving out, engaging the population. Art, whether making use of computers or plastics, now attempts to envelop the "viewer." He is no longer a viewer – he is an *experiencer*. The art swallows him, envelops him. He must step into it. Architects as well as sculptors are devising ways and means of snaring the unsuspecting passer-by, of taking him through consciousness-altering experiences. Interior decorators, clothes designers, even some town planners, have got into the act. People are no longer being allowed to keep their distance from art and structures. They are being forced, holus bolus, to wear the art, to step into it, to be gobbled up by it. They are chewed up in the process, virtually brainwashed. The effort is concentrated always on the experiencer's consciousness. It deliberately seeks to break down his reticular system, to open his head up and his eyes and his ears.

Marshall McLuhan has been our greatest prophet. "If literate Western man were really interested in preserving the most creative aspects of his civilization," McLuhan said, "he would not cower in his ivory tower bemoaning change but would plunge himself into the vortex of electric technology and, by understanding it, dictate his new environment – turn ivory tower into control tower."[68] This, exactly, is what is happening. The artists are moving out, taking up positions behind TV cameras, delivering mindbombs into the livingrooms of technological society. They have been behind almost all the new stereo sound environments which are coming into being. They are putting together the most explosive mindbombing movies. They have taken over the control panels of the rock radio stations. They are the engineers of the most visually-hallucinogenic TV shows and commercials. Others are involved, through advertising, in turning the pages of glossy magazines into visual trips. Certainly, they have been the designers and photographers and collage-makers who have been putting together the covers for the LPs of the new consciousness music groups and singers. One has only to look at a record rack in the nearest available store to have one's mind bombed at least slightly. And the thing which gets overlooked to a large extent is that most of this art, this music, these sound environments and art experiences, are designed to work even better if the experiencer is under the influence of psychedelic drugs. These drugs have already become the medium after the medium of television, and television as well as movies and recordings, is in the process of redefining itself in relation to drugs just as radio, at an earlier stage, had to redefine itself in relation to television.

This is a revolutionary strategy which was not possible in any previous historical context. No society before modern technological society provided such perfect "delivery systems" as television sets, movie houses, record stores, art galleries, and psychotherapeutic centers and retreats. The new consciousness has begun to move into the control tower, firing salvo after salvo smack into the heads of the population. And there is nothing that can be done to check this assault. Voluntarily, individuals plant themselves right in front of the "cannon" of their TV set. Voluntarily they go into a movie house. Voluntarily, they try on new clothes. Voluntarily, they submit to group encounters or step into an art gallery or walk past a building designed to mindbomb them. Voluntarily they turn on the radio, often unaware that it is the radio which is turning *them* on.

Moreover, with every move, the old order increases the pressures which were causing the change to take place spontaneously. Every report of an oil spill, every smog alert, every bomb raid, every leak of poison gas, every escalation of the war, brings the possibility of our collective extinction closer to home. Each time, the pressure mounts. There is nothing the old order can do to prevent the emergence of the new consciousness – except to abandon its own technology. To ban its own commercials. To refuse its own corporations permission to manufacture money-making programs, or money-making movies. "Censorship" is trivial. For even if the old order sets up watchdogs to make sure, for instance, that no "advertisements" for drugs are allowed in popular music, the watchdogs themselves will be incapable of even *recognizing* the advertisements. Devised largely under the influence of drugs, these songs are mainly aimed at people who will be listening to them while under drugs. Only the censors will listen to them "unstoned." Without the "stoned" perspective, they will not be able to see the message, the inferences, the suggestions, and the advice.

All the music would have to be banned. All the movies would have to be cut. All the clothes and architecture and TV shows and commercials and radio programs would have to be clamped under the most totalitarian controls imaginable. Certainly the state has the power to do that but, once it does, the situation automatically reverts from "post-colonial" to "colonial." The millions of new consciousness people suddenly are catapulted into the past where the cause of oppressed minorities becomes *their* cause. Suddenly they have a "master race" of old consciousness people standing over them. Suddenly, their weapons arsenal is no longer functional. At that stage, the repression is hyped up to such a level that the "old" revolutionary mechanism is activated, and the artists, therapists, group leaders, actors, musicians, architects, designers, producers, cartoonists, hip advertising men, decorators, programmers, cameramen, poets, and writers, who have attained the new consciousness, must leave their incredible new weapons and resort to the *old* weapons. The difference between the new weapons and the old is this: the new weapons do not *kill*, they simply liberate. The old weapons kill. It is on a thread this fine, balanced between the old revolutionary option and the new, that the United States of America today is trembling. To clamp an iron curtain down between the population and the new consciousness revolutionaries who are now hurling mindbombs through the delivery systems of the mass media is to leave no alternative for the new revolutionaries except the grenade. Such an increase in the level of repression would end one of history's greatest experiments: a physically non-violent revolution. It would also block man's first effort to take control of the evolutionary process.

For it is the artists, not the laboratory technicians, who are undertaking this incredible engineering project, a revelation which should surprise no one. Artists, after all, are the true innovative psychologists. As a group, "social engineers," like psychiatrists and sociologists, are mere technicians who have found a way of getting their hands on a tool a bit like the one which artists all along have had at their disposal: intuition. It is this same tool which the new consciousness has adopted. The new consciousness brings "non-artists" to a level of awareness which in the past was limited to the artist. The new consciousness lives its art, embodies it, *is* art.

And now all these super-psychologists are reaching out, deliberately, for the minds of the unliberated majority, reaching with their power vastly extended by the mass media. Formerly, they could only raise the level of mindbombing high enough to have any real effect on a one-to-one basis, as Kesey suggests. But with their hands on the levers of the mass media, they may begin to operate on a million-to-one basis. The "enemy" is picked off, bombed, his mind blown open. The "atomic bomb" of LSD is not the only weapon, as we have seen. Millions of small "mind-bullets" are unleashed every hour, as often as not by the "enemy" himself. (Commercials.) These take longer to do their work, but they do it nevertheless.

It is a basic condition of the psychic regions now being entered that the inner landscape becomes as vivid as the outer. In the future now coming down like an avalanche on our heads, the "night life" recognized by Freud will be experienced in the broad daylight of awareness. It will be as though street lamps had been erected along the avenues and back roads of the mind. Electricity lit up the darkness of cities and caused the planet to glitter in space. Now the long night of the psychic world is being interrupted. Electricity is again the main agent of the transformation. But now chemicals are critical factors as well, working with electricity to make the face of the invisible world glow, to make mapping possible, allow courses to be charted, resources to be made use of, to bring the whole mysterious subconscious region into sharp focus. Electricity makes it possible to see into areas once blacked-out entirely. Chemicals make us mobile. We may begin to travel in the dawn light, explore, become settlers, frontiersmen, even pirates and commanders of small armies. (Ken Kesey comes to mind.) We can go adventuring and come back to tell of our discoveries, our experiences, our bad moments and good, the monsters we saw and the valleys flowing with honey. We are at the beginning of it. The Christopher Columbuses are mostly dead or locked up or fled. The first reconnaisance crews have gone out and come back. Reports and diaries are available. Even maps. The first wave of pioneers have gone up the beach and disappeared into the woods. We may see in the distance the smoke from their encampments. It tells us we are on the right course. But we know we may advance even further. Certainly our children will. And are doing it now.

The psychedelic drugs are just catalysts. They free minds. Most of them are crude vehicles, primitive, like logs strung together with vines to make rafts. The great chemical railways of the future have not yet been built. Neither have the truly supersonic jets. It may be that the transportation devices will be necessary for a long time – possibly forever. After all, having built airplanes, we have not noticeably begun to grow wings or sprout feathers. Our natural inability to fly has not been diminished in the least. So it is possible that chemicals will continue to be depended upon for transportation into the deeps of consciousness. It is "unnatural," certainly, but so is flying a plane or riding in a car. The human mind, on the other hand, is more flexible, more unexplored in terms of its potential, than the human body. No doubt we have "wings" inside us and we only need to learn how to use them. So the drugs, too, may be transcended.

# NINETEEN NOT ONE SAINT, BUT MILLIONS

Two questions remain which have been formulated herein but which have not been answered:

Where may the new consciousness be expected to "take over" first?

And where is the "fourth" stage, the "post-environmental" stage, in its development?

The first answer can only be this: I am a Canadian. From here, inside *my* cultural space, it seems as though much change is being effected. Little of it has found any political expression, which should not be surprising. It is from the positions of power that the view of the new world will seem the most threatening and mad. In view of the unhistorical nature of this revolution (there is no precedent), it will not be taken "seriously" until it is virtually over. What is "serious" is judged in our society by a relative handful, exactly those persons in power: statesmen, judges, moral and cultural authorities of every kind. The power elite or Establishment, whatever they are called.

In relative terms, the authority of the powers-that-be in Canada would seem to be weaker than, for instance, in America. The press is liberal, even slightly leftward. Much rhetoric is invested in the *demonstration* of democratic procedure. This would seem a healthy situation. Change might proceed rapidly under such favorable circumstances. Prior to October, 1970, I would quickly have suggested Canada as the first likely "host" of the new consiousness. The implementation of the War Measures Act changed all that. It was not just the fact that the federal government chose to implement the act which did damage to the structure of the country, it was the *reaction* aroused. Moby Dick sounded quickly. The most regressive elements in the country were allowed to seize the fear (of change) that was in the air, and had been in the air for a while, and make themselves into heroes in the frightened eye of the masses. Thus, the country shifted backwards as a whole, coming closer to fit the malfunctioning, growth-resisting American model. (Which, if it is allowed to continue on its "normal," business-as-usual course, will inevitably trigger either a war or an environmental collapse.) We have seen what the fear-suppression pattern has led to in the U.S.: vastly increased numbers of "niggers," violent counter-attack, counter-counter-attack, a vicious upward spiral toward armed conflict. I can only stress again that the new consciousness has *spontaneously* come into existence, it is a necessary evolutionary change. And the pressures which are creating it are getting stronger all the time (as the stockpiles get bigger and the oil spills get more numerous and the "peace talks" go on and on, accomplishing at the most only miniscule shifts in the arrangements of power which are *themselves* the sources of danger of a nuclear confrontation). The change can only be resisted so long – at the most, up until the moment the Bomb goes off. The longer Canada resists, the more it gets like America, the less chance there is that the new consciousness will emerge as the dominant, more sane pattern of behavior in at least *one* country. That country, large or small, might make some revolutionary changes in its own behavior, thus beginning to set off chain reactions within other countries.

October, 1970, was one small step for Pierre-Elliott Trudeau and one giant (backward) leap for Canadians.

Yet – it might not make much difference. For, at the same time, the current regime is moving rapidly in the direction of opening the gates to allow in the consciousness along the environmental avenue. The Quebec situation is different from the black situation in the U.S. The Quebecois are in the same basic "colonial" situation, but they are not spread in ghettoes throughout every major city. Their struggle does not communicate itself so directly to other Canadians, the young particularly. Quebecois might have been oppressed and exploited for centuries, but they were never slaves. They were never lynched. More than their share might have been shipped off to war, but, individually, their experience with other Canadians has not been of an "inferior race" dealing with a "master race." Racism has been gentle toward the French in Canada, and it has never (at least so far as Quebecois are concerned) been of the mob variety.

Young English-speaking Canadians do not find themselves quite so intimately, out of collective guilt or simple charity or whatever, bound up in the Quebec struggle. Moreover, it is a struggle which still shows signs of being able to resolve itself without a full-blown civil war. As for the Native people in Canada, their struggle, also a genuine anti-colonial struggle, has only begun to come self-consciously into focus at a time when the power structure has become sophisticated enough to make adjustments, to involve itself in more Marcusean methods of control. The struggle of the Native people will likely never be allowed to flare to such an intensity (as the black struggle has in the States) where the rage demands blood vengeance.

Canada would therefore still seem to be one of the first nations likely to experience the change in consciousness. Certainly, the delivery system exists.

As for other nations, the consciousness will come most quickly into focus where repression is least. That would disqualify the totalitarian states. Countries like Norway, Denmark, Sweden would appear to be well on their way to achieving it – well ahead of Canada or Britain. They are "freer," more open societies, and the new consciousness will likely surface first there. Britain, too, would appear to be well ahead of Canada, at least in terms of the number of artists who have got to the control tower. (The Beatles, obviously, but there are many, many others.)

Neither Australia nor New Zealand has shown much sign of any rapidly accelerated growth.

As for Japan, first-hand reports of the country suggest that the rapid and brutal transition from feudal to technological society has been accomplished at tremendous cost. Japanese society holds itself together only by exerting the greatest force. In order to express itself in Japan, the new consciousness would have to untangle a lot more psychic knots than it would have to even in

Europe. For the aftermath of the Second World War lies over the Japanese spirit like hardened gum.

It is possible, as McLuhan suggests, that it is in the unindustrialized regions that we will see the change take place first. Laying their hands on the new electric technologies, these nations may bypass entirely the stage of industrialization. Their consciousness, more holistic in the old pre-technological sense, may more readily attain the new level. Individuals need not experience the body-mind split which finds its most extreme expression in adoption of the operationalistic mode. But there are massive and rapidly accelerating problems to be overcome: overpopulation, famine, depletion of resources. Moreover, most of the governments in the Third World are repressive, brutal, even totalitarian. Some are not, but it is difficult to estimate their chances.

As for the second unanswered question, the direction implied by the "stages" in the growth of the new consciousness is clear: at each stage it has been organically expanding, growing out of the old frames of reference. First, it transcended purely personal psychological boundaries, then it transcended purely cultural boundaries, and then political boundaries – attaining at last a truly "natural," or environmental, level of awareness. Now it has grounded itself in existence, in the relationship of life to its world. Beyond that elemental contact with the ground of physical being, the new consciousness can only become *transcendental*, what we usually call spiritual. The trend is unmistakable. It will be through the force and clarity of its vision at the transcendental stage that the new consciousness will finally succeed in bringing all men into one embrace. Not one saint, but thousands and millions – funky, earthy, young saints, more Zen-like than righteous, will lead it. It has all begun.

# APPENDIX

It is not really enough to describe the new consciousness as being "holistic." While the word itself is accurate enough – "holism" refers to the tendency in nature to form wholes that are more than the sum of the parts *by creative evolution* – it is not quite the full story. In using that word, we are speaking only of the general character of the consciousness, the basic nature of the beast. This is like referring to an individual as being Caucasian or Negro: having said that, one has said very little. More specifically, this holistic consciousness exhibits a strong phenomenological tendency. Also, while the conflict between the old and the new basic modes of consciousness is posed here in terms of operationalism versus holism, to leave the discussion at that would be to miss one of the distinctive qualities of the new consciousness. What we have been posing so far is a very generalized conflict. While, in its basic orientations, the new consciousness remains holistic, it does not achieve its final form merely *in opposition* to the reductionist, operational mode. Rather, it *transcends* operationalism. This does not mean that all operationalistic orientations are rejected. As a tool for cognition, operationalism has its obvious powers and advantages; lots of bread and linen may be provided through application of the operationalistic mode. The new consciousness has at its base the concept of length. It is a firm foundation (although it makes a terrible "roof"). In transcending that concept, the consciousness does not have to reject it. It simply demotes the tool from the status of a totem. This is a key distinction. Otherwise, the emergence of a new consciousness at this stage would amount to nothing more than slippage, a return to levels of awareness which had been achieved in the past. To speak, as McLuhan does, of "retribalization" is to recognize the communal characteristics of the new consciousness, to recognize its holistic outline, perhaps even to suggest its phenomenological tendencies, but it is a potentially misleading word nevertheless. For it leaves the impression, at any rate, that some sort of a regression is taking place. Also, holistic modes of the past lacked the existential dimension which is so clearly a facet of the New Holism. Personal responsibility in primitive societies was strictly defined in terms of submission to a higher, if unseen, authority. This is definitely not the case with the new consciousness. The full "name" of this consciousness, therefore, would be: the new holistic, existential, post-operationalistic, phenomenological consciousness. NHEPOP? Only a semantics professor could love such a name. Accordingly, I have chosen to refer to it simply as the "new consciousness," or the new "holistic consciousness."

# REFERENCES

1 John R. Platt, "What We Must Do," *Science*, Nov. 28, 1969, pp. 1115-1121.
2 Loren Eiseley, "Evolution & Ego," *Psychology Today*, Oct., 1970, p. 94.
3 Ludwig von Bertalanffy, *Robots, Men and Minds*, George Braziller, Inc., 1967, p. 50.
4 Julian Silverman, "When Schizophrenia Helps," *Psychology Today*, Sept., 1970, p. 63.
5 Anton Boisen, *Exploration of The Inner World: A Study of Mental Disorder and Religious Experience*, Harper, 1936.
6 Arthur Koestler, *The Ghost in The Machine*, Macmillan, 1968; Hutchinson & Co. Ltd., 1967, p. 324.
7 Lister Grinspoon, paper presented at the 1962 meeting of the American Association for the Advancement of Science, quoted in *Manas*, Vol XXIII, No. 47, p. 2, Nov. 25, 1970.
8 Charles A. Reich, *The Greening of America*, Random House, 1970, p. 18.
9 John R. Platt, Hierarchical Growth, *Bulletin of the Atomic Scientists*, Nov., 1970, pp. 2-4, 46-48.
10 This and all further descriptions of technique are drawn from Jacques Ellul, *The Technological Society*, translated by John Wilkinson, Alfred A. Knopf, Inc., 1964.
11 Herbert Marcuse, *One-Dimensional Man*, Beacon Press, 1964, p. 158.
12 *Ibid.*, pp. 158-159.
13 Allen Ginsberg, *Howl and Other Poems*, City Lights Books, 1956.
14 Edward T. Hall, Cities and Culture, *The Hidden Dimension*, Doubleday & Co., Inc., 1966, reprinted in *Beyond Left and Right*, edited by Richard Kostelanetz, William Morrow & Co., Inc., 1968, p. 154.
15 Eldridge Cleaver, *Soul on Ice*, Dell Publishing Co., Inc., 1968, p. 197.
16 Frantz Fanon, *Studies in a Dying Colonialism*, Monthly Review Press.

232

[17] See Mark Gerzon, *The Whole World is Watching*, Paperback Library, 1970, p.18.

[18] Havelock Ellis, *The Dance of Life*, Random House, 1923, pp. 58-61.

[19] See Reginald Whitaker's *Drugs and The Law, The Canadian Scene*, Methuen Publications, 1969.

[20] Alfred Korzybski, *Science and Sanity*, The International Non-Aristotelian Library Publishing Co., 1933, 1941, 1948, p. 57.

[21] See *Drugs and the Law*.

[22] *Science and Sanity*, p. xiii.

[23] *Psychic*, The Bolen Co., Jan.-Feb., 1970.

[24] Plants Are Only Human, *Argosy*, June, 1969.

[25] *Psychic*, Jan.-Feb., 1970.

[26] *Psychology Today*, March, 1969, p. 23.

[27] Quoted by P. G. Stafford and B. H. Golightly, *LSD: The Problem-Solving Psychedelic*, Award Books, 1967, pp. 160-161.

[28] William Willoya and Vinson Brown, *The Soul of The Indian*, quoted in *Warriors of The Rainbow*, Naturograph Co. 1962.

[29] *Your Environment*, Vol. 1, No. 3, 1970.

[30] N. J. Berrill, *Inherit The Earth*, Fawcett Publications, Inc. 1966, p. 111-114.

[31] Martin H. Fischer, *Ill. Medical Journal*, Dec. 1928.

[32] Quoted in *LSD: The Problem-Solving Psychedelic*, p. 256.

[33] *Ibid*, pp. 172-173.

[34] *Ibid*, pp. 161-162.

[35] *One-Dimensional Man*, p. x.

[36] See my *The Enemies of Anarchy*, Part One.

[37] Loren Eiseley, *The Firmament of Time*, Atheneum, 1960.

[38] Ward Shepard, *The Subversive Science, Essays Toward Ecology of Man*, Houghton Mifflin, 1968.

[39] *Manas*.

[40] The Subsersive Science.

[41] Quoted in *One-Dimensional Man*, p. 149.

[42] *Quotations From Chairman Mao*, Foreign Language Press, Peking, 1967, pp. 95-97.

[43] J. K. Galbraith, *The New Industrial State*, Houghton Mifflin Co., p. 255.

[44] Copyright 1969, Time, Inc.

[45] J. G. Frazer, *The Golden Bough*, Abridged Edition, MacMillan & Co., 1963, p. 2.

[46] *The Technological Society*.

[47] Copyright 1968, The New York Times Co.

[48] Copyright 1970, Cowles Communications, Inc.

[49] Theodore Roszak, *The Making of a Counter Culture*, Doubleday & Co. Ltd., 1969, p. 101.

[50] Frederick S. Perls, *Gestalt Therapy Verbatim*, 1969, Real People Press, p. 16.

[51] Martin Esslin, *Theatre of The Absurd*, Doubleday Anchor Books, 1961, p. 7.

[52] Mark Gerzon, *The Whole World Is Watching*, Paperback Library, 1970, p. 41.

[53] Copyright 1968, HMH Publishing Co., Inc.

[54] Ronald Segal, *The Race War*, 1966, The Viking Press.

[55] *Soul On Ice*, pp. 194-195.

[56] Eldrige Cleaver, *Post-Prison Writings and Speeches*, 1969, Ramparts Magazine, Inc., p. 20.

233

[57] *Gestalt Therapy Verbatim,* p. 19

[58] Rudolf Arnheim, *Visual Thinking*, 1969, University of California Press.

[59] From his Minaki address, "The Relation of Welfare and Development in the Transition to Post-Industrialism: A Social Science Appreciation," Background paper prepared for The Canadian Centre for Community Studies, to be published in a memorial volume, honoring the late William Baker, *Innovations in Science.*

[60] *Ibid.*

[61] *Ibid.*

[62] Philip E. Slater, *The Pursuit of Loneliness. American Culture at the Breaking Point,* 1970, Beacon Press.

[63] Ibid.

[64] Martin Faber, *The Foundation of Phenomenology*, Antioch Press, 1970. Reviewed in *Manas*, Vol. XXI, No. 47.

[65] Sam Keen, Sing the Body Electric, *Psychology Today*, Oct., 1970, p. 56.

[66] The Politics of Immortality, *Psychology Today*, Nov., 1970.

[67] *The Ghost in The Machine*, p. 305.

[68] Copyright HMH Publishing Co., Inc., Vol. 16, No. 3, March, 1969.

Hum
BF
311
H84 ✓

DATE DUE

| MAY 3 1 1976 | JUN 4 1981 |
| JUL 2 5 1977 | APR 30 1983 |
| AUG 1 5 1977 | AUG 08 1984 |
| SEP 3 1977 | |
| SEP 1 9 1977 | |
| APR 9 1979 | |
| DEC 4 1980 | |
| MAR 3 0 1981 | |
| | |
| | |
| | |